THE AMERICAN CIVIL WAR

LA GUERRE CIVILE
LA GUERRA CIVIL
DER BÜRGERKRIEG

James E. and Dean S. Thomas

THOMAS PUBLICATIONS
Gettysburg PA 17325

Copyright © 1996 by James E. and Dean S. Thomas

Printed and bound in the United States of America

Published by THOMAS PUBLICATIONS
P.O. Box 3031
Gettysburg, Pa. 17325

ISBN-0-939631-29-6

Cover design by Ryan C. Stouch

THE TRANSLATORS

Thomas Publications is indebted to the following individuals for their assistance and guidance in providing the translations for this work:

French (Francais)   — Marie Jo Arey, Gettysburg, PA
                         Howard Koser, Shippensburg, PA

Spanish (Español) — Carmen and Herbert Brown, Gettysburg, PA

German (Deutsch) — Alwine and Hans Henzel, Fairfield, PA
                         David Crowner, Gettysburg, PA

The translations of the Gettysburg Address are courtesy of the National Park Service, Gettysburg National Military Park.

CONTENTS

THE AMERICAN
CIVIL WAR

INTRODUCTION

The problems that led to the American Civil War (1861-1865) started long before the 1860s. Differences in economy, lifestyle, and politics caused a split between the North and South. The states in the north had a more balanced economy, and with small farms and growing industry in the cities, there was no need or use for slavery. The Southern economy, however, was based largely on one crop—cotton. The large plantations where the cotton was grown depended on slaves as a source of labor, thus slavery was protected by the South as an economic necessity. Another difference was that most Southerners believed in State's Rights—that the state, not the central government, should hold ultimate power over its citizens.

The split grew wider as the years passed and westward expansion brought the admission of new states into the Union. With each new state, there were fierce arguments in Congress over whether it should be admitted as a slave (pro-South) or a free (pro-North) state. Two important events of this period that affected NorthNSouth relations were the Dred Scott case and the Compromise of 1850. Dred Scott was a slave who sued for his freedom in 1846. In 1857, the Supreme Court finally decided that Scott was considered property, not a citizen with rights, and was therefore not entitled to his freedom. The Compromise of 1850 called for the admission of California as a free state. However, any future states from the Mexican Territory (lands won in the Mexican War) could determine their own slave policy. The North also agreed to return escaped slaves. This compromise temporarily settled the "slavery question," thereby postponing the inevitable civil war by over a decade.

The election of Abraham Lincoln as President in 1860 was the turning point for the southern slave-holding states. Lincoln was a member of the Republican party, which did not support slavery. Fearing their whole way of life was in danger, South Carolina seceded (left the Union), believing that because they had voluntarily entered the Union, they should be able to leave it. Within 43 days six additional states seceded. The United States government did not acknowledge these states' right to secede and attempted to maintain control of its military posts, most notably Fort Sumter in Charleston Harbor. South Carolina saw this as an intrusion by foreign troops and was determined to regain the fort. On April 12, 1861, South Carolina militiamen fired on Fort Sumter after Federal attempts to reinforce its garrison. The fort surrendered after 34 hours of bombardment. President Lincoln then called for 75,000 volunteers to protect the Union. Lincoln's call for troops caused four more southern states to follow South Carolina's lead and the Confederate States of America had eleven states.

The American Civil War has been called the last "gentleman's war." It was a chivalrous time filled with much pomp and glamour. In the North and South, young men, believing their cause would be victorious after only a single battle, rushed to join the army before the war was over. The spring of 1861 found Union and Confederate volunteers marching off to fight a war in brightly colored uniforms with bands playing and crowds cheering.

The next four years, however, turned out to be a sad time of death and destruction. The wide-ranging armies foraged, raided and battled through anything in their way, causing millions of dollars worth of damage to farms, towns and whole cities. Atlanta and Richmond were among those cities that were devastated. Technical and industrial advances produced weapons that had greater accuracy and faster rates of fire. Coupled with obsolete infantry tactics and poor medical practices, they meant death and suffering for unprecedented numbers of American soldiers and their families.

About 3,000,000 men served in the Union and Confederate armies. More than 620,000 of them died from disease and battle, a loss that almost equals those of all other U.S. wars combined. Thousands more were limbless or otherwise scarred for life—physically and mentally.

Between 1861 and 1865, more than 2,400 engagements were fought, ranging from small skirmishes to sieges and battles involving massive armies. The bloody sacrifices made at these places are remembered and honored to this day. This book discusses 42 of the most significant of these battles. The commanders, armies, number of soldiers, and casualties are listed for each battle. This is followed by a concise description of the battle, its significance, and a listing of buildings and geographic features that were prominent in the battle.

INTRODUCTION

Les problèmes qui causèrent la Guerre Civil eurent leur génèse longtemps avant les années 60 du dernier siècle. Les différances économiques, culturelles, et politiques amenèrent un schisme entre le Nord et le Sud. L'économie des états du Nord etait plus équilibrée, et puisque les fermes était petites, les industries dans les villes croissantes, les esclaves n'étaient pas nécessaires. L'économie du Sud était basée sur une seule récolte le coton. Les grandes "plantations" dependaient des esclaves pour leur main d'oeuvre. Donc l'eclavage tait protégé par le Sud comme nécessité écomomique. Un autre différend était la croyance qu'avaient le Sudistes en la doctrine des Droits des Etats, à savoir que c'est l'état et non le gouvernement central qui doit gouverner directement ses citoyens.

L'abîme qui séparait les deux régions devint de plus en plus large avec le passage du temps. L'expansion vers l'ouest aboutit à l'admission de nouveaux états dans l'Union. L'entrée de chaque nouveau venu sollicita des débats féroces dans le congrès pour déterminer s'il dut être admis comme un état esclavagiste ou un état non-esclavagiste. Deux événements importants de cette periode fut la décision Dred Scott et le Comprmis de 1850. Dred Scott fut un esclave qui avait demand sa liberté devant le tribunaux des Etats-Unis en 1846. Enfin, en 1857, la Cour Suprême décida qu'il fut un bien de son maître, non un citoyen.

Le Compromis de 1850 admit la Californie comme état non-esclavagiste. Cependant, les territoires cedés aux Etats-Unis par le Mexique (résultat de la Guerre de Mexique) auraient le droit de décider pour eux-mêmes s'ils voudraient être esclavagistes ou anti-ésclavagistes. Le compromis résolut le problème temporairement, différant jusqu'à la décade suivante l'inévitable guerre civil.

L'élection d'Abraham Lincoln fut le point décisif en 1860 pour les états esclavagistes. Lincoln appartenait au parti Républicain, parti anti-esclavagiste. Craignant que leurs us et coutumes, leur culture, furent en danger, la Caroline du Sud sucéda, soutenant que puisqu'il fut entré dans l'Union volontaiement, il eut le droit d'en séceder. Dans 43 jours six autres etats sudistes le suivirent. Le gouvenement des Etats-Unis, au contraire, soutint qu'un état n'eut pas le droit de sucéder, et essaya de maintenir son contrôle de ses bases militaires dans le Sud, notamment Fort Sumter dans le port de Charlston (Caroline du Sud). Aux yeux des sudistes, ce fut une occupation par des troupes étrangères, et ils se décidèrent de le reprendre. Le 12 avril, les sudistes ouvrit le feu, après des tentatives de la part des Nordistes de renforcer la garnison. Le fort capitula après 34 heures de bombardements. Lincoln fit appel à 75 000 volontzaires pour protéger l'Union. L'áppel de Lincoln suscita la sécession de quatre états sudistes de plus, et alors les Etats Confédérés d'Amerique avaient onze états.

On appelle souvent la Guerre Civil "la dernière guerre entre gentlemen." Ce fut une ère chevaleresque pleine de pompe et splendeur. Dans les deux régions de jeunes hommes croyant que leur cause serait victorieuse après une seule bataille voulaient s'engager dans l'armée avant la fin de la guerre. Le printemps de 1861 vit Unionistes et Confédérés vêtus de beaux uniformes en marche vers les champs de bataille au son des fanfares et des applaudissements des foules.

Cependant les quatre années suivantes se montrènt un temps de mort et de destruction. Partout les armées se battaient, fourrageaient, et faisaient des razzias, dévastant fermes et villes et causant des millions de dollars de dommages. Atlanta et Richmond furent parmi les villes dévastées. Des progrès technologigues et industriels produirent des armes de tire plus précis et plus rapide. Les tactiques perimées et les practiques médicales de la période condamnèrent un nombre sans précédent de soldats et leurs familles à la souffrance et la mort.

A peu près 3 000 000 hommes servirent dans les armées Unionistes et Confédérees. Plus de 620 000 morurent de maladies ou dans les batailles. D'autres milliers furent mutilés ou autrement blessés-physiquement et mentalement.

Entre 1861 et 1865, il y eut 2 400 combats à partir de petits accrochages jusqu'aux sièges et de batailles rangées comportant des armées massives. Les sacrifices sanglants faits dans ces lieux sont rappelés et honorés de nos jours. Ce livre décit 42 des plus importantes de ces batailles. Il y a une liste de commandants, d'armés, le nombre de soldats, et les pertes de chaque bataille, suivi d'une courte description des batailles. Il y a aussi une liste de points de repère géographiques et de bâtiments qui jouèrent un rôle dans les batailles.

INTRODUCCION

Los problemas que llevaron a la guerra civil americana empezaron antes de los años de 1860. Diferencias en la economía, el estilo de vida, y las políticas causaron la división entre el Norte y el Sur. Los estados en el notre tenían una economía más equilibrada, y con pequeñas fincas y una industria creciente en las ciudades, no había necesidad o uso de la esclavitud. La economía sureña, sin embargo estaba basada extensamente en un cultivo-algodón. Las grandes plantaciones donde el algodón era cultivado dependía de los esclavos como fuente de labor, así que la esclavitud fue protegida por el Sur como una necesidad económica. Otra diferencia fue que la mayoría de los sureños creían en los Derechos del Estado—que el estado, no el gobierno central, debía sostener el poder último sobre los ciudadanos.

La división creció más vastamente así como los años pasaban y la expansión del occidente trajo la admisión de nuevos estados dentro de la Unión. Con cada nuevo estado, hubo intensas discusiones en el Congreso sobre si debía ser admitido como un estado de esclavo (a favor del Sur) o como un estado libre (a favor del Norte). Dos sucesos importantes de este período que afectaron las relaciones Norte-Sur fueron el caso de Dred Scott y el Compromiso de 1850. Dred Scott fue un esclavo que demandó por su libertad en 1846. En 1857 La Corte Suprema finalmente decidió que Scott era considerado propiedad, no un ciudadano con derechos, y por lo tanto no tenía derecho a su libertad. El Compromiso de 1850 llamado así por la admisión de California como un estado libre. Sin embargo, cualquier estado venidero del Territorio Mexicano (tierras grandes en la guerra mexicana) podía determinar su propia política de esclavo. El Norte también acordó devolver a los esclavos escapados. Este compromiso temporalmente puso orden "al problema de la esclavitud," de modo que pospuso la inevitable guerra civil casi por una década.

La elección de Abraham Lincoln como Presidente en 1860 significó el giro para los estados sureños que tenían esclavos. Lincoln era un miembro del Partido Republicano, el cual no apoyaba la esclavitud. Temiendo que todo su estilo de vida estaba en peligro, South Carolina se separó (dejó la Unión), creyendo que como ellos se habían unido voluntariamente a la Unión, podrían dejarla. En cuestión de 43 días seis estados más se separaron. El gobierno de los Estados Unidos no reconoció el derecho de estos estados a separarse e intentó mantener el control de sus guarniciones militares, el más notable el Fuerte Sumter en el puerto de Charleston. South Carolina vio esto como intrusión por las tropas extranjeras y fue determinado recobrar el Fuerte. El 12 de abril, 1861, la milicia de South Carolina abrió fuego al Fuetre Sumter después de los esfuerzos federales de reforzar sus guarniciones. El Fuerte se rindió después de 34 horas de bombardeo. El presidente Lincoln, entonces, pidió a 75,000 voluntarios para proteger la Unión. La llamada de Lincoln a las tropas provocó que cuatro estados sureños más siguieran la primacía de South Carolina y los Estados Confederados de América tuvieron once estados.

La guerra civil americana ha sido llamada la última "guerra de caballeros." Fue una época caballerosa llena de ostentación y fascinación. En el Norte y en el Sur, hombres jóvenes, creyendo que su causa sería victoriosa después de sólo una batalla, se apresuraron a alistarse en el ejército antes de que la guerra se acabara. La primavera de 1861 encontró a los voluntarios de la Unión y a los Confederados marchando para luchar en la guerra con uniformes de colores brillantes, bandas tocando y multitudes vitoreando.

Los próximos cuatro años, sin embargo, resultó ser un tiempo triste de muerte y destrucción. Los ejércitos más esparcidos saquearon, invadieron y batallaron cualquier cosa en su camino, causando millones de dólares de daño a las fincas, pueblos y ciudades enteras. Atlanta y Richmond estuvieron entre esas ciudades que fueron devastadas. Avances técnicos e industriales produjeron armas que tenían una precisión más grande y una velocidad de disparo más rápida. Unido a antiguas tácticas de infanteria y prácticas médicas pobres, esto significó la muerte y el sufrimiento a números inauditos de soldados americanos y a sus familias.

Sobre 3,000,000 de hombres sirvieron en los ejércitos de la Unión y de los Confederados. Más de 620,000 de ellos murieron de enfermedades y en batalla, una pérdida que casi iguala a todas aquellas de las otras guerras de los Estados Unidos combinadas. Miles más fueron desmembrados o de otro modo cicatrizados por vida—física o mentalmente.

Entre 1861 y 1865 más de 2,400 combates fueron luchados, variando de escaramuzas a asedios y batallas envolviendo grandes ejércitos. Los sangrientos sacrificios hechos en estos lugares son recordados y honorados haste hoy en día. Este libro discute 42 de las batallas más significantes. Los comandantes, ejércitos, número de soldados, y pérdidas están alistadas para cada batalla. Esto viene seguido de una descripción concisa de la batalla y sus consecuencias, y una lista de edificios y puntos geográficos que tuvieron significación en la batalla.

EINLEITUNG

Die Probleme, die zum Amerikanischen Zivilkrieg (1861-1865) leiteten, hatten ihren Anfang lange ehe das Jahr 1860 begann.

Unterschiede in der Ökonomie, im Lebensstiel, und Politik, brachten eine Spaltung zwischen Nord und Süd. Die Staaten des Nordens hatten eine besser ausgeglichene Ökonomie, und mit kleinen Farmen und wachsender Industrie in den Städten, weder Bedürfnis noch Gebrauch von Sklaven entstand. Im Gegensatz, die Ökonomie des Südens bestand hauptsächlich aus einem Ertrag—Baumwolle. Die großen Plantagen, auf welchen die Baumwolle gepflanzt und geerntet wurde, waren auf Sklaven als Arbeitsquelle angewiessen. Aus diesem Grunde war Sklaverei als eine ökonomische Notwendigkeit im Süden angesehen. Ein weiterer Unterschied zwischen beiden Staaten war, daß beinahe der ganze Süden sich an Staatsrechte hielt—was dem Staat, nicht der zentralen Regierung, die endgültige Macht über seine Bevölkerung gab.

Die Spaltung erweiterte sich über die Jahre, während die Erschließung des Westens neue Staaten in die Union mit sich brachte. Hitzige Debatten fanden im Kongress statt, um eine Entscheidung zu treffen, ob ein neuer Staat als Sklaven-(pro Süden), oder Freistaat (pro Norden), aufgenommen werden sollte. Zwei wichtige Ereignisse dieser Zeit, welche den Norden-Süden Verhältnis beeinflußte, war der Dred Scott Fall und der Kompromiß von 1850. Dred Scott war ein Sklave, der, in 1846, für seine Freiheit klagte. Das Oberste Bundesgericht faßte, im Jahre 1857, den endgültigen Entschluß, daß Scott als Eigentum, nicht als ein Bürger mit Rechten, angesehen werden konnte, und war deshalb nicht zu seiner Freiheit berechtigt. Der Kompromiß von 1850 verlangte den Eintritt von Californien als freien Staat. Jedoch in der Zukunft konnten weitere Staaten vom Mexikanischen Gebiet (Land welches im Mexikanischen Krieg gewonnen war) ihre eigene Verfahrungsweise in Bezug auf Sklaven festsetzen. Dieser Kompromiß entschied einstweilen die "Sklaven Frage" und verschob die Unvermeidlichkeit eines Zivilkrieges über eine Dekade.

Die Wahl, in 1860, für Lincoln als Präsident, bezeichnete einen Wendepunkt für die Festhaltung von Sklaven in den Südstaaten. Lincoln, als ein Mitglied der Republikanischen Partei, unterstützte Sklaverei nicht. In der Furcht, daß ihr ganzer Lebensstiel in Gefahr war, trennte sich Südcarolina von der Union ab, in dem Glauben, dass ihr einst freiwilliger Anschluß an die Union ihnen nun ebenson erlaubte, sie wieder zu verlassen. Innerhalb 43 Tagen verließen weitere sechs Staaten die Union. Die Vereinigten Staaten verweigerten die Anerkennung der Rechte dieser Staaten und deren Abtrennung und versuchten, weiterhin die Kontrolle über ihre Militärposten, insbesondere Fort Sumter im Charleston Hafen, zu behalten. Südcarolina sah dies als einen Eindrang ausländischer Truppen an und war fest entschlößen, das Fort wieder unter ihre Kontrolle zu bringen.

Am 12. April 1861, Föderalistische Versuche, ihre Garnison zu verstärken, folgte mit der Beschießung von Fort Sumter bei Südcarolinas Landwehr. Das Fort ergab sich nach einem 34 stündigen Bombardement. Präsident Lincoln folgte diesem Vorkommen mit seinem Aufruf von 75,000 Freiwilligen zur Verteidigung der Union. Lincolns Truppenaufruf brachte zur Folge, daß vier weitere südliche Staaten dem Beispiel Südcarolinas folgten, und mit ihrem Anschluß an die Konföderierten Staaten von Amerika, deren Zahl zu elf vergrößerte.

Der Amerikanische Zivilkrieg wurde, zu Unrecht, als der letzte Krieg von Galantrie, Pomp und Glanz bezeichnet. Im Norden und Süden eilten die jungen Männer, um sich den Armeen anschließen zu können der Krieg zu Ende käme. Sie waren der Überzeugung, daß die Veranlaßung zum Krieg durch die einzige siegreiche Schlacht dessen sofortiges Ende bringen würde. Im Frühjahr 1861, Freiwillige der Union und Konföderation, marschierten, in ihren glänzenden Uniformen, begleitet bei Kapellenmusik und der ansporenden Bevölkerung, in den Kampf.

Jedoch, wie die folgenden vier Jahre bewiessen, dies war eine traurige Zeit, mit Tod und Zerstörung im Land. Die weit ausgedehnten Armeen durchstöberten, plünderten und durchkämpften alles, was in ihren Weg kam, und brachten Millionen von Schaden auf Farmen, in Dörfern und Städten. Atlanta und Richmond waren unter den Städten, die vollkommen zerstört wurden. Technische und industrielle Fortschritte produzierten Waffen, die größere Präzision und schnelleres Feuer gewährten. Veraltete Infanterietaktien und schlechte medizinische Verfahren brachten Tod und Leiden für zahllose amerikanische Soldaten und deren Familien.

Ungefähr 3,000,000 Truppen waren im Dienst der Union und Konföderierten Armeen. Über 620,000 fielen auf den Schlachtfeldern, oder starben durch Krankheiten—ein Verlust, der nahezu Verlusten aller anderen U.S. Kriege gleichkommt. Weitere tausende waren amputiert oder auf irgendeine andere Weise lebenslang verkrüppelt—entweder körperlich oder in ihrer Mentalität.

Zwischen 1861 und 1865 fanden über 2,400 Angriffe statt—von kurzen Gepländen zu Belagerungen und weiter zu Schlachten, die massierte Armeen einbegriffen. Die blutigen Opfer, und die Orte, auf denen sie gefordert wurden, bleiben in Erinnerung und werden geehrt bis auf den heutigen Tag.

Dieses Buch erörtert 42 von den bedeutendsten dieser Schlachten. Die Kommandeure, die Armeen, Truppenstärken und Verluste, alle sind verzeichnet für jede Schlacht. Eine kurze Beschreibung jeder Schlacht, und seiner Bedeutung, folgt, mit einer Liste von Orientierungspunkten und Gebäuden, die eine wichtige Rolle in jeder Schlacht spielten.

FORT SUMTER
April 12-14, 1861

State: South Carolina

U.S.
Commander:
  Maj. Robert Anderson
U.S. Army: 1st U.S. Artillery
  No. of Troops: 128
  (85 + 43 Civilian Engineers)
Casualties:
  Killed: 1
  Wounded: 3 (1 Died Several Days Later)
  Captured or missing: 0

C.S.
Commander:
  Brig. Gen. P.G.T. Beauregard
C.S. Army:
  No. of Troops: 6,700
Casualties:
  Killed: 0
  Wounded: 0
  Captured or missing: 0

COMMENTS

After repeated demands for surrender by South Carolina and several attempts at reinforcement by the North, a mortar shell burst over Fort Sumter signalling the start of a Confederate bombardment and the beginning of the Civil War. This "first shot" of the Civil War was at 4:30 a.m. on April 12, 1861. The bombardment that followed lasted for 34 hours. During that time, Major Anderson's men caused little or no damage to their enemy. The Confederates, however, battered the fort, setting fires and dismounting guns. By afternoon on April 13th, Major Anderson agreed to surrender the fort to General Beauregard. The surrender was due as much to lack of food, supplies, and men as to the Confederate bombardment. Under the terms of the surrender, the men of the fort were allowed to fire a 100 gun salute to the American flag. On the 47th shot, a pile of ammunition exploded causing the only casualties of the battle. Major Anderson's men boarded a ship heading north and the Confederates took possession of the fort.

SIGNIFICANCE

The attack on Fort Sumter was the start of the American Civil War.

On April 15, 1861, one day after the evacuation of Fort Sumter, President Lincoln issued a call for 75,000 men to protect the Union.

In response to Lincoln's call for troops, Virginia, Arkansas, Tennessee, and North Carolina joined the Confederacy.

With Sumter in Southern hands, Charleston Harbor became an important port for blockade runners.

Etat: Caroline du Sud

Etats-Unis
Commandant:
  Major Robert Anderson

Armée: Ière U.S. Artillerie
  128 soldats
  (85 + 43 ingénieurs civils)
Pertes:
  Tué: 1
  Blessés: 3 (1 mourut quelques jours plus tard)
  Prisonnier ou disparu: 0

Estats Confédérés
Commandant:
  Général de Brigade
  P.G.T. Beauregard
Armée: 6700 soldats

Pertes:
  Tué: 0
  Blessé: 0
  Prisonnier ou disparu: 0

COMMENTAIRE

Après plusieurs appels à la reddition de l'Union par la Caroline du Sud et plusieurs essais de renforcement par le Nord, l'explosion d'un mortier au Fort Sumter était le signal du début de la Guerre Civile. Le premier coup fut lancé à 4h30 le 12 avril 1861. Le bombardement qui suivit dura 34 heures. Durant cette période, les hommes du major Anderson causèrent peu ou nul dommage à leurs ennemis. Les Confédérés cependant battirent le fort à coups de canon et alumant des incendies et en démontant les canons. Dans l'après-midi du 13 avril, le major Anderson avait accepté de rendre le Fort au général Beauregard. La reddition était due autant au manque de nourriture, d'équipement et d'hommes, qu'au bombardement des Confédérés. Dans les clauses de la réddition figurait l'autorisation donnée aux hommes du Fort de "saluer" le drapeau américain par 100 coups de canon. Au 47éme, un paquet de munitions explosa, causant la seule mort de cette bataille. Les hommes d'Anderson repartirent vers le Nord, et les Confédérés prirent possession du Fort.

CONSEQUENCES

L'attaque au Fort Sumter fut le point de départ de la Guerre Civile.

Le 15 avril, un jour après l'évacuation du Fort, le président Lincoln lanca un appel pour obtenir 75 000 hommes pour la protection de l'Union.

En réponse à l'appel de Lincoln, la Virginie, l'Arkansas, le Tennessee et la Caroline du Nord joignirent la Confédération.

Sumter étant entre les mains du Sud, le port de Charleston devint une cible majeure pour les forceurs de blocus.

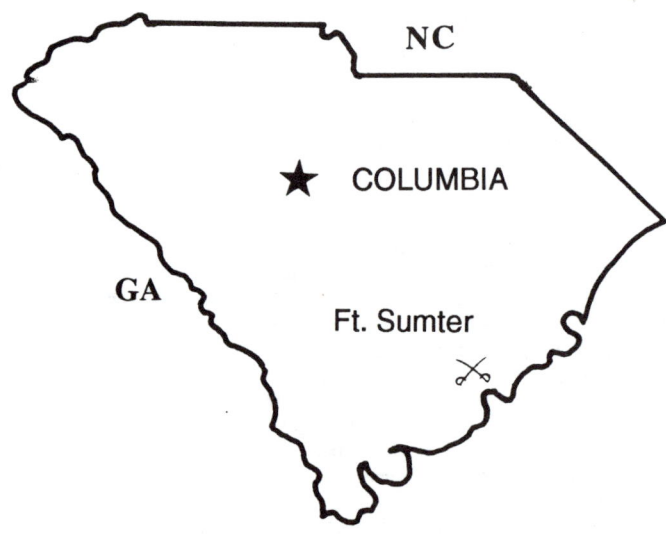

Major Robert Anderson

Important Landmarks
Fort Moultrie
Fort Johnson
Castle Pinckney
Cummings Point (Morris Island)

Estado: South Carolina

U.S.	C.S.
Comandante:	Comandante:
Maj. Robert Anderson	Brig. General P.G.T. Beauregard
U.S. Ejército: 1 U.S. Artillería	C.S. Ejército:
No. de Tropas: 128	No. de Tropas: 6,700
(85 + 43 Ingenieros ciudadanos)	
Pérdidas:	Pérdidas:
Muertos: 1	Muertos: 0
Heridos: 3	Heridos: 0
(1 se murió unos días depués)	Capturados o desapa recidos: 0
Capturados o ausentes: 0	

COMENTARIOS

Después de repetidas demandas para la rendición por la parte de South Carolina y varios atentados por el Norte de reforzarse, una bomba de cañón explotó encima de Fuerte Sumter, lo que fue la señal para el comienzo de un bombardeo Confederado y también el comienzo de la guerra civil norteamericana. Este "primer tiro" de la guerra civil fue a las cuatro y media de la mañana, el 12 de abril de 1861. El bombardeo resultó duró por 34 horas. Durante ese tiempo, las tropas del Major Anderson no hicieron ningún daño a sus enemigos. Los Confederados, sin embargo, demolieron el fuerte, causando muchos fuegos y desmontando muchos cañones. Al llegar al 13 de abril, el Major Anderson acordó rendir el fuerte al General Beauregard. La rendición fue tanto por la falta de tropas, comida y otras provisiones como por el bombardeo. Bajo los términos de la rendición, se dejó que los hombres en el fuerte dispararan una salva de cien cañonazos a la bandera americana. Cuando se disparó el 47 cañonazo, una pila de municiones explotó, causando las únicas pérdidas de la batalla. Las tropas del Major Anderson se fueron por barco para el Norte y los Confederados ganaron posesión del fuerte.

CONSECUENCIAS

El ataque de Fort Sumter fue el comienzo de la guerra civil americana.

El 15 de abril, 1861, un día después de la evacuación de Fort Sumter, el Presidente Lincoln pidió 75,000 voluntarios para proteger la Unión.

En reacción a este pedido de tropas por Lincoln, los estados de Virginia, Arkansas, Tennessee, y North Carolina se juntaron con la Confederación.

Con Fort Sumter en las manos de los Confederados, el puerto de Charleston llegó a ser un asilo importante para los que traían armas y provisiones para el bloqueo de la costa sureña.

Staat: Süd Carolina

Befehlshaber der US:	Befehlshaber der CS:
Major Robert Anderson	Brigadiergeneral
Armee der US: 1. U.S. Artillerie	P.G.T. Beauregard
Truppenstärke: 128	Armee der CS: Provisorische
(85 + 43 Zivil Ingenieure)	Streitkräfte der Konföderierten Staaten
	Truppenstärke: 6,700
Verluste:	Verluste:
Gefallen: 1	Gefallen: 0
Verwundet: 3	Verwundet: 0
(1 starb einige Tage später)	Gefangengenommen oder
Gefangengenommen oder vermißt: 0	vermißt: 0

KOMMENTAR

Südcarolina hatte wiederholt die Kapitulation des Fort's gefordert. Etliche Verstärkungsversuche des Nordens waren erfolglos. Es war der 12. April 1861 — um 16.30 Uhr explodierte eine Granate über Fort Sumter, mit der Ankündigung einer bevorstehenden Bombardierung bei Konföderierten und damit dem Beginn des Bürgerkrieges. Eine 34-stündige Bombardierung folgte. Während dieser Zeit fügten Fort Sumter's Truppen, unter Major Anderson, dem Feind wenig oder keinen Schaden zu. Andererseits, die Konföderierten zerstörten das Fort, Brände entstanden und Geschütze wurden aus den Lafetten geschlagen. Endlich, am Nachmittag des 13. April gab Major Anderson seine Einwilligung, das Fort General Beauregard zu übergeben. Die Entscheidung zur Kapitulation war nicht nur wegen des Bombardements getroffen, weiterer Einfluß kam vom Mangel an Proviant, Nachschub und Truppen. Unter den Bedingungen der Kapitulation wurde dem Kommandeur und den Truppen des Forts ein Abschiedssalut von 100 Salven an ihre Amerikanische Flagge gewährt. Nach der 47. Salve explodierte ein Munitionsstapel. Dies brachte den einzigen Verlust (1 Soldat) in diesem Kampf.

Ein Schiff, auf dem Weg nach Norden, nahm Major Anderson und seine Truppen auf, und die Konföderierten übernahmen das Fort.

BEDEUTUNG

Der Angriff auf Fort Sumter kündete den Anfang des amerikanischen Bürgerkrieges an.

Am 15. April 1861, ein Tag nach der Evakuierung von Fort Sumter, rief Präsident Lincoln 75,000 Männer zur Verteidigung der Union auf.

Die Antwort auf Lincoln's Truppenaufruf war der Anschluß der Staaten Virginia, Arkansas, Tennessee und Nordcarolina an die Konföderierten Staaten.

Mit Fort Sumter in südstaatlichen Händen, wurde der Hafen von Charleston sehr wichtig für Blockadebrecher.

The interior of Fort Sumter after the bombardment. The Confederate flag defiantly flies on the makeshift flagpole.

State: Virginia

U.S.

Commander:
Brig. Gen. Irvin McDowell

U.S. Army: Army of Northeastern Virginia
No. of Troops: 35,000
Casualties:
Killed: 460
Wounded: 1,124
Captured or missing: 1,312

C.S.

Commander:
Gen. P.G.T. Beauregard
Gen. J.E. Johnston

C.S. Army: Army of the Potomac
Army of the Shenandoah
No. of Troops: 32,000
Casualties:
Killed: 387
Wounded: 1,582
Captured or missing: 13

COMMENTS

The Union Army under General McDowell advanced from Washington and camped around Centerville, VA. The Confederates were spread out over 8 miles along the southern bank of Bull Run.

General McDowell started the battle with a feint attack on the Confederate left at the Stone Bridge. At the same time, his main column marched northwest and crossed Bull Run at Sudley Ford in order to attack the Confederate flank and rear. The Confederates in this area, learning of McDowell's flank march, turned to face the Federal attack. Their small force made a gallant stand, but were finally overwhelmed and driven back by the troops of Burnside, Porter, Heintzelman, and Sherman. General T.J. Jackson, marching from another part of the Confederate line, arrived at the Henry House hill in time to halt the Federal advance. (It was here that he got his famous nickname, "Stonewall.") At the height of this attack, McDowell advanced two artillery batteries to fire into Jackson's lines. In desperate fighting, these guns were captured and recaptured several times. Eventually the Confederates were able to take and keep control of the Henry House hill. With the arrival of more reinforcements from Winchester, it was now the Confederates' turn to attack. The Southern attack was aimed at McDowell's right flank and rear. The Federal line staggered and fell back slowly at first but soon the Army was in full retreat. Confederate artillery continued to fire on the retreating columns. This caused a panic which sent the Federal army running back to Washington.

SIGNIFICANCE

This loss did more for the Federals than the victory did for the Confederacy. The Southerners, reassured that they could "whip the Yankees" still believed that it would all be over soon. While the Northerners geared up for a long bloody war and became more determined than ever to put down the rebellion.

Etat: Viginie

Etats-Unis

Commandant:
Général de Brigade Irvin McDowell

Armée: du Nord-Est de Virginie
35 000 soldats
Pertes:
Tués: 460
Blessés: 1 124
Prisonniers ou disparus: 1 312

Etats Confédérés

Commandants:
Général P.G.T. Beauregard
Général G. E. Johnston

Armées: du Potomac et de Shenandoah
32 000 soldats
Pertes:
Tués: 387
Blessés: 1 582
Prisonniers ou disparus: 13

COMMENTAIRE

L'armée de l'Union, aux ordres du général McDowell, avança depuis Washington et campa près de Centerville en Virginie. Les troupes des Confédérés s'étalaient sur une douzaine de kilomètres le long de la rive sud de Bull Run.

Le général McDowell commença la bataille par une fausse attaque contre les Confédérés restés à Stone Bridge. En même temps, le gros de son armée partit en direction nord-ouest et traversa le Bull Run pour attaquer le flanc et l'arrière garde des Confédérés. Avertis de cette manoeuvre, ces derniers firent face à l'attaque fédérale. Leur petite force fit un brave effort mais succomba, finalement forcée à la retraite sous les coups des troupes de Burnside, Porter, Heintzelman et Sherman. Le général T.J. Jackson, arrivant d'une autre direction de la ligne confédérée, atteignit Henry House Hill juste à temps pour arrêter l'avance fédérale (d'où le surnom de "Stonewall"). A l'apogée de cette attaque, McDowell lança deux batteries d'artillerie qui firent feu sur les lignes de Jackson. Dans un combat désespéré, ces canons furent capturés et repris plusieurs fois. Finalement, les Confédérés purent prendre et garder le contrôle de Henry House Hill. Quand arrivèrent les renforts venus de Winchester, les Confédérés prirent l'offensive. L'attaque des Sudistes était dirigée sur les troupes situées à la droite et à l'arrière de McDowell. La ligne fédérale chancela, commença à désintégrer, et bientôt battit en retraite. L'artillerie des Confédérés continua à faire feu sur les troupes en retraite. L'armée fédérale, prise de panique, revint à Washington.

CONSEQUENCES

Cette défaite eut plus d'importance pour l'armée fédérale que la victoire pour les Confédérés. Les Sudistes, certains qu'ils pourraient vaincre les Yankees croyaient encore que tout serait bientôt fini. Mais les Nordistes s'organisèrent pour une longue et dure guerre et furent plus résolus que jamais à éteindre la rébellion.

Important Landmarks

Henry House Hill
Sudley Ford
Cub Run Bridge
Bull Run
Blackburn's Ford
Manassas-Sudley Road
Warrenton Turnpike
Stone Bridge
Chinn Ridge

Important Buildings

Henry House
Sudley Church
Chinn House
"Portici"
Stone House
Robinson House
Mathews House
"Pittsylvania"

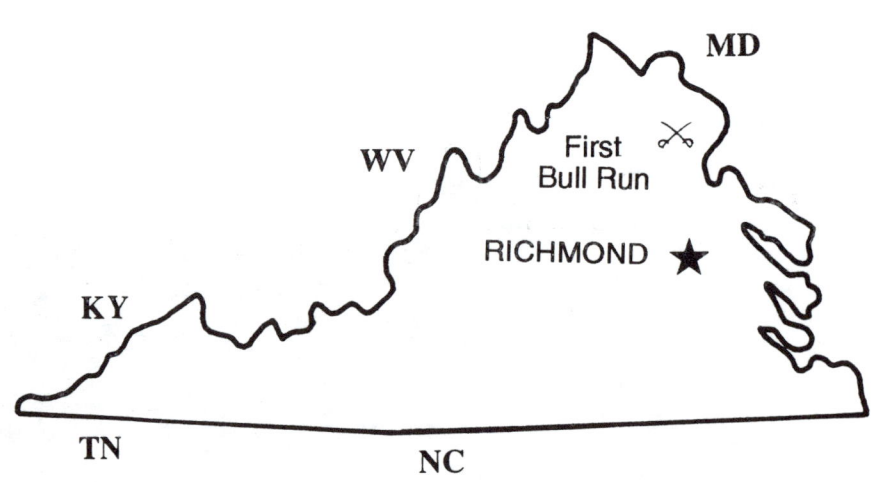

Estado: Virginia

U.S.

Comandante:
Brig. Gen. Irvin McDowell

U.S. Ejército: Army of Northeastern Virginia
No. de tropas: 35,000
Pérdidas:
Muertos: 460
Heridos: 1,124
Capturados o ausentes: 1,312

C.S.

Comandantes:
Gen. P.G.T. Beauregard
Gen. J.E. Johnston

C.S. Ejército: Army of the Potomac
Army of the Shenandoah
No. de tropas: 32,000
Pérdidas:
Muertos: 387
Heridos: 1,582
Capturados o ausentes: 13

COMENTARIOS

El ejército del Norte bajo el General McDowell avanzó desde Washington y acampó cerca de Centerville, Virginia. Los Confederados estuvieron esparcidos por ocho millas al lado de la orilla sureña de Bull Run.

El General McDowell empezó la batalla con un pequeño ataque en la izquierda Confederada en Stone Bridge (Puente de Piedra). Al mismo tiempo, su columna principal marchó para el noroeste y cruzó Bull Run al Vado Sudley para atacar la retaguardia y el flanco de los Confederados. Los Confederados en esta área, aprendiendo de esta marcha de McDowell, hicieron frente al ataque Federal. Su fuerza pequeña hizo una resistencia valiente, pero al final fueron abrumados y empujados para atrás por las tropas de Burnside, Porter, Heintzelman, y Sherman. El General T.J. Jackson, marchando desde otra parte de la línea Confederada, llegó a la colina de Henry House a tiempo para parar el avance Federal. (Fue aquí donde llegó a tener su nombre famoso "Stonewall".) Durante la parte más violenta de este ataque, McDowell avanzó dos baterías de artillería para disparar a las líneas de Jackson. En una lucha desesperada, estos cañones fueron capturados y recapturados varias veces. Eventualmente los Confederados pudieron tomar y mantener control de la colina de Henry House. Con la llegada de más refuerzos de Winchester, les tocaba a los Confederados atacar. El ataque de los Sureños se dirigía para el flanco de la derecha y la retaguardia de McDowell. La línea Federal se tambaleó y retrocedió lentamente al principio, pero pronto el ejército corría en retiro completo. La artillería siguió disparando a estas columnas. Esto causó un pánico que mandó el ejército a Washington corriendo.

CONSECUENCIAS

Esta derrota hizo más para los Federales que la victoria para los Confederados. Los Sureños, asegurados que podían derrotar a los Yanquis, todavía creían que todo iba a acabar pronto. Los Norteños, sin embargo se prepararon para una guerra larga y sangrienta y se pusieron más determinados para aplastar la rebelión.

Staat: Virginia

Befehlshaber der US:
Brigadegeneral Irvin McDowell

Armee der US: Armee von Nordostvirginia
Truppenstärke: 35,000
Verluste:
Gefallen: 460
Verwundet: 1,124
Gefangengenommen oder vermißt: 1,312

Befehlshaber der CS:
General P.G.T. Beauregard
General J.E. Johnston
Armee der CS: Armee des Potomac, Armee des Shenandoah
Truppenstärke: 32,000
Verluste:
Gefallen: 387
Verwundet: 1,582
Gefangengenommen oder vermißt: 13

KOMMENTAR

Unter General McDowell rückte die Unionarmee aus Washington vor und lagerte sich in der Nähe von Centerville in Virginia. Entlang dem südlichen Ufer von Bull Run hatten sich die Konföderierten über mehr als 13 Kilometer verteilt.

General McDowell begann die Schlacht mit einem Scheinangriff auf die linke Seite der Konföderierten an der Stone Bridge. Zur gleichen Zeit marschierte seine Hauptcolonne nordwestlich und durchwatete den Bull Run am Sudley Ford, um die Konföderierten an der Flanke und im Rücken anzugreifen. Die Konföderierten in dieser Gegend bekamen Kenntnis von McDowell's Flankenmarsch und kehrten sich dem Föderalistenangriff zu. Ihre kleine Zahl leistete tapferen Widerstand, aber am Ende waren sie überwältigt von Burnside's, Porter's und Sherman's Truppen und zurückgetrieben. General T.J. Jackson, der von einem anderen Teil der Linie der Konföderierten hermarschierte, erreichte beizeiten den Henry Haus Hügel, um den Vormarsch der Föderalisten aufzuhalten. (Hier erhielt er seinen berühmten Spitznamen "Stonewall"). Als der Kampf am heftigsten tobte, rückte McDowell zwei Artilleriebatterien vor, um in Jackson's Reihen feuern zu können. Im verzweifelten Gefecht ging die Eroberung der Geschütze von einer Seite zur anderen. Schließlich gelang es den Konföderierten, den Henry Haus Hügel zu erobern und beherrschen. Mit der Ankunft von Verstärkungstruppen aus Winchester waren die Konföderierten jetzt imstande, anzugreifen. Sie zielten auf die rechte Flanke und den Rücken von McDowell. Die Reihe der Föderalisten schwankte und wich zunächst langsam zurück, war aber bald ganz auf dem Rückzug. Die Artillerie der Konföderierten feuerte ununterbrochen auf die zurückziehenden Unionkolonnen, die nun panicartig die Flucht zurück nach Washington ergriffen.

BEDEUTUNG

Die Niederlage lehrte den Föderalisten mehr als der Sieg den Konföderierten. In dem Sicherheitsgefühl, sie könnten "die Yankees in die Pfanne hauen", glaubten die Südstaatler an ein schnelles Ende des Krieges. Im Gegensatz, die Nordstaatler bereiteten sich auf einen langen, blutigen Krieg vor, und waren fester entschloßen denn je, die Rebellion niederzuschlagen.

The Stone House (Matthews) on the Warrenton Turnpike. Used as a Federal field hospital in 1861 and 1862.

State: Missouri

U.S.

Commander:
  Brig. Gen. Nathaniel Lyon
U.S. Army: Volunteer Forces
  No. of Troops: 5,400

Casualties:
  Killed: 258
  Wounded: 873
  Captured or missing: 186

C.S.

Commander:
  Brig. Gen. Ben McCulloch
C.S. Army: Missouri, Arkansas, and
  C.S. volunteer forces
  No. of Troops: 10,125

Casualties:
  Killed: 277
  Wounded: 945
  Captured or missing: ?

COMMENTS

The Confederate Army, Commanded by Brig. General Ben McCulloch, wanted to attack Brig. General Nathaniel Lyon's Union Army in Springfield, Missouri.

On August 6th Confederates marched to Wilson Creek, 10 miles from the city, where they camped and planned their attack for morning. However, at 5 a.m., the Union Army made a surprise attack on the Confederate camp. In the initial assault Confederate cavalry was pushed back and General Lyon took possession of Bloody Hill. Soon the Southern infantry arrived at the front and stopped the advance. At the same time Col. Sigel attacked at the other end of the Confederate camp, driving the Southerners toward the fighting on Bloody Hill.

Now both armies settled down to a morning long series of attacks and counterattacks—back and forth over the South slope of Bloody Hill which achieved nothing. In one of these attacks Lyon was killed and the Union command fell upon Maj. Samuel Sturgis.

Meanwhile the Confederates in the rear launched an attack on Sigel, who was soon routed and driven from the field.

The Union Army, tired, short of ammunition, and concerned about Sigel's failure to exert pressure on the Confederate rear, withdrew toward Springfield around 11:30 a.m.

The Southerners, disorganized and low on ammunition did not pursue the Yankees.

SIGNIFICANCE

General Lyon's death was a loss to the Union Army.
This battle was part of a campaign by both armies to gain control of Missouri.

Etat: Missouri

Etats-Unis

Commandant:
  Général de Brigade Nathaniel Lyon
Armée: Enrôlés Volontaires
  5 400 soldats

Pertes:
  Tués: 258
  Blessés: 873
  Prisonniers ou disparus: 186

Etats Confédérés

Commandant:
  Général de Brigade Ben McCulloch
Armées: Missouri, Arkansas, Enrôlés
  Volontaires
  10 125 soldats

Pertes:
  Tués: 277
  Blessés: 945
  Prisonniers ou disparus: ?

COMMENTAIRE

L'armée des Confédérés, commandée par le brigadier général Ben McCulloch, voulait attaquer l'armée de l'Union dirigée par le général Nathaniel Lyon à Springfield dans le Missouri.

Le 6 août les Confédérés s'installèrent à Wilson Creek, à 16 kilomtres de la ville, où ils mirent sur pied leur attaque du matin suivant. Cependant, à 5 heures du matin, l'armée de l'Union attaqua par surprise le camp des Confédérés. Lors de l'assaut initial, la cavalerie confédérée fut repoussée et le général Lyon prit Bloody Hill. Bientôt, l'infanterie sudiste arriva au front où elle mit fin à l'avantage de l'Union. En même temps, le colonel Sigel attaquait l'autre bout de l'armée confédérée, attirant les Sudistes vers la combat de Bloody Hill.

Toute cette matinée les deux armées s'affrontèrent en une longue série d'attaques et de contre-attaques, sur la pente sud de Bloody Hill, pour un résultat nul. Durant l'une de ces attaques le général Lyon fut tué et le major Samuel Sturgis prit en charge le commandement de l'armée de l'''nion.

Pendant ce temps les troupes confédérés derrière sigel lancèrent une attaque sur Sigel qui fut bientôt mis en déroute.

Epuisée, à court de munitions, inquiétée par l'échec de Sigel essayant d'attaquer les arrières des Confédérés, l'armée de l'Union se retira vers 11h30.

Désorganisés et prêts à manquer de munitions, les Sudistes ne poursuivirent pas les Yankees.

CONSEQUENCES

La mort du Général Lyon fut une perte pour l'armée de l'Union.
Cette bataille faisait partie d'une campagne de la part des deux armées pour prendre le contrôle du Missouri.

Important Landmarks
Bloody Hill
Wilson Creek
Telegraph (Wire) Road
Sharp's Cornfield

Important Buildings
Ray House
Gibson's Mill
Ray Spring-house

Estado: Missouri

U.S.	C.S.
Comandante:	Comandante:
Brig. Gen. Nathaniel Lyon	Brig. Gen. Ben McCulloch
U.S. Ejército: Voluntarios	C.S. Ejército: Voluntarios de Missouri
No. de tropas: 5,400	y Arkansas y otros voluntarios
	Confederados
	No. de tropas: 10,125
Pérdidas:	Pérdidas:
Muertos: 258	Muertos: 277
Heridos: 870	Heridos: 945
Capturados o ausentes: 186	Capturados o ausentes: ?

COMENTARIOS

El ejército Confederado, mandado por el Brig. General Ben McCulloch, quería atacar las fuerzas Federales del Brig. General Nathaniel Lyon en Springfield, Missouri.

El 6 de agosto los Confederados marcharon a Wilson Creek, a diez millas de la ciudad, donde acamparon y planearon su ataque para la mañana siguiente. Sin embargo, a las cinco de la mañana, el ejército Federal hizo un ataque de sorpresa en el campamento Confederado. En el primer asalto la caballería fue empujada para atrás y el General Lyon tomó posesión de Bloody Hill. Llegó pronto la infantería sureña al frente y paró el avance. Al mismo tiempo el Col. Sigel atacó al otro lado del campamento Confederado, manejando a los rebeldes hacia la lucha en Bloody Hill.

Ahora los dos ejércitos se pusieron a una série de ataques y contrataques que duraron por toda la mañana–de aquí para allá por la cuesta sureña de Bloody Hill, lo que no resultó en nada. En uno de estos ataques Lyon murió y la comandancia cayó en manos de Maj. Samuel Sturgis.

Mientras tanto, los Confederados en la retaguardia lanzaron un ataque a Sigel, quien fue rápidamente derrotado y empujado del campo de batalla.

El ejército Federal, cansado, faltando municiones, y preocupado por el fracaso de Sigel de ejercer presión en la retaguardia de los Confederados, salió para Springfield a las once y media de la mañana.

Los Sureños, desorganizados y con pocas municiones, no persiguieron a los Yanquis.

CONSECUENCIAS

La muetre del General Lyon fue una gran pérdida para el ejército del Norte.

La batalla fue parte de una campaña de los dos ejércitos para obtener control de Missouri.

Staat: Missouri

Befehlshaber der US:	Befehlshaber der CS:
Brigadegeneral Nathaniel Lyon	Brigadegeneral Ben McCulloch
Armee der US: Freiwilligenheer	Armee der CS: Freiwilligenheer von
Truppenstärke: 5,400	Missouri, Arkansas und andere
	Truppenstärke: 10,125
Verluste:	Verluste:
Gefallen: 258	Gefallen: 277
Verwundet: 873	Verwundet: 945
Gefangengenommen oder	Gefangengenommen oder
vermißt: 186	vermißt: ?

KOMMENTAR

Die unter Brigadegeneral Ben McCulloch stehende Konföderationsarmee plante, die Unionarmee unter Brigadegeneral Nathaniel Lyon in Springfield, Missouri, anzugreifen.

Am 6. August marschierten die Konföderierten bis an Wilson's Creek, 16 Kilometer von der Stadt, in der sie lagerten, und ihren Angriff für den nächsten Morgen planten. Um 5.00 Uhr setzte die Unionarmee jedoch zum Überraschungsangriff auf das Lager der Konföderierten an. Beim ersten Angriff wurde die Kavallerie der Südstaatler zurückgedrängt, und General Lyon eroberte Bloody Hill. Kurz danach erreichte die südstaatliche Infanterie die Front und hielt den feindlichen Vormarsch auf. Um die gleiche Zeit stürmte Oberst Sigel die andere Seite des Lagers der Konföderierten und trieb sie in Richtung Bloody Hill.

Für den Rest des Morgens beschränkten sich beide Armeen zu einer Reihe von Angriffen und Gegenangriffen - hin und her über den südlichen Hang des Hügels, ohne entscheidende Resultate. In einem dieser Angriffe fiel Lyon und das Kommando der Unionstreitkräfte fiel Major Samuel Sturgis zu.

Die Konföderierten im Rücken gingen inzwischen zum Angriff gegen Sigel über. Er war bald in die Flucht geschlagen und räumte das Feld.

Die Unionarmee, ermüdet, und knapp an Munitionen, war weiterhin beunruhigt, daß der erwartete Druck von Sigel auf den Rücken der Konföderierten fehlgeschlagen hatte. Sie zogen sich um etwa 11.30 Uhr nach Springfield zurück.

Die Konföderierten verfolgten die Yankees nicht: sie waren desorganisiert und es mangelte ihnen and Munitionen.

BEDEUTUNG

Der Tod von General Lyon war ein schwerer Verlust für die Unionarmee.

Diese Schlacht war ein Teil der Kampagne beider Armeen, Missouri in ihre Gewalt zu bringen.

Nathaniel Lyon, 1818-1861, was killed in action during the battle. He was the North's first military hero.

Ben McCulloch, 1811-1862, was later killed in action at the Battle of Pea Ridge (March 7, 1862).

State: Tennessee

U.S.
Commander:
 Brig. Gen. Ulysses S. Grant
U.S. Army:
 No. of Troops: 27,000
Casualties:
 Killed: 510
 Wounded: 2,152
 Captured or missing: 224

C.S.
Commander:
 Brig. Gen. John B. Floyd
C.S. Army:
 No. of Troops: 15,500
Casualties:
 Killed: 250
 Wounded: 1,250
 Captured: 13,000

COMMENTS

On Feb. 12 Grant reached Fort Donelson and deployed his Army south and west of the Confederate fort. On the 13th, he attacked the center of the works. The attack failed, only resulting in heavy casualties for the Northerners.

On February 14 Commodore Foote's flotilla of Union Gunboats arrived to bombard the fort from the river. The duel between the gunboats and Fort Donelson's water battery lasted for two hours. However, the high ground the Confederates had chosen for their gun positions gave them the advantage. Every Union ship took direct hits and most were seriously damaged. Foote, realizing he was defeated, ended the assault.

Grant, seeing that direct assaults were not successful and cost too many lives, was considering a siege of the fort. Meanwhile Floyd, fearing such a move by the Federals, planned a surprise attack.

The next morning the Confederates assaulted the Union right and pushed it back. An escape route to Nashville was now open. But then Gen. Pillow, for unknown reasons, ordered the Confederates back to the trenches. Grant regrouped, counterattacked and regained all he had lost.

During the night the Southerners decided to surrender. Gen. Floyd and Gen. Pillow escaped during the night, leaving Gen. Buckner in command.

On the morning of Feburary 16 Buckner requested terms for surrender. Grant responded with his famous ultimatum, "unconditional and immediate surrender." Buckner accepted.

SIGNIFICANCE

After a year of war in which the Confederates had been mostly successful, this was a major victory and greatly raised the sagging morale of the Northern people.

Forts Henry and Donelson were the center of the Confederacy's northwestern line of defense. After their capture, the Confederates were forced to fall back. In doing so, control of Kentucky and western Tennessee fell into Union hands. The greatest loss to the Confederacy in this area was Nashville, an important depot and manufacturing town.

The victory greatly increased Grant's prestige and launched his career.

Etat: Tennessee

Etat-Unis
Commandant:
 Général de Brigade Ulysses S. Grant
Armée: 27 000 soldats
Pertes:
 Tués: 510
 Blessés: 2 152
 Prisonniers ou disparus: 224

Etats Confédérés
Commandant:
 Général de Brigade John B. Floyd
Armée: 15 500 soldats
Pertes:
 Tués: 250
 Blessés: 1 250
 Prisonniers ou disparus: 13 000

COMMENTAIRE

Le 12 février, Grant atteignit le Fort Donelson et déploya son armée au sud et à l'ouest du fort. Le 13, il attaqua au centre des travaux. Ce fut un échec qui se solda par de lourdes pertes pour les Nordistes.

Le 14 février, la flotille de chaloupes canonnières de l'Union, menée par le commodore Foote bombarda le Fort depuis la rivière. La lutte dura deux heures. Cependant, l'avantage revint aux Confédérés grâce aux positions de leurs canons sur un terrain choisi pour sa hauteur tactique. Chaque bateau de l'Union reçut des coups directs et la plupart furent sérieusement endommagés. S'apercevant de sa défaite, Foote mit fin àl'assaut.

Voyant l'insuccès et le prix humain des assauts directs, Grant pensa à assiger le fort. Cependant, Floyd, craignant cette action même, prépara une attaque surprise.

Le lendemain, les Confédérés assaillirent et forcèrent la droite de l'Union. La route de Nashville était libre. Mais le général Pillow, pour des raisons inexpliquées, renvoya les Confédérés dans leurs tranchées. Grant récupéra ses forces, contre-attaqua et regagna tout ce qu'il avait perdu.

Pendant la nuit, les Sudistes décidèrent de se rendre. Les génèraux Floyd et Pillow s'échappèrent pendant la nuit, laissant leur armée sous les ordres du général uckner.

Le matin du 16 février, Buckner s'enquit des clauses de la reddition. Grant réondit par son célèbre ultimatum: "Reddition immdiate et sans conditions!" Buckner accepta.

CONSEQUENCES

Apérs un an de guerre où le Confédérés avaient été le plus souvent les vainqueurs, cette bataille fut une victoire d'importance pour l'Union et remonta considérablement le moral ébranlé des Nordistes.

Le Forts Henry et Donelson étaient les points majeurs de la ligne de défense nord-ouest de la Confédération. Ces forts pris, le Confédérés durent se replier. Ainsi, le Kentuky et le Tennessee de l'Ouest tombaient entre les mains de l'Union. La plus grande perte pour la Confédération dans cette région fut Nashville, ville de dépôt et de manufactures.

Cette victoire accrut le prestige de Grant et lança sa carrière militaire.

Important Landmarks
Water Batteries
Cumberland River
Indian Creek
Forge Road
Charlotte Road
Hickman's Creek

Important Buildings
Dover Hotel
Mrs. Crisp's
Rollins House
Cherry House
Rowlett's Mill
William's House
J. Crisp's House

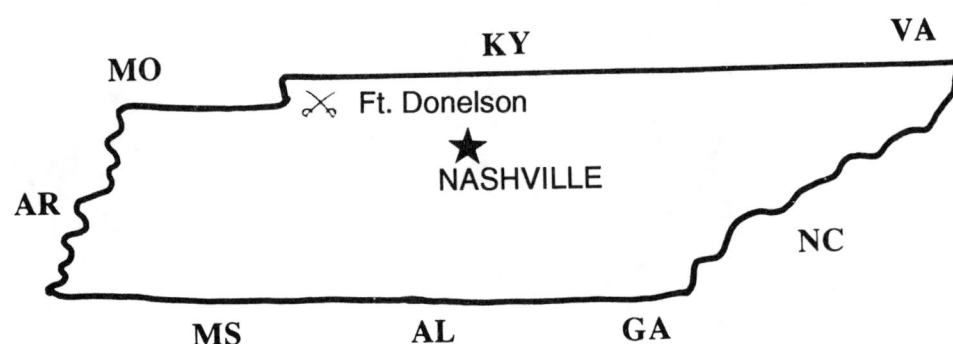

Estado: Tennessee

U.S.

Comandante:
 Brig. Gen. Ulysses S. Grant
U.S. Ejército:
 No. de tropas: 27,000
Pérdidas:
 Muertos: 510
 Heridos: 2152
 Capturados o ausentes: 224

C.S.

Comandante:
 Brig. Gen. John B. Floyd
C.S. Ejército:
 No. de tropas: 15,500
Pérdidas:
 Muertos: 250
 Heridos: 1250
 Capturados o ausentes: 13,000

COMENTARIOS

El 12 de febrero Grant llegó a Fort Donelson y puso sus fuerzas al sur y al oeste del fuerte Confederado. El 13, él atacó el centro de las defensas. El ataque fracasó, resultando en muchas pérdidas para los Norteños.

El 14 de febrero una flotilla de barcos armados, bajo el mando de Commodore Foote, llegó para bombardear el fuerte desde el río. El duelo entre los barcos armados y las baterías del fuerte duró dos horas. Sin embargo, la tierra alta elegida por los Confederados para sus cañones les dieron la ventaja. Todos los barcos Federales sufrieron golpes directos y la mayoría fue sériamente dañada. Foote, dándose cuenta de que había sido derrotado, terminó el asalto.

Grant, viendo que los asaltos directos no tuvieron éxito y costaron demasiadas vidas, consideró un cerco del fuerte. Mientras tanto, Floyd, temiendo una estrategia así por los Federales, planeó un ataque de sorpresa.

Por la mañana siguiente los Confederados asaltaron la derecha de los Federales y la empujó para atrás. Una ruta de escape a Nashville se abrió por este ataque. Pero el General Pillow, por razones desconocidas, mandó que los Confederados volvieran a sus trincheras. Grant reoraganizó sus fuerzas y reganó todo lo que se había perdido.

Durante la noche, los Confederados decidieron rendirse. Los Generales Floyd y Pillow se escaparon durante esta noche, dejando al General Buckner el mando.

El 16 de febrero, por la Mañana Buckner pidió los términos de rendición. Grant respondió con su respuesta famosa, "rendición inmediata sin condiciones." Buckner aceptó.

CONSECUENCIAS

Después de un año de guerra en la que los Confederados, por la mayor parte, habían tenido éxito, ésta fue una victoria importante y levantó el espíritu de la gente del Norte.

Los fuertes Henry y Donelson eran el centro de la línea noroeste de defensa de los Confederados. Después de su captura, los Confederados tuvieron que retroceder. Al hacer eso, el control de Kentucky y el oeste de Tennessee cayó en las manos de los Norteños. La pérdida más grave para los Confederados en este área fue Nashville, una estación de ferrocarriles muy importante y una ciudad de mucha fabricación.

La victoria aumentó el prestigio de Grant y lanzó su carrera.

Staat: Tennessee

Befehlshaber der US:
 Brigadegeneral Ulysses S. Grant
Armee der US: Armee des
 Cumberland
 Truppenstärke: 27,000
Verluste:
 Gefallen: 510
 Verwundet: 2,152
 Gefangengenommen oder
 vermißt: 224

Befehlshaber der CS:
 Brigadegeneral John B. Floyd
Armee der CS: Armee von Tennessee
 Truppenstärke: 15,500

Verluste:
 Gefallen: 250
 Verwundet: 1,250
 Gefangengenommen oder
 vermißt: 13,000

KOMMENTAR

Am 12. Februar erreichte Grant Fort Donelson in Tennessee. Er stellte seine Armee südlich und westlich vom Konföderierten Fort auf. Am 13. Februar stürmte er die Mitte der Befestigung, aber der gescheiterte Angriff brachte ihm nur schwere Verluste.

Am 14. Februar erreichte Kommodore Foote's Union Kanonenbootflotille das Fort und öffnete, vom Fluss her, seine Bombardierung. Das Duell zwischen den Kanonenbooten und der Wasserbatterie von Fort Donelson dauerte zwei Stunden. Die Konföderierten auf der hohen Lage, die sie sich für ihre Geschützstellungen ausgewählt hatten, waren im Vorteil. Jedes Boot der Union erlitt einen Volltreffer, und die Mehrzahl der Schiffe waren schwer beschädigt. Angesicht der Niederlage beendete Kommodore Foote den Angriff.

Als Grant zu der Erkenntnis kam, daß direkte Angriffe erfolglos waren, und viel zu viele Menschenleben gefordert hatten, zog er eine Belagerung des Forts in Betracht. Brigadegeneral Floyd, der solch eine Strategie von Seiten der Unionarmee befürchtete, plante einen Überraschungsangriff.

Am nächsten Morgen griffen die Konföderierten die rechte Seite der Unionarmee an und drängten sie zurück. Ein Fluchtweg nach Nashville war jetzt frei. Aus unbekannten Gründen befahl jedoch General Pillow die Konföderierten in die Schützengräben zurück. Grant gruppierte um, ging zum Gegenangriff über und gewann zurück was vorher verloren war.

In der Nacht trafen die Konföderierten den Entschluß sich zu ergeben. Generale Floyd und Pillow waren während der Nacht entflohen — General Buckner übernahm das Kommando.

Am Morgen des 16. Februar ersuchte Buckner die Kapitulations bedingungen. Grant antwortete mit seinem berühmten Ultimatum: "bedingungslose und sofortige Kapitulation." Buckner's Annahme war prompt.

BEDEUTUNG:

Nach einem Kriegsjahr, das im Großen Ganzen für die Konföderierten erfolgreich war, bekam dies ein bedeutender Sieg für die Nordstaatler, der ihre Stimmung bedeutend hob.

Forts Henry und Donelson bildeten den Mittelpunkt der nordwestlichen Verteidigungslinie der Konföderation. Nach deren Eroberung wurden die Konföderierten dazu gezwungen, zurückzuweichen, wodurch die Kontrolle über Kentucky und West Tennessee in die Hände der Union kam. In diesem Gebiet lag die Stadt Nashville, eine industrielle Stadt mit einem wichtigen Depot. Der schwerste Verlust für die Konföderation.

Der Sieg förderte Grant's Prestige und gab seiner Karriere einen guten Start.

The charge of Smith's Division on the Confederate defenses.

State: Arkansas

U.S.	C.S.
Commander:	Commander:
Maj. Gen. Samuel R. Curtis	Maj. Gen. Earl Van Dorn
U.S. Army:	C.S. Army:
No. of Troops: 10,500	No. of Troops: 16,200
Casualties:	Casualties:
Killed: 203	Killed: 1,000
Wounded: 980	Wounded:
Captured or missing: 201	Captured or missing: 300

COMMENTS

General Curtis with 11,000 Federals, chased Confederate General Price out of Missouri and into Arkansas. Once there, Price was joined by General McCulloch and Maj. Gen. Earl Van Dorn. Van Dorn assumed command of the Army. He ordered the army North again, planning an attack on the Federals. When Curtis learned of the advance, he formed a defensive position on Pea Ridge.

On March 6 the Southerners were joined by Gen. Pike's three regiments of Cherokee Indians. Van Dorn planned diversions against the Federal right and center while the main thrust would be made by Gen. Price on the Federal left.

At about 7 a.m. on the 7th, shooting started along the lines. However, Price took over three hours to get his attack organized. When his Missourians finally charged, the Federal artillery was waiting, the shot and shell stopping this charge and a second. The third charge, however, swept the Union left, commanded by Gen. Carr, westward beyond Elkhorn Tavern. Gen. Pike's Cherokees advanced and broke another Union division, but a Federal counterattack soon regained all that was lost. A fourth attack by Price pushed Carr's men back farther. As darkness fell over the battlefield Union reserves moved up and stabilized the line.

On the 8th Gen. Sigel was ordered to attack the Confederates around Elkhorn Tavern. His two divisions of infantry smashed into the Missourians and sent them running. Gen. Carr then attacked the left of the Confederate line, driving them back also. With his whole line broken, Gen. Van Dorn ordered a retreat.

SIGNIFICANCE

This was the first decisive victory for the Union in a battle west of the Mississippi.

Confederate hopes of carrying the fighting into Missouri were crushed for the time being.

Etat: Arkansas

Etat-Unis	Etats Confédérés
Commandant:	Commandant:
Général de division Samuel R. Curtis	Général de division Earl Van Dorn
Armée:	Armée:
10 500 soldats	16 200 soldats
Pertes:	Pertes:
Tués: 203	Tués: 1 000
Blessés: 980	Blessés:
Prisonniers ou disparus: 201	Prisonniers ou disparus: 300

COMMENTAIRE

L'armée du général Curtis, avec 11 000 hommes, chassa l'armée confédérée du général Price du Missouri et la poursuivit jusqu'en Arkansas. Price y fut rejoint par le général McCulloch el la général Earl Van Dorn. Celui-ci prit la commande de l'armée. Il préparait une attaque contre l'Union. Quand Curtis apprit son avance, il organisa une position de défense sur Pea Ridge.

Le 6 mars, les Sudistes étaient rejoints par 3 régiments de Cherokee Indians du général Pike. Van Dorn prévoyait des attaques de diversion contre la droite et le centre de l'armée fédérale, tandis que l'attaque principale serait lancée par le général Price sur la gauche de l'armée fédérale.

Vers 7 heures du matin, le 7 mars, les bombardements commencèrent, Cependant, il fallut plus de trois heures au général Price pour organiser son attaque. Quand ses Missouriens chargèrent, l'artillerie fédérale attendait et réduisit rapidement l'adversaire. Mais la troisième attaque balaya la gauche de l'Union, commandée par le général Carr, à l'ouest d'Elkhorn Tavern. Les Cherokees de Pike avancèrent et brisèrent une autre division de l'Union, mais une contre-attaque fédérale permit de regagner aussitôt tout ce qui avait été perdu. Une quatrième attaque de Price repoussa les hommes de Carr. Au crépuscule, les troupes de réserves montèrent et les lignes de front furent stabilisées.

Le 8, le général Sigel reçut l'ordre d'attaquer les Confédérés près d'Elkhorn Tavern. Ses deux divisions d'infanterie foncèrent dans les Missouriens qui s'efuirent. Le général Carr attaqua alors la gauche de la ligne confédérée dont les hommes s'enfuirent également. Ses troupes battues, le général Van Dorn ordonna la retraite.

CONSEQUENCES

Ceci était la première victoire décisive de l'Union à l'ouest du Mississipi.

Les espoirs des Confédérés de poursuivre la lutte jusque dans le Missouri étaient alors anéantis.

Important Landmarks
Big Mountain
Telegraph Road
Bentonville & Keetsville Road
Little Mountain

Important Buildings
Elkhorn Tavern
Clemen's House
Pratt's Store

Estado: Arkansas

U.S.	C.S.
Comandante:	Comandante:
Maj. Gen. Samuel R. Curtis	Maj. Gen. Earl Van Dorn
U.S. Ejército:	U.S. Ejército:
No. de tropas: 10,500	No. de tropas: 16,200
Pérdidas:	Pérdidas:
Muertos: 203	Muertos: 1,000
Heridos: 980	Heridos:
Capturados o ausentes: 201	Capturados o ausentes: 300

COMENTARIOS

El General Curtis, con 11,000 Federales, ahuyentó al General Confederado Price fuera de Missouri hasta Arkansas. Una vez allí, los Generales McCulloch y Earl Van Dorn se juntaron con Price. Van Dorn se hizo comandante de todo el ejército. El mandó el ejército al norte de nuevo, planeando un ataque contra los Federales. Cuando Curtis supo de este avance, él formó una posición de defensa en Pea Ridge.

El 6 de marzo a los Sureños se juntaron tres regimientos de indios Cherokee bajo el mando del General Pike. Van Dorn planeó diversiones contra la derecha y centro Federal mientras el empuje principal sería hecho por el General Price contra la izquierda Federal.

Cerca de las siete de la mañana, el 7, empezaron los tiros por las líneas. Sin embargo, Price tardó más de tres horas en organizar su ataque. Cuando por fin sus Missourianos empezaron su embestida, la artillería Federal la esperaba, y las balas y bombas pararon este asalto y un segundo. El tercero, sin embargo, manejó la izquierda Federal bajo el mando del General Carr al oeste más allá de Elkhorn Tavern. Los indios del General Pike avanzaron y rompieron otra división Yanqui, pero un contrataque Federal reganó todo lo que se había perdido. Un cuarto ataque por Price empujó a las tropas de Carr para atrás de nuevo. Al caer la oscuridad sobre el campo de batalla, reservas Federales avanzaron y estabilizaron la línea.

El día 8, el General Sigel mandó atacar a los Confederados alrededor de Elkhorn Tavern. Sus dos divisiones de infantería chocaron con los Missourianos y los manejaron corriendo para atrás. El General Carr entonces atacó la izquierda Confederada, empujándolos para atrás también. Con toda su línea rota, el General Van Dorn mandó un retiro.

CONSECUENCIAS

Esta fue la primera victoria decisiva para la Unión al oeste del río Mississippi.

Las esperanzas de los Confederados de llevar la guerra a Missouri fueron aplastadas por el momento.

Staat: Arkansas

Befehlshaber der US:	Befehlshaber der CS:
Generalmajor Samuel R. Curtis	Generalmajor Earl Van Dorn
Armee der US: Southwest Armee	Armee der CS: Transmississippi Armee
Truppenstärke: 10,500	Truppenstärke: 16,200
Verluste:	Verluste:
Gefallen: 203	Gefallen und Verwundet: 1,000
Verwundet: 980	Gefangengenommen oder
Gefangengenommen oder	vermißt: 300
vermißt: 201	

KOMMENTAR

Mit 11,000 Truppen der Unionarmee jagte General Curtis Konföderationsgeneral Price aus Missouri und in Arkansas hinüber. Nachdem Price in Arkansas angekommen war, schloßen sich ihm General McCulloch und Generalmajor Earl Van Dorn an. Van Dorn übernahm das Kommando der Armee. In der Absicht, die Unionarmee anzugreifen, beorderte er seine Truppen nach Norden vorzurücken. Als Curtis von dem Vormarsch hörte, ging er auf Pea Ridge in Verteidigungsstellung.

Am 6. März schloßen sich General Pike's drei Regimente von Cherokee Indianern den Konföderationstruppen an. Van Dorn hatte es vor, Ablenkungen gegen die Mitte und rechte Seite der Föderalisten durchzuführen, während General Price den Hauptstoß auf die linke Seite der Föderalisten machen sollte.

Am Morgen des 7., etwa um 7.00 Uhr, begann das Schießen entlang den Linien. Ehe Price seinen Angriff organisieren konnte, waren bereits mehr als drei Stunden vergangen. Als seine Missourianer endlich stürmten, wartete die Föderalistenartillerie schon auf sie. Ihre Schüße und Kugeln hielten die erste und zweite Welle auf. Jedoch der dritten Angriff jagte die linke Seite der Union, die unter dem Kommando von General Carr stand, westlich bis jenseits der Elkhorn Tavern. General Pike's Cherokees drängten vorwärts und brachen eine weitere Uniondivision. Ein Gegenangriff bei Uniontruppen eroberte für sie das Gelände, das verloren war. Price's vierter Angriff drängte Carr's Truppen weiter zurück. Als die Nacht über das Schlachtfeld einbrach, rückten die Reserveeinheiten der Union vor und stabilisierten die Linie.

Am 8. wurde General Sigel befohlen, die Konföderierten in der Umgebung der Elkhorn Tavern anzugreifen. Seine beiden Infanteriedivisionen stürzten sich auf die Missourianer und trieben sie zur Flucht. General Carr griff dann die linke Seite der Konföderierten an und trieb sie ebenfalls zurück. Mit seiner ganzen Linie jetzt gebrochen, befahl General Van Dorn den Rückzug.

BEDEUTUNG

Dies war der erste Entscheidungssieg für die Union in einer Schlacht westlich des Mi.ssissippi.

Die Hoffnung der Konföderierten, den Kampf bis nach Missouri hineinzubringen, wurde vorübergehend zunichte gemacht.

The last hour of the battle, General Sterling Price rallies Hill's troops as the Federals advance and retake the position at Elkhorn Tavern.

State: Virginia

U.S.	C.S.
Commander:	Commander:
Lt. John Worden	Lt. Catesby Jones
U.S. Ship: U.S.S. Monitor	C.S. Ship: C.S.S. Virginia
Crew Compliment: 58	Crew Compliment: 250
Casualties:	Casualties:
Killed: 0	Killed: 2
Wounded: 3	Wounded: 19
Captured or Missing: 0	Captured or Missing: 0

COMMENTS

Just after the Civil War began in April 1861, Union forces evacuated the city of Norfolk, Virginia, destroying the ships and port facilities located there. These steps were taken to deny their use by the Confederates. Among the naval vessels destroyed was the 40 gun steam frigate U.S.S. Merrimac, which was in port for engine repair. The destruction was incomplete and the Confederate navy raised the scuttled vessel and rebuilt her as an iron clad. At that time only three iron clad vessels existed. Two in England and one in France.

Work began in the summer of 1861. The wooden sides were angled and covered with iron sheeting 4 inches thick. Above the water line Merrimac's hull was almost impenetrable to shot and shell because an armor piercing shell had not been invented. The Merrimac did have its problems. It could not operate in shallow water, nor was it seaworthy in the open ocean. The engines were unreliable but her weakest point was the rudder and propeller, which were both exposed to fire.

Union authorities were aware of the Confederate work on the Merrimac and searched for a way to counter the threat. An inventor named John Ericsson submitted plans for an iron clad vessel to the Union navy. The vessel was small, could operate in shallow water, and the design left only a low deck and gun turret above the water line. This made the ship less vulnerable to fire. The new ship was named the Monitor and like its Confederate counterpart was not perfect. Its low deck made it very unseaworthy and it had significant ventilation problems. The government accepted the design with the stipulation that the Monitor would be built in only 100 days and if it was unsuccessful Ericsson would receive no money.

On March 8, 1862, the completed Merrimac, renamed the C.S.S. Virginia, steamed toward Union Fort Monroe and Hampton Roads. She engaged three Union warships, the U.S.S. Cumberland, the U.S.S. Congress, and the U.S.S. Minnesota. The wooden warships were helpless. Virginia sank the Cumberland, burned the Congress, and ran the Minnesota aground. The Virginia then retired for the evening, planning to return the next morning and finish the Minnesota.

While the Virginia wrecked the Union navy, the Monitor steamed to help, arriving inside Hampton Roads at darkness on the 8th. The next morning Virginia came back to finish the battle. The fighting began at 8:45 A.M. and the two ships pounded each other unmercifully for 3 and 1/2 hours. The combat was close and at one point the two ships collided with one another. The Monitor was struck no less than 22 times by cannon fire. During the engagement a shell exploded near the viewing port of the pilot house and wounded Lt. Worden, the commander of the Monitor. The combat was indecisive, few casualties were sustained, and neither vessel destroyed the other.

SIGNIFICANCE

It was the first fight between iron clad vessels.
It made the wooden navies of the world obsolete.

Important Landmarks
Fort Monroe
Virginia Peninsula

Etat: Virginie

Etats-Unis	Etats Confédérés
Commandant:	Commandant:
Lieutenant John Woren	Lieutenant Catesby Jones
Vaisseau: U.S.S. Monitor	Vaisseau: C.S.S. Virginia
Equipage: 58	Equipage: 250
Pertes:	Pertes:
Tués: 0	Tués: 2
Blessés: 3	Blessés: 19
Prisonniers ou disparus: 0	Prisonniers ou disparus: 0

COMMENTAIRE

Juste après le comencement de la Guerre Civile, le 12 avril 1861, les forces fédérales evacuèrent la ville de Norfolk en Virginie, détuisant les navives et les facilités du port, afin d'en priver l'usage aux Confédérés. Parmi les vaisseaux détruits fut la frigate à vapeur, l'U.S.S. Merrimac, 40 canons, qui fut là pour la réparation de ses machines. La destruction ne fut pas complète, et la marine confédérée le réleva, le reconstruisit en cuirassé, et le renomma Virginia. A cette époque. Il n'y eut que trois cuirasses existants dans le monde entier, deux en Angleterre et un en France.

Le travaille de reconstruction commença pendant l'été de 1861. La coque en bois fut inclinée et couvete de plaques de fer d'une épaisseur de quatre pouces. Au dessus de la ligne de flottaison, la coque du Virginia fut presqu' impénétrable par les munitions de l'époque. Le Virginia eut ses problèmes. Il ne pouvait pas opérer dans les eaux peu profondes, et il ne tint pas bien la mer. Ses machines ne furent pas assez puissantes, mais ses points les plus faibles furent son gouvernail et son hélice qui ne furent pas protégés par le blindage, et par conséquant, vulnérables au feu ennemi.

Les authorités fédérales savait que les Confédérés travaillaient sur la construction d'un curassé, et ils cherchaient un moyen de le contrcarrer. Un inventeur, John Ericsson, soumit un plan à la marine fédérale d'un cuirassé. Le vaisseau fut petit, de peu de tirant, et seule un pont bas et une tourelle furent visible au dessus de la ligne de flottaison. Donc le vaisseau fut un cible difficile pour les canonniers ennemis. Le nouveau vaisseau s'appela Monitor et ne tint pas bien la mer à cause de son pont bas, et il eut des problèmes de ventilation aussi. Le gouvenement accepta le projet d'Erickson mais stipula que le navire dut être compléter dans 100 jours et qu'au cas d'insuccès, Ericsson ne recevrait rien.

Le 8 mars 1862, le Virginia mit le cap sur Fort Monroe et Hampton Roads. Il attaqua trois navires de guerre: l'U.S.S. Congress, l'U.S.S. Cumberland, et l'U.S.S. Minnesota. Ces vaisseaux en bois ne pouvaient rien contre le curassé confédéré. Le Virginia coula le Cumberland, brûla le Congress et força le Minnesota à s'échouer. Le Virginia, comptant administrer le coup de grâce au Minnesota le lendemain, se retira.

Pendant que le Virginia ruinait la marine fédérale, le Monitor accourait à la rescousse, arrivant à Hampton Roads pendant la nuit du 8. Le matin suivant le Virginia revint pour terminer la bataille. Le combat commença à 8 h 45, et les deux vaisseaux se pilonnaient sans merci pendant 3 1/2 heures. Les deux navires se rapprchaient à tel point qu'ils se sont entrechoqués. Le Monitor reçut 22 impacts. Pendant le combat un obus éclata pres de l'abri de navigation et blessa le lieutenant Worden, commandant du Monitor. Ce fut un engagement indécis; il y eut peu de pertes, et ni l'un ni l'autre des adversaires ne fut victorieux.

CONSEQUENCE

Ce fut le premier combat entre cuirassés de l'histoire.
Les navires de bois sont maintenant périmés.

The C.S.S. Virginia and U.S.S. Monitor engaged in the first battle between ironclad ships.

Estado: Virginia

U.S.	C.S.
Comandante:	**Comandante:**
El teniente John Worden	El teniente Catesby Jones
El buque de U.S.: U.S.S. Monitor	El buque de C.S.: C.S.S. Virginia
Tripulación: 58	Tripulación: 250
Pérdidas:	Pérdidas:
Muertos: 0	Muertos: 2
Heridos: 3	Heridos: 19
Capturados o desaparecidos: 0	Capturados o desaparecidos: 0

COMENTARIOS

Justo después de que la Guerra Civil empezara en abril de 1861, fuerzas de la Unión evacuaron la ciudad de Norfolk, Virginia, destruyendo los barcos y las facilidades del puerto localizadas allí. Estos pasos fueron tomados para negar el uso a los Confederados. Entre los buques destruídos estaba el 40 cañonero de vapor U.S.S. Merrimac, el cual estaba en el puerto para la reparación del motor. La destrucción fue incompleta y la Marina de guerra Confederada sacó la nave barrenada y la reconstruyó como un acorazado. En ese momento sólo tres de esos buques acorazados existían. Dos en Inglaterra y uno en Francia.

El trabajo empezó en el verano de 1861. Los lados de madera fueron angulares recubiertos con láminas de hierro de cuatro pulgadas de grueso. Por encima de la línea del agua el casco del Merrimac era casi impenetrable por balas o balas de cañones porque una bomba que penetrara la coraza no había sido inventada. El Merrimac tenía sus problemas. No podía operar en agua poco profunda, ni era buen navegador en el océano abierto. Los motores eran de poca confianza pero su punto más débil era el timón y el hélice ambos fueron expuestos al fuego.

Autoridades de la Unión sabían que los Confederados trabajaban en el Merrimac y buscaron una forma de responder la amenaza. Un inventor llamado John Ericsson propuso planes para un buque de guerra acorazado a la Marina de guerra de la Unión. El buque era pequeño y podría operar en agua poco profunda y el diseño dejó sólo una cubierta baja y una torre blindada de cañón por encima de la línea del agua. Esto hizo el barco menos vulnerable al fuego. El nuevo barco fue llamado el Monitor y como su doble no era perfecto. Su cubierta baja lo hizo muy mal navegador y tenía problemas significantes de ventilación. El gobierno aceptó el diseño con el acuerdo de que el Monitor sería construído en sólo cien días y si no tenía éxito Ericsson no recibiría dinero.

El 8 de marzo de 1862, el Merrimac terminado, se le renombró el C.S.S. de Virginia, tomó rumbo hacia el Fuerte Monroe de la Unión y las carreteras de Hampton. Entró en combate con tres buques de guerra de la Unión el U.S.S. Cumberland, el U.S.S. Congress, y el U.S.S. Minnesota. Los buques de madera estuvieron imposibilitados. El Virginia hundió el Cumberland, quemó el Congress, y encalló el Minnesota. El Virginia, entonces, se retiró por esa noche, planeando represar a la mañana siguiente y acabar con el Minnesota.

Mientras el Virginia destruía la Marina de la Unión, el Monitor salió para ayudar, llegó al interior de las carreteras de Hampton al oscurecer del día 8. A la mañana siguiente el Virginia regresó para acabar la batalla. La lucha empezó a las 8:45 de la mañana y los dos buques se aporrearon sin misericordia por tres horas y media. El combate estuvo muy reñido y hubo un momento en que los dos buques chocaron. El Monitor fue golpeado no menos de 22 veces por el fuego de los cañones. Durante el enfrentamiento una bomba explotó cerca de la cañonera de la timonera hiriendo al teniente Worden, el comandante del Monitor. El combate fue indeciso, algunas pérdidas fueron sustentadas, y los buques no se destruyeron.

CONSECUENCIAS

Fue el primer combate entre buques con corazas de hierro.
Hizo que los barcos de madera fueran los más anticuados del mundo.

Staat: Virginia

US Kommandant:	CS Kommandant:
Lieutenant John Worden	Lieutenant Catesby Jones
U.S. Ship: U.S.S. Monitor	CS Ship: C.S.S. Virginia
Schiffsmannschaft: 58	Schiffsmannschaft: 250
Verluste:	Verluste:
Gefallen: 0	Gefallen: 2
Verwundet: 3	Verwundet: 19
Gefangengenommen oder vermißt: 0	Gefangengenommen oder vermißt: 0

KOMMENTAR

Im April 1861, unmittelbar nach dem Beginn des Zivilkrieges, evakuierten Unionstreitkräfte die Stadt Norfolk in Virginia, nachdem sie Schiffe und Hafenanlagen zerstört hatten. Diese Schritte waren unternommen, um den Konföderierten deren Benützung zu verweigern. Unter den zerstörten Marineschiffen befand sich die 40 Kanonen Dampf Fregatte Merrimac, die sich für Maschinenreparaturen im Hafen befand. Glücklicherweise gelang es nicht, die Fregatte vollkommen zu zerstören, und die Konföderierte Marine hob das gesunkene Schiff und baute es in ein Panzerschiff um. Nur drei Panzerschiffe existierten zu der Zeit - zwei in England und eines in Frankreich.

Die Arbeit an der Merrimac begann im Somner 1861. Die rechtwinkligen Holzplankenseiten wurden mit 10 cm dicker eiserner Verkleidung bedeckt. Über der Wasserlinie war Merrimac's Rumpf beinahe undurchdringlich für Geschoße — ein Geschoß mit der Kapazität Armorierung zu durchbrechen war zu der Zeit noch nicht erfunden. Aber Merrimac war nicht frei von Problemen. Das Schiff konnte nicht in seichtem Wasser funktionieren, noch war es seetüchtig. Ihre Maschinen waren unzuverläßig, aber der grosste Schwachpunkt waren Steuerruder und Propeller - beide waren der Gefahr von feindlichem Feuer ausgesetzt.

Authoritäten der Union hatten Kenntnis von der Arbeit an Merrimac und suchten für einen Weg, sich dieser Bedrohung entgegenstellen zu können. Ein Erfinder - John Ericsson - legte der Unionmarine einen Entwurf für ein Panzerschiff vor. Das Schiff war klein, konnte in seichtem Wasser operieren, und der Entwurf erlaubte nur ein Niederdeck und einen Geschützturm über der Wasserlinie. Dies setzte die Gefahr durch feindliches Feuer bedeutend niedriger. Das neue Schiff - der Monitor - war, evenso wie sein Konföderiertes Ebenbild, nicht ohne Makel. Sein Niederdeck machte es äusserst seeuntüchtig und bedeutsame Probleme in der Ventilation kamen zum Vorschein. Die Unionregierung nahm den Entwurf an, mit der Bedingung, daß der Monitor innerhalb 100 Tagen erbaut werden könnte. Aber sollte dies erfolglos sein, keine Bezahlung würde an Ericsson gehen.

Vollkommen ausgerüstet, Merrimac - unter ihrem neuen Namen C.S.S. Virginia - dampfte am 8. März in Richtung auf das Union Fort Monroe und Hampton Roads. Sie griff drei Kriegsschiffe der Union an: U.S.S. Cumberland, U.S.S. Congress, and U.S.S. Minnesota. Die Holzplankenschiffe waren hilflos - die Virginia sank Cumberland, setzte Congress in Brand, und strandete Minnesota. Dann zog sie sich zurück für die Nacht, mit dem Plan, am folgenden Morgen zurückzukehren um die Vernichtung der Minnesota zu vervollständigen.

Während des Kampfes, in dem die Virginia die Unionmarine vernichtete, dampfte der Monitor zur Hilfe und erreichte am 8., bei Dunkelheit, Hampton Roads. Am nächsten Morgen kehrte die Virginia zurück, um der Schlacht ein Ende zu machen. Der Kampf begann um 8:45 und beide Schiffe hämmerten sich gegenseitig erbarmungslos für 3 1/2 Stunden. Der Kampf wogte ziemlich im Ausgleich und in einer Phase stießen beide Schiffe zusammen. Der Monitor erhielt nicht weniger als 22 Treffer bei Kanonenfeuer. Während der Schlacht explodierte eine Kugel in der Nähe der Aussichtsluke des Pilotenhauses und verwundete den Kommandant des Monitors, Lt. Worden. Der Kampf lief unentschieden aus, kostete wenige Verluste, und ließ keines der Schiffe kampfunfähig.

BEDEUTUNG

Dies war der erste Kampf zwischen Panzerschiffen.
Die Holzschiffe der Marinen der Welt bekamen rudimentär.

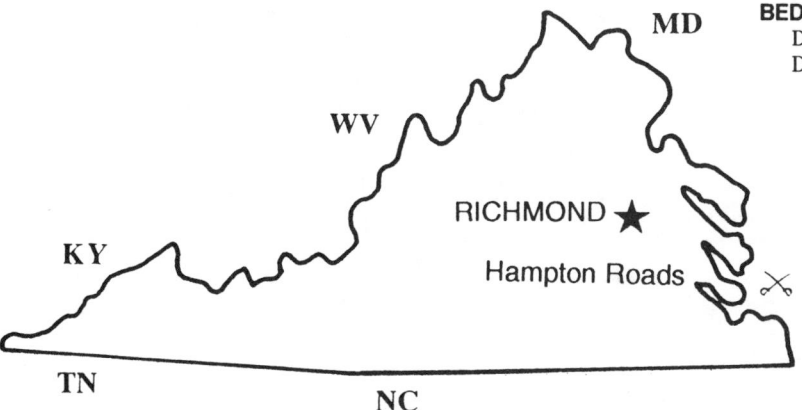

MD

WV

KY

RICHMOND ★

Hampton Roads

TN

NC

State: Tennessee		Etat: Tennessee	
U.S.	**C.S.**	**Etat-Unis**	**Etat Confédérés**
Commander:	Commander:	Commandant:	Commandant:
Maj. Gen. U.S. Grant	Gen. Albert Sidney Johnston	Général de division U.S Grant	Général Albert Sidney Johnston
Maj. Gen. Don Carlos Buell	Gen. P.G.T. Beauregard	Général de division Don Carlos Buell	Général P.G.T. Beauregard
U.S. Army: Army of the Tennessee	C.S. Army: Army of the Mississippi	Armée: du Tennessee et de l'Ohio	Armée: du Mississippi
Army of the Ohio	No. of Troops: 44,000	65 000 soldats	44 000 soldats
No. of Troops: 65,000			
Casualties:	Casualties:	Pertes:	Pertes:
Killed: 1,754	Killed: 1,728	Tués: 1 754	Tués: 1 728
Wounded: 8,408	Wounded: 8,012	Blessés: 8 408	Blessés: 8 012
Captured or missing: 2,885	Captured or missing: 959	Prisonniers ou disparus: 2 885	Prisonniers ou disparus: 959

COMMENTS

Gen. Grant, after his victories at Forts Henry and Donelson, pushed south along the Tennessee River to join Gen. Buell's 20,000 man army and threaten the Confederate railroad center of Corinth, Mississippi, Grant was camped at Pittsburg Landing on the Tennessee River.

On April 6, Johnston opened the battle with a surprise attack at 5 a.m. The Union divisions of Sherman, Prentiss, and McClernand encamped near Shiloh Church were overrun by the initial Confederate attack. Gen. Prentiss' division reorganized itself along a sunken road in a wooded thicket soon to be known as "The Hornet's Nest" because of the great number of bullets "buzzing" through the air. The Confederates charged "The Hornet's Nest" 12 times but could not dislodge the Northerners.

Around 2:30 Gen. Johnston, personally directing the attacks, was shot in the leg and he soon bled to death. Gen. Beauregard assumed command of the Southern Army. He positioned 62 cannons to fire into "The Hornet's Nest." For two hours the Confederate gunners shelled Prentiss' division, and at 5:30, he and 2000 men surrendered. Gen. Prentiss held out long enough to give Gen. Grant time to form a new line on a ridge overlooking the Tennessee River.

With the addition of some heavy artillery and two gunboats, Grant's line was very strong and Beauregard wisely decided not to attack.

During the night Gen. Buell's army reinforced Grant. The morning of April 7 was bloody, but the Federals steadily pushed the Confederates back. By late afternoon Beauregard ordered a withdrawal to Corinth. The Federals did not pursue.

SIGNIFICANCE

This "victory" was another step toward cutting the Confederacy in half. By late May the Southern army moved farther south, leaving Corinth and severing the railroad from Memphis to Chattanooga. This left only the forts near Vicksburg on the Mississippi River in Southern hands.

COMMENTAIRE

Après ses victoires aux Forts Henry et Donelson, le général Grant avança vers le sud le long de la rivière du Tennessee pour rejoindre les 20 000 hommes du général Buell. Il comptait menacer les Confédérés situés sur la voie ferrée au centre de Corinthe, dans le Mississipi. Grant campa à Pittsburg Landing, au bord du Tennessee.

Le 6 avril, Johnston ouvrit la bataille par une attaque surprise à 5 heures du matin. Les divisions de l'Union de Sherman, Prentiss et McClernand, installées près de l'église de Shiloh furent renversées par l'attaque initiale des Confédérés. La division du général Prentiss se réorganisa dans un fourré, appelé bientôt "Le nid de guêpes" à cause du grand nombre de balles qui en echappant et bourdonnaient dans l'air. Les Confédérés attaquèrent le "nid de guêpes" 12 fois sans pourvoir déloger les Nordistes.

Vers 2h30, le général Johnston, qui dirigeait les attaques, fut blessé à la jambe et saigna à mort. Le général Beauregard prit la commande de l'armée sudiste. Il mit 62 canons en position pour tirer sur le "nid de guêpes." Pendant deux heures, les canons des Confédérés bombardèrent la division de Prentiss, qui se rendit à 5h30 avec 2 000 hommes. Le général Prentiss avait tenu assez longtemps pour donner au général Grant le temps de former une nouvelle ligne sur les hauteurs dominant la rivière du Tennessee.

Renforcées par de l'artillerie lourde et deux chaloupes canonnières, les lignes de Grant étaient puissantes, et Beauregard eut la sagesse de ne pas attaquer.

Pendant la nuit, l'armée de Buell renforça celle de Grant. Le matin du 7 avril fut sanglant, mais l'Union repoussa fermement les Confédérés. Dans l'après-midi, Beauregard avait ordonné un repli sur Corinthe. Les Fédéraux n'insistèrent pas.

CONSEQUENCES

Cette victoire fut une nouvelle étape vers la coupure en deux de Confédération. A la fin du mois de mai, les armées sudistes descendirent plus au sud, laissant Corinthe et coupant le chemin de fer de Memphis à Chattanooga. Ceci ne laissait aux mains des Sudistse que les forts proches de Visksburg sur la rivière du Mississipi.

Important Landmarks
"Hornet's Nest"/Sunken Road
Pittsburg Landing
Bloody Pond
Peach Orchard
Tennessee River
Fraley Field

Important Buildings
Shiloh Church
Cherry Mansion (Savannak, TN)
War Cabin

Estado: Tennessee

U.S.	C.S.
Comandantes:	Comandantes:
Maj. Gen. U.S. Grant	Gen. Albert Sidney Johnston
Maj. Gen. Don Carlos Buell	Gen. P.G.T. Beauregard
U.S. Ejército: Army of the Tennessee	C.S. Ejército: Army of the Mississippi
Army of the Ohio	No. de tropas: 65,000
No. de tropas: 65,000	
Pérdidas:	Pérdidas:
Muertos: 1,754	Muertos: 1,728
Heridos: 8,408	Heridos: 8,012
Capturados o ausentes: 2,885	Capturados o ausentes: 959

COMENTARIOS

El General Grant, después de sus victorias en los fuertes Henry y Donelson, salió para el sur por el río Tennessee para juntarse con el ejército de 20,000 tropas bajo el General Buell. Quería amenazar el centro de ferrocarriles Confederados en Corinth Mississippi. Grant acampaba en Pittsburg Landing al lado del río Tennessee.

El día 6 de abril, Johnston abrió la batalla con un ataque de sorpresa a las 5 de la mañana. Las divisiones Federales bajo Sherman, Prentiss, y McClernand acampando cerca de la iglesia Shiloh fueron dominadas por el primer ataque Confederado. La división del General Prentiss se reorganizó por un camino sumido en un bosquecito que llegó a llamarse "The Hornet's Nest" (Panal de avispón) por el gran número de balas "zumbando" por el aire. Los Confederados atacaron The Hornet's Nest 12 veces pero no pudieron desalojar a los Norteños.

Cerca de las dos y media el General Johnston, personalmente dirigiendo los ataques, recibió un tiro en la pierna y pronto sangró hasta morirse. El General Beauregard se hizo comandante de las fuerzas sureñas. El posicionó 62 cañones para disparar hacia The Hornet's Nest. Por dos horas los artilleros Confederados bombardearon la división de Prentiss, y a las 5:30, él y 2000 hombres se rendieron. Pero el General Prentiss mantuvo su posición por bastante tiempo para que el General Grant tuviera tiempo para formar una línea nueva en un lomo que miraba el río Tennessee.

Con la adición de artillería pesada y dos barcos armados, la línea de Grant era muy fuerte y Beauregard inteligentemente decidió no atacar.

Durante la noche el ejército del General Buell reforzó él de Grant. La mañana del día 7 fue sangrienta, pero los Federales continúamente empujaron a los Confederados para atrás. Por la tarde, Beauregard mandó un retiro a Corinth. Los Yanquis no los persiguieron.

CONSECUENCIAS

Esta victoria fue otro paso hacia el corte de los estados Confederados en dos partes. Al final de mayo el ejército sureño se movió más para el sur, dejando Corinth y cortando la línea de ferrocarril entre Memphis y Chatanooga. Esto dejó sólamente los fuertes cerca de Vicksburg en el río Mississippi en las manos de los Confederados.

Staat: Tennessee

Befehlshaber der US:	Befehlshaber der CS:
Generalmajor Ulysses S. Grant	Generalmajor Albert Sidney
Generalmajor Don Carlos Buell	Johnston
Armee der US: Armee von Tennessee,	Armee der CS: Armee von Mississippi
Armee von Ohio	Truppenstärke: 44,000
Truppenstärke: 65,000	
Verluste:	Verluste:
Gefallen: 1,754	Gefallen: 1,728
Verwundet: 8,408	Verwundet: 8,012
Gefangengenommen oder	Gefangengenommen oder
vermißt: 2,885	vermißt: 959

KOMMENTAR

Nach seinen Siegen über die Forts Henry und Donelson, drängte sich General Grant südwärts am Tennessee Fluß entlang, um sich an General Buell's Armee von 20,000 Mann anzuschließen. Er plante dann Corinth in Mississippi, ein Zentralpunkt der Eisenbahn der Konföderierten, anzudrohen. Grant lagerte sich an Pittsburg Landing am Tennessee Fluß.

Am 6. April, um 5.00 Uhr, eröffnete Johnston die Schlacht mit einem Überraschungsangriff. Die Uniondivisionen von Sherman, Prentiss und McClernand, die ihr Lager nahe der Shiloh Church bezogen hatten, wurden vom ersten Konföderierten Vorstoß überrannt. General Prentiss' Division organisierte sich wieder in einem Dickicht, entlang einer tiefliegenden Straße. In Kürze wurde dieses Gebiet, wegen der großen Zahl von Kugeln, die durch die Luft "summten", "Das Wespennest" genannt. Zwölf Mal stürmten die Konföderierten "Das Wespennest", konnten aber die Uniontruppen nicht verdrängen.

Um 14.30 Uhr wurde General Johnston, der die Angriffe persönlich führte, ins Bein getroffen und verblutete schnell. General Beauregard übernahm das Kommando der Föderalisten Armee. Er stellte 62 Kanonen so auf, daß sie ins "Wespennest" feuern konnten. Zwei Stunden lang stand Prentiss' Division unter Beschuß, und um 17.30 Uhr kapitulierte er mit 2,000 Mann. General Prentiss hatte lange genug ausgehalten, sodaß General Grant eine neue Linie auf den Höhen, mit Blick auf den Tennessee Fluß, aufstellen konnte.

Durch die Zufuhr von schwerem Geschütz, und zwei Kanonenbooten, war Grant's Linie sehr stark geworden, und Beauregard traf die kluge Entscheidung, nicht anzugreifen.

In der Nacht verstärkte General Buell's Armee General Grant. Der Morgen vom 7. April war blutig, aber die Föderalisten drängten die Konföderierten allmählich zurück. Am späten Nachmittag beorderte Beauregard den Rückzug nach Corinth. Die Föderalisten verfolgten sie nicht.

BEDEUTUNG

Dieser "Sieg" war ein weiterer Schritt auf dem Weg zur Spaltung der Konföderation. Die Konföderationarmee zog sich weiter nach Süden, als sie Ende Mai Corinth verließen und die Bahnlinie von Memphis nach Chattanooga unterbrochen hatte. Als Folge davon blieben nur die Forte am Mississippi Fluß, in der Nähe von Vicksburg, in südstaatlichen Händen.

A battery of 24-pdr. siege guns that formed a part of Grant's "Last Line" above Pittsburg Landing.

FORT PULASKI

State: Georgia

U.S.
Commander:
 Brig. Gen. Thomas W. Sherman
 Chief Eng. Capt. Quincy A.
 Gillmore
U.S. Army:
 No. of Troops: 11,100
Casualties:
 Killed: 1
 Wounded: 0
 Captured or missing: 0

C.S.
Commander:
 Col. Charles H. Olmstead

C.S. Army:
 No. of Troops: 385
Casualties:
 Killed: 1
 Wounded: 13
 Captured or missing: 371

COMMENTS

Fort Pulaski is located near the mouth of the Savannah River in Georgia. The port of Savannah was a haven for blockade runners. With the fort guarding the mouth of the river, it became a serious hole in the Federal naval blockade.

In February 1862, an expedition was sent to Tybee Island, near the fort. Gillmore immediately started work on eleven artillery batteries facing Fort Pulaski. Since the batteries were within range of the Confederate guns, the Federals could only work at night. Each night's work was camouflaged before daylight so that the Confederates wouldn't know what was being done. By April 9, the Federals were ready, armed with smoothbore and rifled cannons and mortars. On April 10, a request for surrender was sent to the fort. Col. Olmstead, the commander of the fort, refused to surrender and both sides prepared for battle. A mortar signaled the start of the bombardment at 8:15 a.m. The rate of fire was slow at first but increased as the day progressed. By the end of the day, the fort, although scarred by the shot and shells, still looked solid to the Federals. On the inside, however, the fort was in a shambles. The firing picked up again the next morning. Shortly, several holes in the walls of the fort became visible as the bricks crumbled away from the shot of the rifled cannons. Shells passed over the breach and threatened the fort's powder magazine. Olmstead now had to face being blown up by his own gunpowder. By 2:30 p.m. on April 11, a white flag was raised over the fort.

SIGNIFICANCE

Savannah was closed as a blockade-running port.

A new way of building "stationary" forts would have to be developed. This battle showed that "old" masonry forts couldn't stand up to the "new" rifled cannons.

Etat: Georgie

Etat-Unis
Commandants:
 Général de Brigade Thomas W.
 Sherman, Chef Ingénier Capitaine
 Quincy A. Gilmore
Armée:
 11 100 soldats
Pertes:
 Tué: 1
 Blessé: 0
 Prisonnier ou disparu: 0

Etat Confédérés
Commandant:
 Colonel Charles H. Olmstead

Armée:
 385 soldats
Pertes:
 Tué: 1
 Blessés: 13
 Prisonniers ou disparus: 371

COMMENTAIRE

Le Fort Pulaski est situé près de l'embouchure de la rivière Savannah, devenait un refuge pour les forceurs de blocus naval unioniste.

En février 1862, une expédition arriva à l'île Tybee, près du fort. Gillmore se mit aussitôt au travail avec 11 batteries d'artilleries faisant face au fort Pulaski. Les batteries étant à portée des coups des Confédérés, l'armée fédérale ne pouvait travailler que la nuit. La travail de chaque nuit était camouflé avant le lever du jour pour que les Confédérés ne sachent pas ce qui avait été fait. Le 9 avril, les troupes de l'Union étaient prêtes, armées de lance-bombes, de canons à âme lisse et de canons rayés. Le 10 avril, le fort futt sommé de se rendre. Le colonel Olmstead, commandant le fort, refusa, et les deux armées se préparèrent pour la bataille. Un lance-bombe signala le commencement du bombardement à 8h15. Durant la journée, le rythme des feux s'intensifia. A la fin de ce jour, le fort, bienqu'endommagé par les obus et les boulets, conservait pour l'Union un air solide. A l'intrieur du fort, cependant, c'était un désastre. Les feux reprirent le matin suivant. En peu de temps, plusieurs trous devinrent visibles dans les murs du fort tandis que les briques s'écroulaient sous les coups des canons rayés. Des obus passèrent par-dessus la brèche menaçant la poudrière du fort. Olmstead voyait maintenant le risque d'explosion du fort par sa propre poudre à canon. Le 11 avril à 14h30, le drapeau blanc flottait au-dessus du fort.

CONSEQUENCES

Comme port de forcement de blocus, Savannah fut fermé.

Il devenait nécessaire de trouver un nouveau moyen de construire les forts stationnaires. Cette bataille montra que la vieille maçonnerie ne pouvait pas résister aux nouveaux canons rayés.

TN   NC

ATLANTA   SC

AL

Ft. Pulaski

FL

Important Landmarks
Cockspur Island
Savannah River
Big Tybee Island

Important Buildings
Tybee Light House
Martello Tower
(destroyed during World War II)

The breach and ruins in the southeast angle of the fort.

Estado: Georgia

U.S.	C.S.
Comandante:	Comandante:
Brig. Gen. Thomas W. Sherman	Col. Charles H. Olmstead
Jefe de Ingenieros:	
Capt. Quincy A. Gillmore	
U.S. Ejército:	C.S. Ejército:
No. de tropas: 11,100	No. de tropas: 385
Pérdidas:	Pérdidas:
Muertos: 1	Muertos: 1
Heridos: 0	Heridos: 13
Capturados o ausentes: 0	Capturados o ausentes: 371

COMENTARIOS

Fort Pulaski está localizado cerca de la boca del río Savannah en Georgia. El puerto de Savannah era un asilo para los que pasaban por el bloqueo para traer municiones y otros materiales al sur. Por el hecho de que el fuerte guardaba la boca del río, llegó a ser un problema grave para la armada Federal.

En febrero de 1862 una expedición fue enviada a la isla de Tybee, cerca del fuerte. Gillmore inmediatamente comenzó a trabajar poniendo 11 baterías a entrentarse con Fort Pulaski. Como las baterías estaban en el alcance de la artillería Confederada, los Federales sólamente podían trabajar por la noche. El trabajo de cada noche fue camuflado antes del amanecer para que los sureños no supieran lo que se estaba haciendo. Por la tarde, los Federales estaban listos, armados con morteros, y cañones rayados y barrenos lisos. El 10 de abril, una demanda para la rendición fue mandada al fuerte. El Col. Olmstead, comandante del fuerte, rehusó rendirse, y los dos lados se prepararon para la batalla. Un mortero señaló el comienzo del bombardeo a las 8:15 de la mañana. Al principio tiraban despacio, pero durante el curso del día la proporción creció. Al final del día, el fuerte, aunque marcado con grietas, todavía les parecía sólido a los Yanquis desde afuera. Dentro del fuerte, sin embargo, el fuerte era un desastre. Los tiros empezaron de nuevo por la mañana siguiente. Pronto, varios agujeros aparecieron en las paredes como los ladrillos se desmenuzaban por los tiros de los cañones rayados. Las bombas pasaban por encima de la brecha y amenazaban el polvorín. Ahora Olmstead tuvo que enfrentarse con el problema de morir por su propia pólvora. A las 2:30, el día 11 de abril, una bandera blanca se levantó encima del fuerte.

CONSECUENCIAS

Savannah se cerró como puerto de proveedores.

Una nueva manera de construir fuertes de estacionamiento tendría que ser desarrollada. Esta batalla mostró que los fuertes antiguos de ladrillos no podían resistir los tiros de los cañones rayados.

Staat: Georgia

Befehlshaber der US:	Befehlshaber der CS:
Brigadegeneral	Oberst Charles H. Olmstead
Thomas W. Sherman	
Hauptingenieur:	
Hauptmann Quincy A. Gilmore	
Armee der US:	Armee der CS:
Truppenstärke: 11,000	Truppenstärke: 385
Verluste:	Verluste:
Gefallen: 1	Gefallen: 1
Verwundet: 0	Verwundet: 13
Gefangengenommen oder vermißt: 0	Gefangengenommen oder vermißt: 371

KOMMENTAR

Fort Pulaski liegt nahe der Mündung des Savannah Flußes in Georgia. Der Hafen von Savannah war ein Zufluchtsort für Blockadebrecher. Da das Fort die Flußmündung schützte, bekam der Hafen eine bedeutende Lücke in der Seeblockade der Föderalisten.

Im February 1862 wurde eine Expedition auf Tybee Island, in der Nähe des Forts gesandt. Hauptmann Gillmore machte sich sofort an die Arbeit and den elf Artilleriebatterien, die auf Fort Pulaski gerichtet waren. Da die Batterien in Schußweite der Kanonen der Konföderierten lagen, konnten die Föderalisten nur bei Nacht arbeiten. Vor Tagesanbruch wurde die Nachtarbeit wieder getarnt, sodaß die Konföderierten nicht wußten, was vorging. Am 9. April waren die Föderalisten bereit. Ihre Geschütze waren mit glattem und gerilltem Lauf, und mit Minenwerfern bewaffnet. Am 10. April wurde eine Kapitulationsforderung auf das Fort gesandt. Oberst Olmstead, Kommandant des Forts, verweigerte sich zu ergeben, und beide Seiten bereiteten sich zum Kampf auf. Um 8.15 Uhr meldete ein Kanonenschuß den Beginn der Bombardierung an. Am Anfang kamen die Salven langsam, aber das Tempo steigerte sich im Laufe des Tages. Am Tagesende trug das Fort zwar Spuren der Bombardierung, doch schien es den Föderalisten, immer noch standfest zu halten. Innerhalb des Fortes war allerdings ein heilloser Durcheinander. Am nächsten Morgen setzte sich das Bombardement fort, und in kurzer Zeit waren Löcher in den Mauern sichtbar, als Backsteine unter dem Feuer der gerillten Kanonen bröckelten. Granaten flogen über die Bresche und drohten dem Pulvermagazin. Jetzt mußte sich Olmstead mit der Möglichkeit befaßen, daß er durch sein eigenes Pulvermagazin in die Luft gesprengt werden könnte. Am 11. April wurde um 14.30 Uhr eine weisse Fahne über dem Fort hochgezogen.

BEDEUTUNG

Savannah wurde als Hafen für Blockadebrecher geschlossen.

Man mußte eine neue Bautechnik für "feste" Forte entwickeln. Diese Schlacht zeigte, daß das "alte" Mauerwerk den "neuen" gezogenen Kanonen nicht standhalten konnte.

Captain Quincy A. Gillmore, Chief Engineer

Colonel Charles H. Olmstead

State: Virginia

U.S.

Commander:
  Maj. Gen. John C. Fremont
  Maj. Gen. Nathaniel P. Banks
  Brig. Gen. James Shields
U.S. Army: separate commands
  No. of Troops: 34,000
Casualties:
  Killed: 398
  Wounded: 1,808
  Captured or missing: 2,463

C.S.

Commander:
  Maj. Gen. Thomas J. Jackson

C.S. Army: Army of the Valley
  No. of Troops: 16,000
Casualties:
  Killed: 230
  Wounded: 1,373
  Captured or missing: 232

COMMENTS

Gen. McClellan's Union army had been advancing toward Richmond since April. In May, Gen. "Stonewall" Jackson started an offensive campaign in the Shenandoah Valley planned to prevent McClellan from getting additional reinforcements from the Union armies in the valley.

Jackson opened the campaign by marching his troops toward the Allegheny mountains. On May 8 the Confederates attacked Maj. Gen. John Fremont at the Battle of McDowell. The Federals were defeated and withdrew to the west. Jackson then marched his troops to engage Maj. Gen. Nathaniel Banks. On May 23 the Southerners overwhelmed a small part of Bank's army at Front Royal. The remainder of Bank's force was pursued to Winchester where it was attacked and defeated on May 25.

President Lincoln, wanting to end Jackson's reign in the Shenandoah Valley, ordered Gen. Fremont to advance toward Jackson from the south. Lincoln also ordered Banks to advance from the north while Gen. McDowell marched toward the valley from Fredericksburg. Jackson's army turned south, and, with several forced marches which earned them the nickname "Foot Cavalry," escaped the Federals trap.

The Confederates then attacked these converging armies separately. On June 8 Gen. Ewell defeated Fremont at Cross Keys. The next day, Jackson and Ewell beat McDowell's troops in the Battle of Port Republic. That ended the Valley Campaign as Jackson's army boarded trains for Richmond to aid Lee's army on the Peninsula.

SIGNIFICANCE

Jackson's lightning marches tied up 3 separate armies which otherwise could have reinforced McClellan on the Peninsula.

Jackson also captured supplies and inflicted heavy casualties on the Union armies.

Etat: Virginie

Etat-Unis

Commandants:
  Général de division John C. Frémont, Général de division Nathaniel P. Banks, Général de Brigade James Shields
Armée: commandements indépendants
  34 000 soldats
Pertés:
  Tués: 398
  Blessés: 1 808
  Prisonniers ou disparus: 2 463

Etats Confédérés

Commandant:
  Général de division Thomas J. Jackson

Armée: de la Vallée
  16 000 soldats
Pertés:
  Tués: 230
  Blessés: 1 373
  Prisonniers ou disparus: 232

COMMENTAIRE

Depuis avril, l'armée du général McClellan avançait vers Richmond. La général Jackson surnommé "Stonewall" (mur de pierre) commença une campagne offensive dans la vallée Shenandoah pour empêcher McClellan de recevoir des renforts supplémentaires des armées de l'Union.

Jackson ouvrit la campagne en faisant marcher ses troupes vers les montagnes Allegheny. Le 8 mai, les Confédérés attaquèrent le major général John Frémont à la bataille de McDowell. Les Fédéraux furent défaits et se retirèrent vers l'ouest. Le 23 mai les Sudistes arrivèrent en masse sur une petite portion de l'armée de Banks à Front Royal. Le reste des forces de Banks fut poursuivi jusqu'à Winchester, puis attaqué et défait le 25 mai.

Le président Lincoln, qui voulait en finir avec le règne de Jackson dans la vallée Shenandoah, donna l'ordre au général Frémont d'avancer vers Jackson pour l'attaquer au sud. Lincoln ordonna aussi à Banks d'avancer depuis le nord tandis que le général McDowell marchait vers la vallée depuis Fredericksburg. L'armée de Jackson vira au sud, et échappa au piege de l'armée fédérale par plusieurs marches forcées. Cela lui valut le surnom de "cavalerie à pied."

Les Confédérés attaquèrent alors ces deux armées convergentes séparément. Le 8 juin, le général Ewell défit Frémont à Cross Keys. Le jour suivant Jackson et Ewell battirent les troupes de McDowell dans la Bataille de Port Republic. Cela mit fin à la campagne de la Valley. Les troupes de Jackson prirent le train pour Richmond où elles allaient aider l'armée de Lee sur la Péninsule.

CONSEQUENCES

Les marches rapides de Jackson occupèrent 3 armées séparées qui auraient autrement renforcé McClellan sur la Péninsule.

Jackson s'empara aussi de l'approvisionnement et infligea de lourdes pertes aux armées de l'Union.

Important Landmarks

Shenandoah River
Massanutten Mountain
Valley Turnpike
Fisher's Hill
Signal Knob
Setlington's Hill
Bull Pasture River
White Oak Ridge
Abraham's Creek
Hall's Ridge

Important Buildings

Jackson's HQ – Winchester
McDowell Presbyterian Church
Lewis Farm – Port Republic

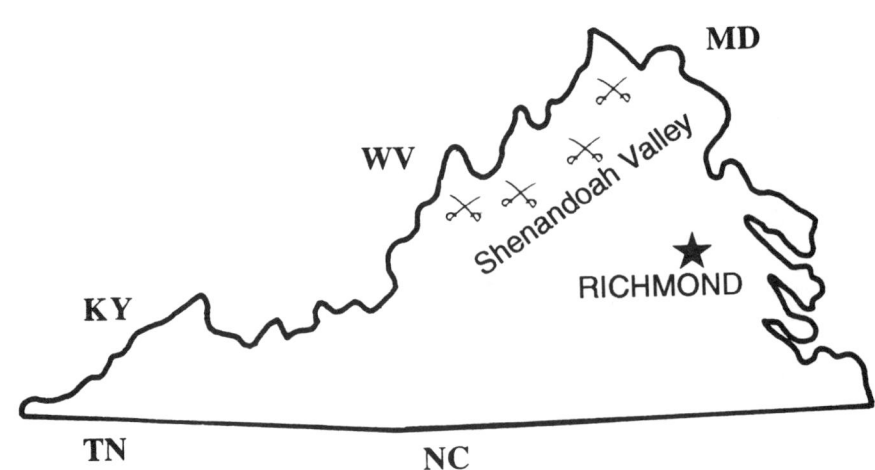

Estado: Virginia

<table>
<tr><td align="center">U.S.</td><td align="center">C.S.</td></tr>
</table>

Comandantes:
Maj. Gen. John C. Frémont
Maj. Gen. Nathaniel P. Banks
Brig. Gen. James Shields
U.S. Ejército: varias comandancias
No. de tropas: 34,000
Pérdidas:
Muertos: 398
Heridos: 1,808
Capturados o ausentes: 2,463

Comandante:
Maj. Gen. Thomas J. Jackson

C.S. Ejército: Army of the Valley
No. de tropas: 16,000
Pérdidas:
Muertos: 230
Heridos: 1,373
Capturados o ausentes: 232

COMENTARIOS

El ejército Federal del General McClellan había estado avanzando hacia Richmond desde abril. En mayo, el General "Stonewall" Jackson empezó una campaña ofensiva en el valle Shenandoah para que McClellan no recibiera más refuerzos de los ejércitos Federales en el valle.

Jackson abrió la campaña marchando sus tropas hacia las montañas Allegheny. El 8 de mayo los Confederados atacaron las fuerzas del General John Frémont en la batalla de McDowell. Los Federales fueron derrotados y se retiraron hacia el oeste. Jackson, entonces, marchó con su ejército para dar batalla al General Nathaniel Banks. El 23 de mayo los sureños aplastaron una pequeña parte del ejército de Banks en Front Royal. Los que quedaban de la fuerza de Banks fueron perseguidos hasta Winchester donde fueron atacados y derrotados el 25 de Mayo.

El Presidente Lincoln, deseando terminar el dominio de Jackson en el valle, mandó al General Frémont que avanzara hacia Jackson desde el sur. Lincoln también ordenó que el General Banks avanzara desde el norte mientras el General McDowell marchaba hacia el valle desde Fredericksburg. El ejército de Jackson se volvió para el sur, y, con varias marchas forzadas que les ganaron el nombre de "Foot Cavalry" (Caballería de pie), se escaparon de la trampa Federal.

Los Confederados, entonces, atacaron estos dos ejércitos uno a la vez. El 8 de junio el General Ewell derrotó a Frémont en Cross Keys. El próximo día Jackson y Ewell derrotaron a las tropas de McDowell en la batalla de Port Republic. Esto acabó la campaña del valle porque el ejército de Jackson fue por tren a Richmond para ayudar al ejército de Lee en la Península.

CONSECUENCIAS

Las marchas rápidas de Jackson ató tres ejércitos seperados que pudieran haber estado con McClellan en la Península.

Jackson también capturó municiones y otras provisiones e infligió muchas pérdidas a los ejércitos de la Unión.

Staat: Virginia

Befehlshaber der US:
Generalmajor John C. Fremont
Generalmajor Nathaniel P. Banks
Brigadegeneral James Shields
Armee der US: Unter einzelnen
Befehlshabern
Truppenstärke: 34,000
Verluste:
Gefallen: 398
Verwundet: 1,808
Gefangengenommen oder
vermißt: 2,463

Befehlshaber der CS:
Generalmajor Thomas J. Jackson

Armee der CS: Armee des Tales
Truppenstärke: 16,000

Verluste:
Gefallen: 230
Verwundet: 1,373
Gefangengenommen oder
vermißt: 232

KOMMENTAR

Seit April rückte General McClellan's Unionarmee in Richtung Richmond vor. Im Mai begann General "Stonewall Jackson" mit einem offensiven Feldzug im Shenandoah Tal, um zu verhindern, daß weitere Verstärkungstruppen der Unionarmee McClellan im Tal erreichen konnten.

Jackson's Kampagne öffnete mit dem Marsch seiner Truppen in Richtung der Allegheny Berge. Am 8. Mai griffen Konföderierte Truppen Generalmajor John Freemont bei McDowell Preshyterian Church - Schlacht bei McDowell (McDowell Presbyterianer Kirche). Die Föderalisten wurden besiegt, und sie zogen sich nach Westen zurück. Nachfolgend setzte Jackson seine Truppen in Marsch, um General Banks in einen Kampf zu verwickeln. Am 23. Mai überwältigten die Konföderierten einen kleinen Teil von Banks' Armee bei Front Royal. Banks' übrige Truppen wurden nach Winchester verfolgt, und am 25. Mai im Angriff dort besiegt.

Um die Herrschaft Jackson's im Shenandoah Tal zu beenden, befahl Präsident Lincoln General Fremont, vom Süden her gegen Jackson vorzurücken. Zur gleichen Zeit gab Lincoln General Banks den Befehl, vom Norden vorzurücken, während General McDowell von Richtung Fredericksburg nach dem Tal marschierte. Jackson's Armee wendete sich nach Süden und, durch mehrere Zwangsmärsche, entkam der Föderalistenfalle. Durch dieses Manöver bekamen sie den Spitznamen "Fusskavallerie."

Die Konföderierten griffen dann einzeln diese sich annähernden Armeen an. Am 8. Juni wurde General Fremont bei Cross Keys von General Ewell besiegt. Am folgenden Tag schlugen Jackson und Ewell McDowell's Truppen in der Schlacht von Port Republic. Das beendete die Kampagne im Tal. Jackson's Truppen stiegen dann in die Züge nach Richmond ein, um auf der Halbinsel Lee's Armee zu unterstützen.

BEDEUTUNG

Jackson's Blitzmärsche feßelten drei separate Armeen, die andernfalls McClellan auf der Halbinsel hätten verstärken können.

Jackson eroberte Provianten und fügte gleichzeitig der Unionarmee schwere Verluste zu.

Post-war view of the town of Port Republic on the south fork of the Shenandoah River.

SEVEN PINES
May 31 - June 1, 1862

State: Virginia

U.S.	**C.S.**
Commander:	Commander:
Maj. Gen. George B. McClellan	Gen. Joseph E. Johnston
	Maj. Gen. Gustavus W. Smith
U.S. Army: Army of the Potomac	C.S. Army: Army of Northern Virginia
No. of Troops: 51,000	No. of Troops: 39,000
Casualties:	Casualties:
Killed: 790	Killed: 980
Wounded: 3,594	Wounded: 4,749
Captured or missing: 647	Captured or missing: 405

COMMENTS

By the end of May 1862 Maj. Gen. McClellan's Union army had worked its way up the peninsula, between the York and James Rivers, to within six miles of the Confederate capitol at Richmond, VA.

At that point, McClellan divided his army, leaving two army corps under Generals Keyes and Heintzelman south of the Chickahominy River. The remaining three army corps crossed the river expecting to hook up with Gen. McDowell's army ordered south from Fredericksburg.

Confederate Gen. Johnston seized this opportunity and devised a plan to attack the two army corps left isolated south of the Chickahominy. The Union line, with Heintzelman's III corps at Fair Oaks, ran south to Seven Pines, where Gen. Keyes' IV corps was located. Johnston planned to attack the Federals from three directions with Generals Longstreet, D.H. Hill, and Huger. the fighting didn't start until 1:00 p.m. due to confusion and misunderstood orders. At that time General Hill attacked alone, but succeeded in driving the Federals back. A bayonet charge by the Federals gave them time to form a second line. Constant pressure by the Confederates was crushing parts of the Union line, forcing some Federals north to Fair Oaks. Late in the day a part of Longstreet's force supported Hill who attacked again. After a failed counterattack, the IV corps was forced to fall back to a third line. By 6:00 p.m. the fighting at this end of the field had ended.

At Fair Oaks, meanwhile, the Confederates finally launched their attack at 4:00 p.m. This attack was repulsed by parts of the II corps which crossed the Chickahominy to reinforce Heintzelman. Around dusk Gen. Johnston was severely wounded. Gen. G.W. Smith replaced him and ordered a renewal of the attacks at dawn. As had happened the day before, confusion hindered the Southern attack. Longstreet only attacked with two brigades. This weak attack was easily repulsed and concluded the Battle of Seven Pines/Fair Oaks.

SIGNIFICANCE

The wounded Johnston was replaced by Gen. Robert E. Lee. Lee became the North's greatest adversary.

The Confederate attacks unnerved the already cautious McClellan and put the Union army on the defensive. This situation led to the Seven Days Campaign and the eventual withdrawal of McClellan's force from the peninsula.

Etat: Virginie

Etats-Unis	**Etats Confédérés**
Commandant:	Commandants:
Général de division George B. McClellan	Général Joseph E. Johnston
	Général de division Gustavus W. Smith
Armée: du Potomac	Armée: de Virginie du Nord
51 000 soldats	39 000 soldats
Pertes:	Pertes:
Tués: 790	Tués: 980
Blessés: 3 594	Blessés: 4 749
Prisonniers ou disparus: 647	Prisonniers ou disparus: 405

COMMENTAIRE

A la fin de mai 1862, l'armée unioniste du général McClellan avait atteint la péninsule, entre les rivières York et James, à moins de 10 km du capitole confédéré à Richmond, en Virginie.

A ce moment, McClellan divisa son Armée, laissant deux corps d'armée sous les ordres des généraux Keyes et Heintzelman au sud de la rivière Chickahominy. Les ttrois autres corps d'armée traversèrent la rivière, espérant se rallier à l'armée du général McDowell arrivant de Frdericksburg.

Le général Johnston, confédéré, saisit cette occasion en formant un plan d'attaque contre les deux corps d'armée isolés au sud de la rivière Chickahominy. La ligne de l'Union, avec le corps III de Heintzelman à Fair Oaks, fonça vers le sud sur Seven Pines, y rejoignant le corps IV du général Keyes. Johnston prévoyait d'attaquer les Fédéraux de trois directions avec les généraux Longstreet, D. H. Hill et Huger. La bataille ne commença pas avant 13h par suite de confusion et de malentendus. Ainsi le général Hill attaqua seul, mais il réussit à repousser les Fédéraux. Une charge à la baionnette des Fédéraux leur donna le temps de former une deuxième ligne. La pression constante des Confédérés écrasa des parties de la ligne de l'Union, forçant les Fédéraux au nord de Fair Oaks. Une partie des forces de Longstreet soutint tardivement Hill qui attaquait à nouveau. Après l'échec d'une contre-attaque, le corps IV dut se rabattre sur une troisième ligne. A 18 heures, la lutte avait cessé sur cette partie du champ de bataille.

Cependant, à Fair Oaks, les Confédérés avaient lancé leur attaque à 16 heures. Celle-ci avait été repoussée par le corps II qui avait traversé la rivière Chickahominy pour aider Heintzelman. Au cérpuscule, le général Johnston était sévèrement blessé. Le général G. W. Smith le remplaça et ordonna de nouvelles attaqua à l'aube. Comme le jour précédent, le manque de coördination entrava le mouvement de l'attaque des Sudistes. Seul Longstreet fit front avec deux brigades. Cette faible attaque fut aisément repoussée et servit de conclusion à la Bataille de Seven Pines/Fair Oaks.

CONSEQUENCES

Johnston blessé fut remplacé par le général Robert Lee qui allait devenir l'adversaire le plus redoutable du Nord.

Les attaques des Confédérés démontèrent le prudent McClellan et mirent l'armée de l'Union sur la défensive. Cette situation amena la Campagne de Sept Jours et finalement le retrait des forces de McClellan de la péninsule.

Important Landmarks
Chickahominy River
White Oak Swamp
Casey's Redoubt
Richmond & York River R.R.
"Grapevine" Bridge
Fair Oaks
Seven Pines
Williamsburg Stage Road

Important Buildings
Twin Houses
Adams House
Allen's Farm-House

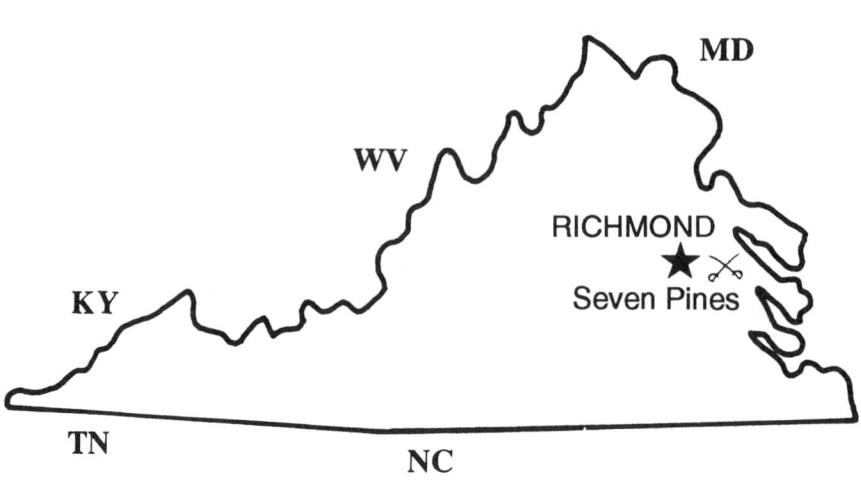

Estado: Virginia

U.S.	C.S.
Comandante:	Comandante:
Maj. Gen. George B. McClellan	Gen. Joseph E. Johnston
	Maj. Gen. Gustavus W. Smith
U.S. Ejército: Army of the Potomac	C.S. Ejército: Army of Northern Virginia
No. de tropas: 51,000	No. de tropas: 39,000
Pérdidas:	Pérdidas:
Muertos: 790	Muertos: 980
Heridos: 3,594	Heridos: 4,749
Capturados o ausentes: 647	Capturados o ausentes: 405

COMENTARIO

A finales de mayo de 1862 el Maj. General McClellan, con su ejército, había progresado por la Península, entre los ríos York y James, hasta estar dentro de seis millas de la capital Confederada, Richmond, Virginia.

En ese punto McClellan dividió su ejército, dejando dos cuerpos armados bajo los Generales Keyes y Heintzelman al sur del río Chickahominy. Los tres cuerpos militares que quedaban cruzaron el río esperando juntarse con el ejército de McDowell que había sido mandado al sur desde Fredericksburg.

El General Confederado Johnston cogió esta oportunidad e inventó un plan para atacar a los dos cuerpos que se habían dejado a isolados al sur del Chickahominy. La línea Federal, con el Cuerpo I de Heintzelman en Fair Oaks, tenía posición hasta el sur a Seven Pines, donde estaba el IV cuerpo del General Keyes. Con los Generales Longstreet, D.H. Hill, y Huger, Johnston pensaba en atacar a los Federales desde tres direcciones. La pelea no empezó hasta la una de la tarde por confusión y mandatos mal comprendidos. En ese momento el General Hill atacó solo, pero tuvo éxito en empujar a los Yanquis para atrás. Un ataque de bayoneta por los Federales les dio tiempo para formar una segunda línea. Presión constante por los Confederados aplastó partes de la línea Federal, forzando a algunos de los Federales al norte a Fair Oaks. Tarde en el día una parte de la fuerza de Longstreet apoyó a Hill quien atacó otra vez. Después de un contraataque fracasado, el IV cuerpo fue forzado a retirarse a una tercera línea. A las seis de la tarde la batalla en esta parte del campo había terminado.

En Fair Oaks, mientras tanto, los Confederados finalmente lanzaron su asalto a las cuatro de la tarde. Este ataque fue repulsado por partes del Cuerpo I que cruzó el río Chickahominy para reforzar al General Heintzelman. Alrededor del anochecer el General Johnston fue sériamente herido. El General G.W. Smith lo reemplazó y mandó que los ataques comenzaran de nuevo al amanecer. Como pasó el día antes, la confusión impidió el ataque sureño. Longstreet atacó con sólamente dos brigadas. Este ataque débil fue fácilmente repulsado y concluyó la Batalla de Seven Pines/Fair Oaks.

CONSECUENCIAS

El General Johnston herido fue reemplazado por el General Robert E. Lee quien llegó a ser el adversario más grande del Norte.

Los ataques Confederados enervaron al General McClellan quien ya era demasiado cauto y puso al ejército Federal en la defensa. Esta situación inició la campaña de Seven Days y causó el retiro eventual de la fuerza de McCllan de la Península.

Staat: Virginia

Befehlshaber der US:	Befehlshaber der CS:
Generalmajor George B. McClellan	General Joseph E. Johnston
	Generalmajor Gustavus W. Smith
Armee der US: Armee des Potomac	Armee der CS: Armee von Nordvirginia
Truppenstärke: 51,000	Truppenstärke: 39,000
Verluste:	Verluste:
Gefallen: 790	Gefallen: 980
Verwundet: 3,594	Verwundet: 4,749
Gefangengenommen oder vermißt: 647	Gefangengenommen oder vermißt: 405

KOMMENTAR

Bei Ende Mai 1862 hatte Generalmajor McClellan's Unionarmee, zwischen dem York Fluß und James Fluß auf der Halbinsel, die Strecke zurückgelegt, die sie auf 10 Kilometer vor die Hauptstadt der Konföderierten, Richmond, im Staat Virginia, brachte.

Hier verteilte McClellan seine Armee, und ließ zwei Armeekorps, unter den Generalen Keyes und Heintzelman, südlich des Chickahominy Flußes zurück. Die drei übrigen Armeekorps überquerten den Fluß, in der Erwartung, sich südlich von Fredericksburg der Armee von General McDowell anschließen zu können.

Konföderationsgeneral Johnston ergriff diese Gelegenheit und faßte den Plan, die beiden isolierten Armeekorps, die südlich des Chickahominy zurückgelassen wurden, anzugreifen. Die Unionlinien mit Heintzelman's 3. Korps bei Fair Oaks, liefen südlich nach Seven Pines, wo sich das 4. Korps von General Keyes befand. Johnston hatte es vor, die Föderalisten aus drei Richtungen, mit Truppen unter Longstreet, D.H. Hill und Huger, anzugreifen. Verwirrung und mißverstandene Befehle verzögerten den Beginn des Angriffs bis 13.00 Uhr.

General Hill machte den Vorstoß allein, und es gelang ihm, die Föderalisten zurückzudrängen. Aber mit einem Bajonettenangriff gewannen die Föderalisten Zeit, eine zweite Linie aufzustellen. Stetiger Druck von den Konföderierten verursachte, Teile der Unionlinie zu brechen, und zwang einen Teil der Föderalisten nordwärts nach Fair Oaks. Spät am Tage unterstützte ein Teil von Longstreet's Truppen Hill, der noch einmal angriff. Nach einem gescheiterten Gegenangriff wurde das 4. Korps gezwungen, auf eine dritte Linie zurückzufallen. Um 18.00 Uhr war das Gefecht auf dieser Seite des Feldes zu Ende.

Mittlerweile waren die Konföderierten endlich, um 16.00 Uhr, bei Fair Oaks zum Angriff übergegangen. Dieser Ansturm wurde von Teilen des 2. Korps, die den Chickahominy überquert hatten, um Heintzelman zu verstärken, zurückgeschlagen. Bei Einbruch der Dunkelheit wurde General Johnston schwer verwundet. General G. W. Smith ersetzte ihn und beorderte, bei Tagesanbruch, erneute Angriffe. Wie am vorigen Tag verzögerte Verwirrung den Angriff. Longstreet griff mit nur zwei Brigaden an. Dieser Angriff wurde sofort zurückgeschlagen, und bedeutete den Schluß der Schlacht von Seven Pines/Fair Oaks.

BEDEUTUNG

Der verwundete Johnston wurde von General Robert E. Lee ersetzt. Lee bekam der größte Gegner des Nordens.

Die Konföderationsangriffe entnervten den bereits übervorsichtigen McClellan und zwangen die Unionarmee in die Defensive. Diese Situation führte zur Seven Days Campaign, und am Ende zum Rückzug von McClellan's Streitkräften von der Halbinsel.

The twin farm-houses as seen from Casey's Redoubt; an 8-in. siege howitzer is in the foreground.

Maj. Gen. George B. McClellan

Gen. Joseph E. Johnston

State: Virginia

U.S.
Commander:
  Maj. Gen. George B. McClellan
U.S. Army: Army of the Potomac
  No. of Troops: 105,000
Casualties:
  Killed: 1,734
  Wounded: 8,062
  Captured or missing: 6,053

C.S.
Commander:
  Gen. Robert E. Lee
C.S. Army: Army of Northern Virginia
  No. of Troops: 85,000
Casualties:
  Killed: 3,478
  Wounded: 16,261
  Captured or missing: 875

COMMENTS

The Seven Days' Campaign started with Lee's bold move to attack Gen. Porter's V Corps, the only corps remaining north of the Chickahominy River.

Lee's plan was to leave a small part of his army to defend Richmond while the rest of his army along with Jackson's army, arriving from the Shenandoah Valley, would attack Porter's isolated corps. On June 25, while Lee was preparing to attack Porter, Gen. Hooker was sent on reconnaissance toward Richmond. Following a short engagement at Oak Grove, Hooker was ordered back.

The next day, at the Battle of Mechanicsville or Beaver Dam Creek, A.P. Hill and D.H. Hill attacked Porter's entrenched position with no success and lost about four men to every one lost by Porter. During the night, Porter moved back to another strong position at Boatswain's Creek.

On the 27th Lee launched a series of strong attacks against the Federals, who held on, but both sides suffered heavy casualties. At dark the Confederates finally pierced the Union lines, forcing Porter to withdraw south of the Chickahominy River. During the next three days Lee tried to destroy McClellan's retreating army, but due to a faulty staff and uncoordinated attacks, his plans failed.

At Savage Station on the 29th and at Glendale on the 30th McClellan's rear guard repulsed all Confederate attacks. At Malvern Hill McClellan halted and formed a strong defensive line. Lee ordered an attack on July 1 hoping to finally destroy the Army of the Potomac. Lee watched as the advancing lines of his assault were erased by the massed Union artillery. This bloody defeat brought an end to the campaign and McClellan retreated to Harrison's Landing under the protection of Union gun boats.

SIGNIFICANCE

The threat to Richmond was removed.

The Southern army seized the initiative in the Eastern theater. This led to Lee's first plan to invade the North.

Etat: Virginie

Etat-Unis
Commandant:
  Général de division George B. McClellan
Armée: du Potomac
  105 000 soldats
Pertes:
  Tués: 1 734
  Blessés: 8 062
  Prisonniers ou disparus: 6 053

Etats Confédérés
Commandant:
  Général Robert E. Lee
Armée: Virginie du Nord
  85 000 soldats
Pertes:
  Tués: 3 478
  Blessés: 16 261
  Prisonniers ou disparus: 875

COMMENTAITE

La Bataille des Sept Jours (Seven Days' Campaign) commença par l'audacieuse attaque de Lee contre le seul corps qui restait au nord de la rivière Chickahominy, le corps V du général Porter.

Le projet de Lee était de laisser une petite portion de l'armée à défendre Richmond, tandis que le reste de son armée, avec celle de Jackson qui arrivait de la vallée du Shenandoah attaquerait le corps d'armée isolé de Porter. Le 25 juin, alors que Lee se prparait à attaquer Porter, le général Hooker était envoyé en mission de reconnaissance sur Richmond. Après un court combat à Oak Grove, Hooker reçut l'ordre de se retirer.

Le jour suivant, à la bataille de Mechanicsville ou Beaver Dam Creek, A. P. Hill et D. H. Hill attaquèrent sans succès la position retranchée de Porter et perdirent une moyenne de 4 hommes pour un perdu par Porter. Pendant la nuit, Porter se replia sur une position plus forte à Boatswain's Creek.

Le 27, Lee lança une série d'attaques serrées contre les Fédéraux qui tinrent bon, mais les deux camps souffrirent de lourdes pertes. Le jour tombé, les Confédérés percèrent finalement les lignes de l'Union, forçant Porter à se retirer au sud de la rivire Chickahominy. Pendant les trois jours suivants, Lee tenta de détruire l'armée en retraite de McClellan, mais échoua par suite de l'incompétence de son état major et d'attaques mal coórdonnées.

Le 29 à Savage Station, et le 30 à Glendale, l'arrière-garde de McClellan repoussa toutes les attaques des Confédérés. A Malvern Hill McClellan s'arrêta pour former une ligne de défense puissante. Espérant détruire définitivement l'armée du Potomac, Lee ordonna une attaque le 1er juillet. Lee vit toutes les lignes de son assaut effacées par l'artillerie massée de l'Union. Cette défaite sanglante mit fin à la campagne et McClellan se retira à Harrison's Landing sous la protection des chaloupes canonnières de l'Union.

CONSEQUENCES

La menace de Richmond avait disparu.

L'armée des Sudistes prit l'initiative dans le théâtre de l'Est. Ceci amena le premier projet de Lee d'envahir le Nord.

Important Landmarks
Chickahominy River
Beaver Dam Creek
Richmond & York R.R.
Harrison's Landing
Boatswain's Creek
Crossroads at New & Old Cold Harbor
White Oak Swamp
White Oak Bridge
Charles City Road
Longbridge Road
Willis Church Road
Darbytown Road
Malvern Hill
James River
Mechanicsville
Grapevine Bridge

Important Buildings
Ellerson's Mill
Gaines Mill
Watt House
Old Cold Harbor Tavern
Dr. Trent's Farmhouse
Westover Mansion
Savage Station
Glendale
Willis Methodist Church
Berkley Plantation
The Parsonage
Crew House
Garthright House
Riddekk's Shop
Malvern House
West House

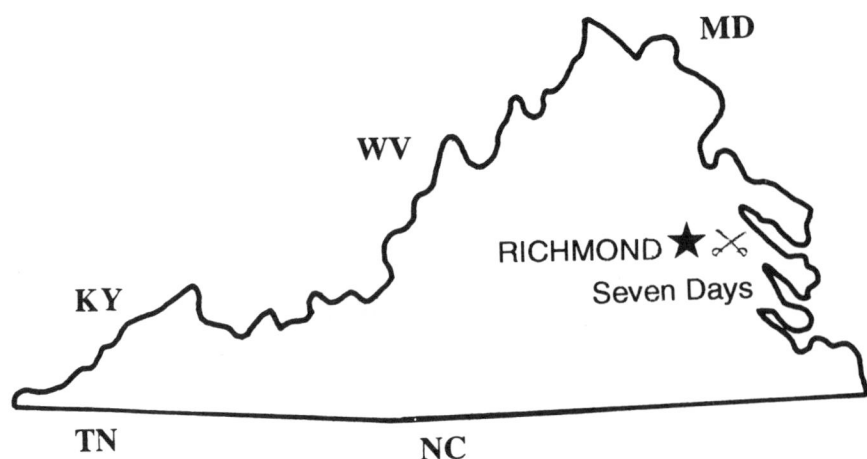

Estado: Virginia

U.S.	C.S.
Comandante:	Comandante:
Maj. Gen. George B. McClellan	Gen. Robert E. Lee
U.S. Ejército: Army of the Potomac	C.S. Ejército: Army of Northern Virginia
No. de tropas: 105,000	No. de tropas: 85,000
Pérdidas:	Pérdidas:
Muertos: 1,734	Muertos: 3,478
Heridos: 8,062	Heridos: 16,261
Capturados o ausentes: 6,053	Capturados o ausentes: 875

COMENTARIO

La campaña de los Seven Days (Siete Días) empezó con el movimiento audaz de Lee de atacar el V cuerpo Federal bajo el General Porter, el único cuerpo que quedaba al norte del río Chickahominy.

El plan de Lee era dejar una pequeña parte de su ejército para defender Richmond mientras el resto del ejército, con el de Jackson, llegando del valle de Shenandoah, atacaría el cuerpo aislado de Porter. El 25 de junio, mientras Lee hacía las preparaciones para atacar a Porter, el General Hooker fue mandado en una misión de reconocimiento hacia Richmond. Después de un pequeño encuentro en Oak Grove, Hooker fue mandado para atrás.

El próximo día, en la batalla de Mechanicsville o Beaver Dam Creek, A.P. Hill y D.H. Hill atacaron la posición atrincherada de Porter sin éxito perdieron cuatro hombres por cada uno de Porter. Por la noche, Porter reformó su línea en otra posición fuerte en Botswain's Creek.

El 27, Lee lanzó una serie de ataques fuertes contra los Federales, quienes mantuvieron su posición, pero los dos lados sufrieron muchas pérdidas. Al oscurecer, los Confederados finalmente perforaron la línea Federal, forzando a Porter a retirarse al sur del Chickahominy. Durante los próximos tres días, Lee trató de destruir el ejército de McClellan que estaba retirándose, pero debido a un cuerpo deficiente y ataques no bien coordinados, sus planes fracasaron.

En Savage Station el 29 y en Glendale el 30, la guardia trasera de McClellan repulsó todos los ataques Confederados. En Malvern Hill McClellan paró y formó una línea fuerte defensiva. Lee ordenó un ataque el 1 de julio, esperando destruir finalmente la Army of the Potomac. Lee vio como sus líneas de asalto fueron borradas por la artillería norteña. Esta derrota sangrienta trajo el final de la campaña y McClellan se retiró a Harrison's Landing bajo la protección de barcos armados.

CONSECUENCIAS

La amenaza a Richmond se removió.

El ejército Confederado cogió la iniciativa en el teatro militar del este. Esto llevó al primer plan de Lee para invadir el Norte.

Staat: Virginia

Befehlshaber der US:	Befehlshaber der CS:
Generalmajor George B. McClellan	General Robert E. Lee
Armee der US: Armee des Potomac	Armee der CS: Armee von Nordvirginia
Truppenstärke: 105,000	Truppenstärke: 85,000
Verluste:	Verluste:
Gefallen: 1,734	Gefallen: 3,478
Verwundet: 8,062	Verwundet: 16,261
Gefangengenommen oder vermißt: 6,053	Gefangengenommen oder vermißt: 875

KOMMENTAR

Die Sieben Tage Kampagne öffnete mit dem kühnen Schritt von Lee, General Porter's 5. Korps anzugreifen. Dieses Korps war das einzige, das nördlich des Chickahominy Flußes verblieb.

Lee's Plan war es, einen kleinen Teil seiner Armee zur Verteidigung von Richmond zurückzulassen, während seine übrigen Truppen, samt der Armee Jackson's, die vom Shenandoah Tal ankam, Porter's isoliertes Korps angreifen sollte. Am 25. Juni, während Lee seinen Angriff auf Porter vorbereitete, wurde General Hooker im Aufklärungseinsatz nach Richmond geschickt. Nach kurzem Gefecht bei Oak Grove, wurde Hooker beordert, zurückzukehren.

In der Schlacht von Mechanicsville oder Beaver Dam Creek, griffen A. P. Hill und D. H. Hill am nächsten Tag Porter's verschanzte Stellung erfolglos an, und verloren vier Mann im Vergleich zu jedem einzelnen, den Porter verlor. In der Nacht zog sich Porter zu einer anderen, starken Stellung am Boatswain's Creek zurück.

Am 27. ging Lee zu einer Reihe von schweren Angriffen gegen die Föderalisten über. Diese hielten fest, aber beide Seiten erlitten schwere Verluste. Beim Einbruch der Dunkelheit durchbrachen die Konföderierten endlich die Unionlinien und zwangen Porter, sich südlich über den Chickahominy Fluß zurückzuziehen. Während der folgenden drei Tage versuchte Lee, McClellan's zurückziehende Armee zu vernichten, aber sein Versuch scheiterte wegen seines unerfahrenen Stabes und unkoordinierten Angriffen.

Die Nachhut von McClellan schlug alle Konföderierten Angriffe zurück — am 29. an Savage Station und am 30. bei Glendale. Am Malvern Hill hielt McClellan an und bezog eine starke Defensivstellung. Lee befahl am 1. Juli den Angriff, und hoffte, die Armee des Potomac endlich vernichten zu können. Lee sah seine vorrückenden Sturmlinien durch die maßierte Unionartillerie eradiert. Diese blutige Niederlage brachte die Kampagne zu Ende, und McClellan zog sich, im Schutz der Unionkanonenboote, nach Harrison's Landing zurück.

BEDEUTUNG

Die Gefahr für Richmond war beseitigt.

Die Konföderierte Armee ergriff die Initiative auf dem östlichen Kriegsschauplatz. Das führte zu Lee's erstem Plan, den Norden zu überfallen.

Union field hospital at Savage's Station, after the battle of Gaines' Mill.

State: Virginia

U.S.	**C.S.**
Commander:	Commander:
Maj. Gen. John Pope	Gen. Robert E. Lee
U.S. Army: Army of Virginia	C.S. Army: Army of Northern Virginia
No. of Troops: 65,000	No. of Troops: 55,000
Casualties:	Casualties:
Killed: 1,747	Killed: 1,553
Wounded: 8,452	Wounded: 7,812
Captured or missing: 4,263	Captured or missing: 109

COMMENTS

The destruction of the Union supply base at Manassas Junction by "Stonewall" Jackson caused Maj. Gen. John Pope to concentrate his Union army in that area.

By Aug. 29 Jackson had formed his battle line in the woods behind an unfinished railroad embankment. During that day Gen. Pope attacked Jackson with Sigel's, Hooker's, Kearney's, and Reynolds' troops. But the attacks, which advanced piecemeal and uncoordinated, gained nothing. In the afternoon Gen. Porter's V Corps took position off to Pope's left. Gen. Pope, believing Porter had a clear avenue of attack on Jackson's right flank, ordered him to advance. Porter prepared for the attack but, learning that Longstreet's 30,000 man wing of Lee's army had arrived on the field opposite him, wisely cancelled the order to advance. Porter's decision ruined his military career but probably saved the army.

During the night Lee tightened his lines. Pope interpreted this as a Southern retreat and planned his pursuit. On the morning of the 30th Porter was again ordered to attack. The Federals advanced three lines deep across the open fields. Artillery and musket fire staggered the blue lines. The first two waves were repulsed but on came a third. This time the Northerners swept up the railroad embankment straining the Confederate line. As hand-to-hand combat raged along the line one group of Southerners, out of ammunition, resorted to throwing rocks at the Federals. After Porter was repulsed, Longstreet ordered his troops forward. Wheeling them to the northeast, the screaming gray lines coming from the south caught the Union army off guard. Jackson ordered his men forward also. Federal units soon dissolved in a sea of blue. Pope's army was in full retreat.

Heavy fighting on Chinn Ridge bought time for Pope to establish a strong defensive position on Henry Hill. A gallant stand there saved the Army from disaster. The Union army retreated to Centerville during the night.

SIGNIFICANCE

The Confederate victory offset losses in the west.
This cleared the way for Lee's invasion of the North.
Porter was court-martialed.

Etat: Virginie

Etat-Unis	**Etats Confédérés**
Commandant:	Commandant:
Général de division John Pope	Général Robert E. Lee
Armée: de Virginie	Armée: de Virginie du Nord
65 000 soldats	55 000 soldats
Pertes:	Pertes:
Tués: 1 747	Tués: 1 553
Blessés: 8 452	Blessés: 7 812
Prisonniers ou disparus: 4 263	Prisonniers ou disparus: 109

COMMENTAIRE

La destruction de la base d'approvisionnement de l'Union à Manassas Junction par "Stonewall" Jackson amena le général Pope de concentrer son armée de l'Union dans cette région.

Le 29 août, Jackson avait formé sa ligne de bataille dans les bois, derrière le remblai d'une voie ferrée en construction. Pendant la journée, le général Pope attaqua Jackson avec les troupes de Sigel, Hooker, Kearny et Reynolds. Mais ces attaques, avançant par morceaux et mal orchestrées, ne gagnèrent rien. Dans l'après-midi, le corps d'armée V de Porter prit position à la gauche de Pope. Croyant que Porter avait le champ libre pour attaquer le flanc droit de Jackson, Pope lui ordonna d'avancer. Porter prépara son attaque, mais, apprenant que l'aile de l'armée de Lee, avec les 30 000 hommes de Longstreet, était arrivée dans le champ opposé, il annula prudemment l'ordre d'avancer. Si la décision de Porter ruina sa carrière militaire, elle sauva vraisemblablement l'armée.

Pendant la nuit, Lee resserra ses lignes. Pope interpreta a ce mouvement comme une retraite des Sudistes, et pérpara sa poursuite. Le matin du 30, Porter reçut à nouveau l'ordred'attaquer. Les Fédéraux avancèrent à travers les champs à découvert. Les feux de l'artillerie et des mousquets ébranlèrent les lignes bleues. Après que les deux premières vagues eurent été repoussées en arriva une trolsième. Cette fois, les Nordistes balayèrent le quai de la voie ferrée, contraignant la ligne confédérée. Tandis que les combats corps à corps faisaient rage, un groupe de Sudistes, à court de munitions, en vint à lancer des pierres aux Fédéraux. Porter repoussé, Longstreet fit avancer ses troupes. Faisant une conversion au nord est, les lignes grises arrivèrent du sud en hurlant, prenant l'armée de l'Union au dépourvu. Jackson fit aussi avancer ses hommes. Les unités fédérales furent dissoutes dans une nuée bleue. L'armée de Pope battit en retraite.

Le combat intense de Chinn Ridge donna à Pope le temps d'établir une forte position de défense sur Henry Hill. L'armée fut sauvée du désastre par une brave résistance. Pendant la nuit, l'armée de l'Union se retira à Centerville.

CONSEQUENCES

Cette victoire des Confédérés compensa les pertes de l'ouest.
Ces évènements donnèrent le champ libre à Lee pour envahir le Nord.
Porter passa en conseil de guerre.

Important Landmarks

Warrenton Turnpike
Manassas-Sudley Road
Unfinished R.R.
Young's Branch
Henry House Hill
Buck Hill
"Deep Cut"
Stuart's Hill
Chinn Ridge

Important Buildings

Dogan House
Chinn House
Stone House
Sudley Church
Brawner Farm
Groveton

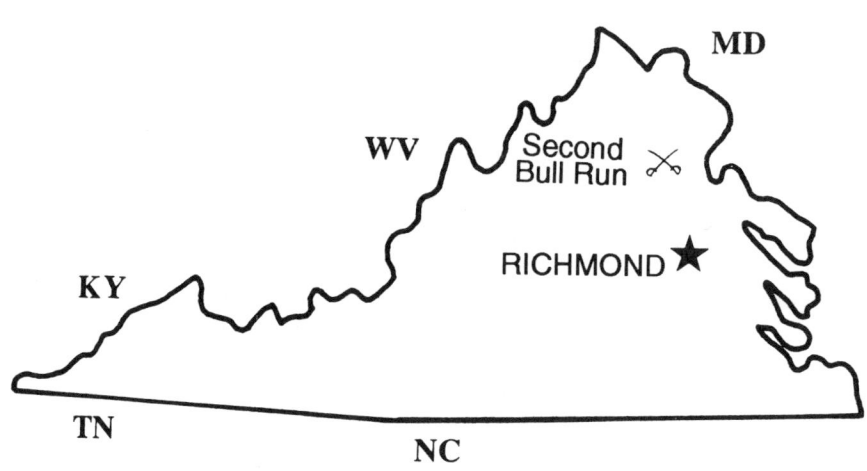

Estado: Virginia

U.S.

Comandante:
 Maj. Gen. John Pope
U.S. Ejército: Army of Virginia
 No. de tropas: 65,000

Pérdidas:
 Muertos: 1,747
 Heridos: 8,452
 Capturados o ausentes: 4,263

C.S.

Comandante:
 Gen. Robert E. Lee
C.S. Ejército: Army of Northern
 Virginia
 No. de tropas: 55,000

Pérdidas:
 Muertos: 1,553
 Heridos: 7,812
 Capturados o ausentes: 109

COMENTARIO

La destrucción de la base Federal de provisiones en Manassas Junction por Stonewall Jackson causó a Maj. Gen. John Pope concentrar a su ejécito en ese área.

El 29 de agosto Jackson ya había formado su línea de batalla en un bosque detrás de un terraplén todavía no completado para railes de ferrocarriles. Durante ese día el General Pope atacó a Jackson con las tropas de Sigel, Hooker, Kearney, y Reynolds. Pero los ataques, que avanzaron hecho de trozos y sin coordinación, no ganaron nada. Por la tarde, el V cuerpo, bajo Porter, tomó posición en la izquierda de Pope. El General Pope, creyendo que Porter tenía un camino abierto para atacar el flanco derecho de Jackson, le ordenó que avanzara. Porter se preparó para el ataque pero, comprendiendo que los 30,000 hombres de Longstreet habían llegado al campo opuesto a él, prudéntemente canceló el avance. Esta decisión de Porter arruinó su carrera militar pero probablemente salvó el ejército.

Durante la noche Lee apretó sus líneas. Pope interpretó esto como una retirada y planeó su perseguimiento. Por la mañana del 30 Porter fue mandado a atacar de nuevo. Los Federales avanzaron en tres líneas por los campos abiertos. Las líneas de azul se tambalearon bajo el fuego de los rifles y artillería. Las primeras dos olas fueron repulsadas pero la tercera siguió. Esta vez los Norteños subieron el terraplén estirando la línea Confederada. Mientras el combate cuerpo a cuerpo ardía por la línea, un grupo de Sureños que ya no tenía municiones recurrió a tirar rocas a los Yanquis. Después de que se repulsó a Porter, Longstreet mandó un avance. Volviendo sus tropas al noreste, las líneas grises vinieron gritando del sur y cogió al ejército Federal desprevenido. Jackson tambíen ordenó que sus tropas avanzaran. Las unidades Federales se disolvieron en un mar de azul. El ejécito de Pope estaba en un estado de retirada completa.

Una pelea fuerte en Chinn Ridge compró tiempo para Pope para establecer una posición defensiva fuerte en Henry Hill. Una lucha valiente allí salvó el ejército del desastre. El ejército de la Unión se retiró para Centerville durante la noche.

CONSECUENCIAS

La victoria Confederada contrapesó las pérdidas en el oeste.
Esto creó un camino para la invasión del Norte.
Porter recibió un consejo de guerra.

Staat: Virginia

Befehlshaber der US:
 Generalmajor John Pope
Armee der US: Armee von Virginia
 Truppenstärke: 65,000

Verluste:
 Gefallen: 1,747
 Verwundet: 8,452
 Gefangengenommen oder vermißt: 4,263

Befehlshaber der CS:
 General Robert E. Lee
Armee der CS: Armee von Nordvirginia
 Truppenstärke: 55,000

Verluste:
 Gefallen: 1,553
 Verwundet: 7,812
 Gefangengenommen oder vermißt: 109

KOMMENTAR

Stonewall Jackson's Vernichtung des Nachschublagers der Unionarmee an der Manassas Junction, veranlaßte Generalmajor John Pope, seine Uniontruppen in dieser Gegend zu konzentrieren.

Beim 29. August hatte Jackson seine Angriffslinie im Wald, hinter einem unfertigen Bahndamm, aufgestellt. An diesem Tag griff General Pope mit Truppen von Sigel, Hooker, Kearney und Reynolds, Jackson an. Jedoch die Angriffe, die verzöttelt und unkoordiniert vorgingen, brachten keine Resultate. Am Nachmittag bezog das 5. Unionkorps von General Porter eine Stellung links von Pope. General Pope befahl Porter vorzurücken, denn er glaubte, daß Porter einen freien Angriffsweg auf Jackson's rechte Flanke hatte. Porter bereitete sich auf den Kampf vor. Vernünftigerweise nahm Porter aber den Befehl zurück, als er lernte, daß Longstreet's Flügel von Lee's Konföderiertenarmee, mit 30,000 Mann, schon auf dem ihm gegenüberliegenden Feld angekommen war. Porter's Entscheidung ruinierte seine Karriere im Militär, aber höchst wahrscheinlich rettete die Armee.

Während der Nacht befestigte Lee seine Linien. Pope sah das als einen Rückzug der Konföderierten an, und plante seine Verfolgung. Die Kolonnen der Föderalisten rückten, in drei Linien tief, über die freien Felder vor. Artillerie- und Musketenfeuer ließ die blauen Linien torkeln. Die ersten beiden Wellen wurden zurückgeschlagen, aber die dritte rückte unaufhaltsam vor. Diesmal überrannten die Föderalisten den Bahndamm und pressten die Linie der Konföderierten. Als der Nahkampf der Linie entlang tobte, griff eine Gruppe von Konföderierten, die nun ohne Munition waren, zu Steinen, die sie auf die Föderalisten schleuderten. Nachdem Porter zurückgeschlagen war, befahl Longstreet seinen Truppen, vorwärts zu gehen. Die schreienden grauen Linien, die aus südlicher Richtung vorrückten, schwenkten nach Nordosten und überraschten die Unionarmee. Jackson ebenfalls befahl seine Truppen vorwärts. Einheiten der Föderalisten lösten sich bald in ein blaues Meer auf. Pope's Armee war auf vollem Rückzug.

Ein schwerer Kampf trug sich auf Chinn Ridge ab. Dies gewann Pope Zeit, eine starke Defensivstellung auf Henry Hügel aufzubauen. Sein tapferer Widerstand dort bewahrte die Unionarmee vor einer Katastrophe.

Während der Nacht zog sich die Unionarmee nach Centerville zurück.

BEDEUTUNG

Der Sieg der Konföderierten glich die Niederlagen im Westen aus.
Der Sieg bahnte General Lee den Weg für seine Invasion des Nordens.
Porter kam for ein Kriegsgericht.

The Warrenton Turnpike crossed Bull Run on the Stone Bridge. It was the main route of the Federal retreat. Temporary wooden bridges were built by Federal engineers on the site during the war. One such bridge, destroyed after the Union retreat, August 31.

State: Virginia (W.VA)

U.S.	C.S.
Commander:	**Commander:**
Col. Dixon S. Miles	Maj. Gen. Thomas J. Jackson
Brig. Gen. Julius White	
U.S. Army: Railroad Brigade	C.S. Army Army of Northern Virginia
No. of Troops: 14,000	No. of Troops: 23,000
Casualties:	Casualties:
Killed: 44	Killed: 39
Wounded: 173	Wounded: 247
Captured or missing: 12,520	Captured or missing: 0

COMMENTS

As Lee moved into Maryland on his first northern invasion, the Union garrison at Harpers Ferry became a threat to the rear of the Confederate army. The capture of this garrison was a key element in Lee's plan so he left the task in the capable hands of "Stonewall" Jackson. Harpers Ferry sits in a hole with Maryland Heights overlooking the town from the north, Loudoun Heights from the south, and Bolivar Heights from the west.

By Sept. 13 Confederate Gen. McLaws was in position on Maryland Heights and Gen. Walker's southerners occupied Loudoun Heights. Jackson sealed the trap by marching his column toward Harpers Ferry form the west. The Federals, under Col. Miles, still retained a position on low-lying Bolivar Heights; and with the arrival of Gen. White's brigade from Martinsburg, Miles bolstered his command to 14,000. With Confederates looking down from two mountains, White waived his rank to Miles—the old army veteran who knew the terrain and disposition of troops about Harpers Ferry.

During the night of Sept. 14 Col. Davis and 1400 Union cavalrymen escaped across the Potomac River by a road left unguarded by the Confederates. On their route to freedom the horsemen even managed to capture some prisoners and wagons.

On the morning of the 15th Jackson was preparing to assault the left flank of the Union line on Bolivar Heights, but the attack became unnecessary when a Confederate artillery barrage forced the Federals to raise the white flag. Col. Miles received a mortal wound during the bombardment, compelling Gen. White to surrender to Stonewall Jackson.

SIGNIFICANCE

With this quick victory Jackson was able to catch up with Lee in time to force a draw with McClellan at Antietam.

Large quantities of much needed supplies, guns and cannons were captured by the Confederates.

Etat: Virginie

Etat-Unis	Etats Confédérés
Commandants:	**Commandant:**
Colonel Dixon S. Miles	Général de division Thomas J.
Général de Brigade Julius White	Jackson
Armée: Brigade du Chemin de Fer	Armée: de Virginie du Nord
14 000 soldats	23 000 soldats
Pertes:	Pertes:
Tués: 44	Tués: 39
Blessés: 173	Blessés: 247
Prisonniers ou disparus: 12 520	Prisonniers ou disparus: 0

COMMENTAIRE

Tandis que Lee entrait dans le Maryland pour sa première invasion du Nord, la garnison de l'Union à Harpers Ferry devint une menace pour l'arrière de l'armée confédérée. La prise de la garnison étant l'élément majeur du plan de Lee, il confia cette mission à la compétence de "Stonewall" Jackson. Harpers Ferry se trouve dans une dépression avec Maryland Heights surplombant la ville au nord, Loudoun Heights au sud, et Bolivar Heights à l'ouest.

Le 13 septembre, le général confédéré McLaws était en position sur Maryland Heights, et les Sudistes de général Walker occupaient Loudoun Heights. Jackson ferma le piège en dirigeant sa colonne de l'ouest vers Harpers Ferry. Commandés par le colonel Miles, les Fédéraux restaient en position enfoncés dans les bas terrains de Bolivar Heights; et quand la brigade du général White arriva de Martinsburg, Miles maintint sa commande de 14 000 soldats. Les Confédérés ayant bonne vue du haut de leurs montagnes, White abandonna son rang à Miles – vétéran de la vieille armée – que connaissait le terrain et la disposition des troupes à Harpers Ferry.

Pendant la nuit du 14 septembre, le colonel Davis et 1 400 hommes de la cavalerie de l'Union s'évadèrent à travers le Potomac par une route non surveillée par les Confédérés. Sur la route de leur liberté, les cavaliers trouvèrent même le moyen de prendre quelques prisonniers et des fourgons.

Le matin du 15, comme Jackson se préparait à mettre l'assaut sur le flanc gauche de la ligne unioniste à Bolivar Heights, l'attaque se révéla inutile car un barrage formé par l'artillerie confédérée força les Fédéraux à lever le drapeau blanc. Le colonel Miles reçut une blessure mortelle pendant le bombardement, ce qui obligea le général White à se rendre à Stonewall Jackson.

CONSEQUENCES

Grâce à sa rapide victoire, Jackson put rejoindre Lee à temps pour aboutir à une partie nulle avec McClellan à Antietam.

Les Confédérés prirent de grandes quantités d'approvisionnements dont ils avaient besoin.

Important Landmarks
Potomac & Shenandoah Rivers
The Point
Jefferson Rock
Maryland, Loudon & Bolivar Heights
Virginius Island
Baltimore & Ohio R.R.
Camp Hill

Important Buildings
John Brown Fort/Engine House
Master Armorer's House
U.S. Armory (site)
Hall's Rifle Works (site)
Arsenal Buildings (site)
Lockwood House
St. John's Episcopal Church
St. Peter's Catholic Church
Harper House
Storer College

Estado: Virginia

U.S.	C.S.
Comandante: Col. Dixon S. Miles Brig. Gen. Julius White U.S. Ejército: Railroad Brigade No. de tropas: 14,000 Pérdidas: Muertos: 44 Heridos: 173 Capturados o ausentes: 12,520	Comandante: Maj. Gen. Thomas J. Jackson C.S. Ejército: Army of Northern Virginia No. de tropas: 23,000 Pérdidas: Muertos: 39 Heridos: 247 Capturados o ausentes: 0

COMENTARIO

Cuando Lee entró en el estado de Maryland en su primera invasión del Norte, la guarnición Federal en Harpers Ferry llegó a ser una amenaza al trasero del ejército Confederado. La captura de esta guarnición fue un elemento principal en el plan de Lee, así dejó el quehacer en las manos capaces de "Stonewall" Jackson. Harpers Ferry está situado en un agujero con los Maryland Heights dominando el pueblo desde el norte, Loudon Heights desde el sur, y Bolival Heights desde el oeste.

El día 13 de septiembre el General McLaws ya estaba en posición en Maryland Heights y los Sureños del General Walker ocupaban Loudon Heights. Jackson cerró la jaula poniendo en marcha su columna hacia Harpers Ferry del oeste. Los Federales, bajo el Col. Miles, todavía retenían una posición en Bolivar Heights; y con la llegada de la brigada del General White de Martinsburg, Miles aumentó su comandancia a 14,000. Con los Confederados mirando para abajo desde dos montañas, White le dio su comandancia a Miles—el veterano viejo del ejército que conocía bien el terreno y la disposición de las tropas alrededor de Harpers Ferry.

Durante la noche del 14 de septiembre, el Col. Davis y 1400 soldados de caballería Federal, se escaparon a través del río Potomac por un camino dejado sin guardias Confederadas. En su ruta a la libertad los soldados lograron capturar algunos prisioneros y carromatos.

Durante la mañana del 15, Jackson se preparó para el asalto de la flanca izquierda de la línea Federal en Bolivar Heights, pero el ataque no fue necesario porque un bombardeo Confederado forzó a los Yanquis a levantar la bandera blanca. El Col. Miles recibió una herida mortal durante este bombardeo, lo que hizo que el General White se rindiera a Stonewall Jackson.

CONSECUENCIAS

Con esta victoria rápida Jackson pudo ponerse al día con Lee a tiempo para forzar un empate con McClellan en la batalla de Antietam.

Cantidades grandes de provisiones, muy necesitadas, armas y cañones se capturaron por los Confederados.

Staat: Virginia (Westvirginia)

Befehlshaber der US:	Befehlshaber der CS:
Oberst Dixon S. Miles Armee der US: Eisenbahnbrigade Truppenstärke: 14,000 Verluste: Gefallen: 44 Verwundet: 173 Gefangengenommen oder vermißt: 12,520	Generalmajor Thomas J. Jackson Armee der CS: Armee von Nordvirginia Truppenstärke: 23,000 Verluste: Gefallen: 39 Verwundet: 247 Gefangengenommen oder vermißt: 0

KOMMENTAR

Als Lee sich auf seiner ersten Invasion des Nordens in den Staat Maryland rückte, bekam die Uniongarnison in Harpers Ferry eine Gefahr für die Nachhut der Armee der Konföderation. Die Eroberung dieser Garnison spielte eine Hauptrolle in Lee's Plänen. Aus diesem Grunde überließ er diese Aufgabe dem fähigen "Stonewall" Jackson. Harpers Ferry liegt in einem tiefen Flußtal - die Maryland Heights überblicken die Stadt vom Norden, die Loudoun Heights vom Suden, und die Bolivar Heights vom Westen.

Am 13. September war Konföderationsgeneral McLaws in Stellung auf Maryland Heights, und die Konföderierten, unter General Walker, besaßen die Loudoun Heights. Jackson stellte der Unionarmee eine Falle, wobei er seine Kolonne nach Harpers Ferry vom Westen anmarschierte. Die Föderalisten, unter Oberst Miles, hielten immer noch eine Stellung auf niedrigen Bolivar Heights, und mit Ankunft der Brigade von General White aus Martinsburg, verbesserte Miles seine Streitkräfte auf 14,000 Mann. Mit Hinsicht auf die Konföderierten Stellungen auf den zwei Bergen, die den Überblick ins Tal beherrschten, überließ White das Kommando Miles, ein alter Veteran, der mit dem Terrain und der Aufstellung der Truppen um Harpers Ferry bekannt war.

In der Nacht vom 14. September entkamen Overst Davis und 1,400 Unionkavalleristen über den Potomac Fluß auf einem von den Konföderierten unbewachten Weg. Auf ihrem Fluchtweg gelang es den Kavalleristen sogar, einige Soldaten gefangen zu nehmen und Wagen zu erobern.

Am Vormittag des 13. bereitete sich Jackson for, die linke Flanke der Unionlinie auf Bolivar Heights zu stürmen. Aber der Angriff wurde unnötig. Sperrfeuer der Südartillerie zwang die Föderalisten, die weisse Fahne zu hissen. Während der Bombardierung wurde Oberst Miles tödlich verwundet, was General White zwang, sich Jackson zu ergeben.

BEDEUTUNG

Durch diesen schnellen Sieg war es Jackson möglich, Lee beizeiten einzuholen, was dazu beitrug, den Kampf gegen McClellan bei Antietam ohne Entscheidung zu Ende bringen zu können.

Unmengen von Proviant, Gewehren und Kanonen, die för die Konföderierten dringend notwendig waren, wurden erobert.

The town of Harpers Ferry as seen from the Maryland side of the Potomac River. The ruined buildings of the U.S. Armory line the river.

State: Maryland

U.S.

Commander:
   Maj. Gen. George B. McClellan
U.S. Army: Army of the Potomac
   No. of Troops: 87,000
Casualties:
   Killed: 2,108
   Wounded: 9,549
   Captured or missing: 753

C.S.

Commander:
   Gen. Robert E. Lee
C.S. Army: Army of Northern Virginia
   No. of Troops: 40,000
Casualties:
   Killed: 1,512
   Wounded: 7,816
   Captured or missing: 1,844

COMMENTS

General Lee's plans for a northern invasion fell short of success, but he was determined to salvage his campaign hoping for a decisive victory as he gathered his army behind Antietam Creek.

The battle started at dawn when Hooker's Union I Corps attacked the Confederate left at the northern end of the battlefield. The Federals poured through the North Woods and into a cornfield where they ran into Jackson's Confederates. The Southerners were slowly pushed back during the vicious fighting. Around 6:00 a.m. Jackson was reinforced and was able to drive the Federals back. An hour later, however, Mansfield's XII Corps advanced in support of Hooker. The XII Corps passed the East Woods and headed through the same cornfield toward the West Woods and the Dunker Church. Here, Jackson managed to hold on as hundreds of soldiers on both sides fell, including Mansfield dead and Hooker wounded. Now the Union II Corps entered the battle also. Its leading division drove deep into the West Woods only to be met by Jackson's remnants and two divisions of fresh reinforcements. The Federal division was hammered on three sides losing 2,200 men out of 5,500 in twenty minutes, or 2 per second. Jackson chased the retreating Federals back across the cornfield only to be repulsed with even heavier losses. The other two divisions of the II Corps veered to the south and hit the Confederate center along a sunken road soon to be named "Bloody Lane." After three hours of furious attacks the Confederates were dislodged, but the Federals were unable to pursue.

The action shifted to the southern end of the field around a bridge where Burnside's IX Corps finally made a crossing by 3:00 p.m. and deployed. Burnside slowly pushed the weakened Confederate right flank back toward Sharpsburg and a Union victory, when suddenly Hill's division arrived from Harpers Ferry, drove the Federals back toward the bridge, and saved the Southern army. The battle was finally over. The Confederates re-crossed the Potomac River to Virginia on the night of the 18th.

SIGNIFICANCE

The bloodiest single day of the Civil War.

Tactically, the battle was a draw, but it was a moral, political, and diplomatic victory for the North which allowed Lincoln to issue of the Preliminary Emancipation Proclamation.

Etat: Maryland

Etat-Unis

Commandant:
   Général de division George B. McClellan
Armée: du Potomac
   87 000 soldats
Pertes:
   Tués: 2 108
   Blessés: 9 549
   Prisonniers ou disparus: 753

Etats Confédérés

Commandant:
   Général Robert E. Lee
Armée: de Virginie du Nord
   40 000 soldats
Pertes:
   Tués: 1 512
   Blessés: 7 816
   Prisonniers ou disparus: 1 844

COMMENTAIRE

Les plans du général Lee d'envahir le Nord faillirent, mais il était résolu à sauver sa campagne, espérant une victoire décisive en rassemblant son armée derrière Antietam Creek.

La lutte commença à l'aube quand le corps d l'Union, commandé par Hooker, attaqua la gauche des Confédérés dans la partie nord du champ de bataille. Les Fédéraux arrivaient en grand nombre à travers North Woods et dans un champ de maïs où ils rencontrèrent les Confédérés de Jackson. Les Sudistes furent lentement repoussés pendant une lutte sans merci. Vers 6 heures du matin, Jackson reçut des renforts et repoussa les Fédéraux. Une heure plus tard, cependant, le corps XII de Mansfield avança pour soutenir Hooker. Le corps XII dépassa les bois de l'est et s'engagea dans le même champ de maïs vers les bois de l'ouest et église Dunker. Jackson restait debout tandis que dans les deux camps les soldats tombaient par centaines; Mansfield mourut et Hooker fut blessé. Enfin le corps II de l'Union entra dans la bataille. Sa division de tête s'engagea dans les bois de l'ouest pour y rencontrer les restes de corps de Jackson et deux divisions de renforts. La division fédérale fut écrasée sur trois côtés, perdant 2 200 hommes sur 5 500 en 20 minutes, soit 2 par seconde. Jackson chassa les Fédéraux en retraite à travers le champ de maïs pour être repoussé avec des pertes encore plus lourdes. Les deux autres divisions du corps II virèrent au sud et frappèrent les Confédérés du centre le long d'un chemin creux bientôt appelé la "Voie Sanglante." Après trois heures de bataille furieuse, les Confédérés furent délogés, mais les Fédéraux étaient incapables de les poursuivre.

L'action fut déplacée vers la partie sud du champ, près du pont que le corps IX de Burnside arriva à traverser à 15 heures pour déployer ses troupes. Peu à peu, Burnside repoussa le flanc droit des Confédérés affaibis vers Sharpsburg donnant l'espoir d'une victoire pour l'Union, quand soudain la division de Hill, arrivant de Harpers Ferry, battit les Fédéraux et sauva l'armée sudiste. La bataille était enfin à son terme. Dans la nuit du 18, les Confédérés retraversèrent le Potomac pour revenir en Virginie.

CONSEQUENCES

Ce fut le jour le plus sanglant de la guerre civile.

Du point de vue tactique, cette bataille était une partie nulle, mais stratégiquement parlant, c'est cette victoire morale, politique et diplomatique pour les Nordistes qui a amené la question de la Preliminary Emancipation Proclamation (Proclamation Préliminaire de l'Emancipation).

Important Landmarks

Miller "Cornfield"
"Burnside" Bridge
"Bloody Lane"
North Woods
East Woods
West Woods
Hagerstown Pike
Nicodemus Hill
Harpers Ferry Road
Blackford's Ford
Snavely's Ford
Antietam Creek

Important Buildings

Dunker Church
Poffenberger Farm
Mumma Farm
Roulette Farm
Piper Farm
Pry House
Miller Farm

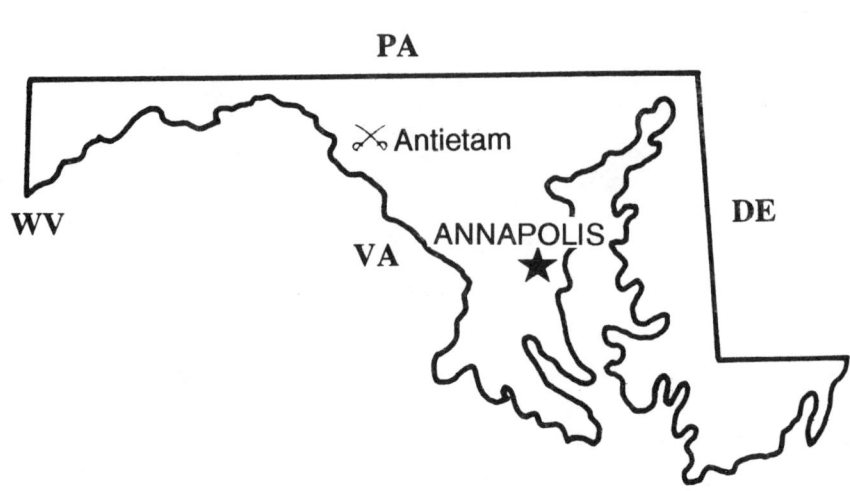

Estado: Maryland

U.S.	C.S.
Comandante:	Comandante:
Maj. Gen George B. McClellan	Gen. Robert E. Lee
U.S. Ejército: Army of the Potomac	C.S. Ejército: Army of Northern Virginia
No. de tropas: 87,000	No. de tropas: 40,000
Pérdidas:	Pérdidas:
Muertos: 2,108	Muertos: 1,512
Heridos: 9,549	Heridos: 7,816
Capturados o ausentes: 753	Capturados o ausentes: 1,844

COMENTARIO

Los planes del General Lee para una invasión del Norte no habían tenido el éxito que él quiso, pero se determinó salvar su campaña esperando una victoria decesiva poniendo a su ejército detrás del arroyo Antietam.

La batalla comenzó al amanecer cuando el cuerpo I del General Hooker atacó la izquierda Confederada al término norteño del campo de batalla. Los Federales entraron por North Woods (bosque del norte) y en un campo de maíz donde encontraron a los Rebeldes de Jackson. Los Confederados fueron poco a poco empujados para atrás durante la lucha violenta. Alrededor de las 6 de la mañana Jackson fue reforzado y pudo empujar a los Federales. Una hora después, sin embargo, el XI Cuerpo I del General Mansfield avanzó para apoyar a Hooker. El XI Cuerpo I pasaron por el East Woods y se dirigió por el mismo campo de maíz hacia el West Woods y la iglesia Dunker. Aquí, Jackson lograba mantener su posición mientras cientos de soldados de los dos lados caían, incluyendo a Mansfield muerto y Hooker herido. Ahora el cuerpo II Federal entró en la batalla. Su primera división se manejó profundamente en el West Woods para encontrarse con los que quedaban de Jackson y dos divisiones frescas de refuerzos. La division Federal fue martillada por tres lados perdiendo 2,200 hombres de 5,500 en 20 minutos, o dos por segundo. Jackson persiguió a los Federales que huían por el campo de maíz y fue repulsado con muchas pérdidas. Las otras dos divisiones del cuerpo II se volvieron al sur y atacaron el centro Confederado en un camino hundido que llegó a tener el nombre "Bloody Lane" (Camino de sangre). Después de tres horas de ataques furiosos los Confederados fueron desalojados, pero los Yanquis no pudieron perseguirlos.

La acción se mudó hacia el sur del campo cerca de un puente donde el cuerpo IX del General Burnside finalmente cruzó sobre las tres y desplegó sus tropas. Poco a poco Burnside empujó al flanco Confederado debilitado para atrás hacia Sharpsburg y una victoria Federal, cuando, de pronto, la división de A.P. Hill llegó de Harpers Ferry, manejó la división Federal hacia el puente y salvó el ejército Confederado. Por fin la batalla se acabó. Los Confederados cruzaron el río Potomac a Virginia la noche del 18.

CONSECUENCIAS

Fue el día más sangrienta de la guerra civil.

Tácticamente la batalla fue un empate, pero estratégicamente fue una victoria moral, política, y diplomática para la Unión. Esto siguió a la Proclamación de Emancipación.

Staat: Maryland

Befehlshaber der US:	Befehlshaber der CS:
Generalmajor George B. McClellan	General Robert E. Lee
Armee der US: Armee des Potomac	Armee der CS: Armee von Nordvirginia
Truppenstärke: 87,000	Truppenstärke: 40,000
Verluste:	Verluste:
Gefallen: 2,108	Gefallen: 1,512
Verwundet: 9,549	Verwundet: 7,816
Gefangengenommen oder vermißt: 753	Gefangengenommen oder vermißt: 1,844

KOMMENTAR

General Lee's Pläne für eine Invasion im Norden gingen nicht in Erfüllung, aber er war fest entschlossen, daß sein Feldzug nicht ohne Erfolg bleiben sollte. Er hoffte doch noch auf einen entscheidenden Sieg und sammelte seine Armee hinter Antietam Creek.

Die Schlacht begann bei Tagesanbruch, als Hooker's 1. Unionkorps die Konföderierten links auf der Nordseite des Schlachtfeldes angriff. Die Föderalisten strömten durch den Nordwald bis auf ein Maisfeld, wo sie auf Jackson's Konföderierte stießen. Während des grauenhaften Gefechts wurden die Konföderierten langsam zurückgedrängt - aber um 6.00 Uhr wurde Jackson verstärkt und konnte die Föderalisten zurücktreiben. Eine Stunde später aber rückte Mansfield's 12. Korps zur Unterstützung Hooker's vor. Das 12. Korps ging am Ostwald vorbei und wendete sich durch dasselbe Maisfeld auf den Westwald und die Dunker Church zu. Hier gelang es Jackson, auszuhalten, als beiderseits Hunderte von Soldaten fielen. Unter ihnen waren Hooker, der verwundet wurde, und Mansfield, der starb. Nun rückte das 2. Unionkorps in die Schlacht ein. Seine führende Division stieß tief in den Westwald ein, wo sie Überreste von Jackson's Truppen und zwei Divisionen von frischen Verstärkungstruppen erwarteten. Die Föderalisten wurden auf drei Seiten geschlagen und verloren, innerhalb 20 Minuten, 2,200 Mann von der 5,500 Truppenstärke, oder zwei Mann pro Sekunde.

Jackson jagte die zurückfliehenden Föderalisten über das Maisfeld, um dann selbst mit schweren Verlusten zurückgeschlagen zu werden. Die beiden anderen Divisionen des 2. Korps drehten sich nach Süden. An einer tiefliegenden Straße, die bald den Namen "Bloody Lane" (Blutiger Weg) bekam, stürmten sie auf die Mitte der Konföderierten ein. Nach drei Stunden wütiger Angriffe wurden die Konföderierten verdrängt, aber die Föderalisten waren nicht imstande sie zu verfolgen.

Die Aktion verlegte sich auf die südliche Seite des Feldes, an eine Brücke, wo das 9. Korps von Burnside endlich um 15.00 Uhr den Fluß überquerte und sich aufstellte. Langsam drängte Burnside die geschwächte rechte Flanke der Konföderierten gegen Sharpsburg zurück. Es schien als ob Burnside sie besiegen würde, aber plötzlich traf Hill's Division von Harpers Ferry ein, trieb die Föderalisten wieder auf die Brücke zurück und rettete die Armee des Südens.

Endlich war die Schlacht beendet. In der Nacht des 18. überquerten die Konföderierten den Potomac Fluß auf ihrem Weg zurück nach Virginia.

BEDEUTUNG

Der blutigste Tag im ganzen Bürgerkrieg.

Taktisch ging die Schlacht unentschieden aus, aber strategisch gesehen, war sie ein psychologischer, politischer und diplomatischer Sieg für den Norden, und führte zur Herausgabe der Vorverkündung der Emanzipation (Preliminary Emancipation Proclamation).

The Confederate dead and limber are possibly from Parker's Virginia Battery. The Dunker Church and West Woods are in the background.

State: Kentucky

U.S.	C.S.
Commander:	Commander:
Maj. Gen. Don Carlos Buell	Gen. Braxton Bragg
U.S. Army: Army of the Ohio	C.S. Army: Army of the Mississippi
No. of Troops: 39,721	No. of Troops: 16,000
Casualties:	Casualties:
Killed: 845	Killed: 510
Wounded: 2,851	Wounded: 2,635
Captured or missing: 515	Captured or missing: 251

COMMENTS

The Battle of Perryville on Oct. 8, 1862, ended Confederate Gen. Braxton Bragg's invasion of Kentucky which began on August 14.

Maj. Gen. Buell's army cautiously pursued Bragg around the state. On Oct. 2 Buell split his army into four parts, three columns headed generally southeast. The fourth headed east to threaten the Provisional Confederate Government set up at Frankfort. The Union soldiers, marching through the drought stricken countryside, suffered form the heat and dust.

By the end of the week, Buell ordered his columns to concentrate west of Perryville in the hopes of getting some water. Gen. Bragg, believing that the real attack would be at Frankfort, had only 16,000 troops at Perryville. By the morning of Oct. 8 only one Union column, commanded by Brig. Gen. Gilbert, faced Perryville. Gilbert's command was under a constant fire until midday. At noon Maj. Gen. Crittenden's corps had arrived extending Gilbert's line to the right and Maj. Gen. McCook's corps just reached the field. Gen. Bragg immediately ordered an attack on the left of the Union army. As McCook was still positioning his troops on the left, they were hit by the advancing Confederates. The Southern charge soon dissolved into desperate close-quarters fighting along the left and center of the Union line. The Confederates found an unguarded ravine between Gilbert and McCook's commands which formed a gap in the Union line. Rushing through it, the Southerners forced McCook to fall back. By late afternoon the Union center was stabilized and the left was reinforced. Although McCook was pushed back more than a mile his lines still held.

Darkness ended the fighting. Gen. Buell planned to renew the fight the next day but the Confederates, in the face of a greatly superior force, withdrew to Harrodsburg during the night.

SIGNIFICANCE

Bragg's defeat at Perryville ended Confederate plans of bringing Kentucky into the Confederacy.

Etat: Kentucky

Etat-Unis	Etats Confédérés
Commandant:	Commandant:
Général de division	Général Braxton Bragg
Don Carlos Buell	
Armée: de l'Ohio	Armée: du Mississipi
39 721 soldats	16 000 soldats
Pertes:	Pertes:
Tués: 845	Tués: 510
Blessés: 2 852	Blessés: 2 635
Prisonniers ou disparus: 515	Prisonniers ou disparus: 251

COMMENTAIRE

La Bataille de Perryville, le 8 octobre 1862, mit fin à l'invasion du Kentucky par le général Bragg qui l'avait commencée le 14 août.

L'armée du major général Buell, avec circonspecion, poursuivit Bragg à travers l'état. Le 2 octobre, Buell divisa son armée en 4; trois colonnes partirent en direction sud, et la quatrième colonne fonça à l'est pour menacer le gouvernement provisoire des Confédérés installé à Frankfort. Les soldats de l'Union, marchant à travers les campagnes frappées par la sécheresse, souffrirent de la chaleur et de la poussière.

A la fin de la semaine, espérant trouver de l'eau, Buell ordonna à ses colonnes de se masser à l'ouest de Perryville. Le général Bragg, croyant que l'attaque réelle serait à Frankfort, n'avait que 16 000 hommes à Perryville. Le matin du 8 octobre, une seule colonne de l'Union, aux ordres du général Gilbert, fit face à Perryville. Jusqu'au milieu du jour, les troupes de Gilbert furent sous les feux de l'ennemi. A midi, le corps d'armée de général Crittenden était arrivé pour soutenir la droite de la ligne de Gilbert, et le corps d'armée du général McCook atteignit le champ de bataille. Immédiatement, le général Bragg ordonna d'attaquer la gauche de l'armée de l'Union. Alors que McCook était encore en train de mettre ses troupes en position à gauche, celles-ci furent frappées par les Confédérés. L'attaque sudiste se réduit à un combat corps à corps désespéré à la gauche et au centre des lignes de l'Union. Les Confédérés trouvèrent un ravin non surveillé qui formait une trouée dans les lignes de l'Union, entre les troupes de Gilbert et de McCook. S'y précipitant, les Sudistes forcèrent McCook à se replier. En fin d'aprés-midi, le centre de l'Union était stabilisé et la gauche était renforcée. Bien que repoussé à environ 2 km, la ligne de McCook tenait bon.

La tombée du jour mit fin au combat. Le général Buell avait l'intention de reprendre la bataille le jour suivant, mais les Confédérés, prévoyant des forces unionistes bien supérieures, se retirèrent à Harrodsburg pendant la nuit.

CONSEQUENCE

La défaite de Bragg à Perryville coupa court à l'espérance des Confédérés d'inclure le Kentucky dans la Confédération.

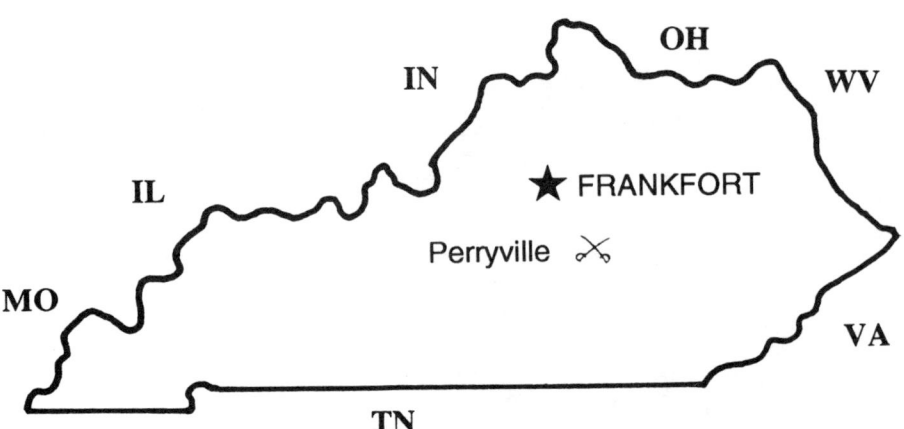

Important Landmarks
Doctor's Creek
Chaplin River
Old Mackville Pike
Springfield Pike
Lebanon Pike

Important Buildings
Russel House
H.P. Bottom Farmhouse

Estado: Kentucky

U.S.
Comandante:
Maj. Gen Don Carlos Buell
U.S. Ejército: Army of the Ohio
No. de tropas: 39,271
Pérdidas:
Muertos: 845
Heridos: 2,851
Capturados o ausentes: 515

C.S.
Comandante:
Gen. Braxton Bragg
C.S. Ejército: Army of the Mississippi
No. de tropas: 16,000
Pérdidas:
Muertos: 510
Heridos: 2,635
Capturados o ausentes: 251

COMENTARIO

La batalla de Perryville, el 8 de 1862, terminó la invasión de Kentucky por el General Braxton Bragg, la cual empezó el 14 de agosto.

El ejército del General Buell persiguió con cuidado al ejército de Bragg por el estado. El 2 de octubre Buell dividió su ejército en 4 partes, tres columnas se dirigieron generalmente para el sudeste. La cuarta fue al este para amenazar el Gobierno Confederado Provisional establecido en Frankfort. Los soldados Federales, marchando por regiones muy áridas, sufrieron del calor y del polvo.

Al final de la semana, Buell mandó que sus columnas se concentraran al oeste de Perryville con la esperanza de encontrar agua. El General Bragg, creyendo que el ataque real sería en Frankfort, sólamente tenía 16,000 tropas en Perryville. Por la mañana del 8 de octubre sólo una columna Federal, bajo el Brig. General Gilbert, se enfrentaba a Perryville. La comandancia de Gilbert estuvo bajo un fuego constante hasta el mediodía. A las 12 el cuerpo del Maj. General Crittenden había llegado, extendiendo la línea de Gilbert a la derecha y el cuerpo del General McCook acabó de llegar al campo. El General Bragg inmediátemente ordenó un ataque a la izquierda Federal. Mientras McCook todavía ponía a sus tropas en posición, ellos fueron golpeados por un avance Confederado. El asalto pronto se convirtió en una lucha desesperada de cuerpo a cuerpo por el centro y la izquierda de la línea Federal. Los Confederados encontraron un barranco no guardado entre las tropas de Gilbert y McCook. Esto era un agujero en la línea Federal. Dándose prisa por el barranco, los Confederados forzaron a McCook para atrás. Tarde por la tarde, el centro de la línea Federal se estabilizó y la izquierda fue reforzada. Aunque, McCook fue empujado por más de una milla sus líneas todavía se mantenían.

La oscuridad terminó la lucha. El General Buell planeó comenzar la batalla de nuevo el próximo día, pero los Confederados, contra una fuerza superior en números, se retiraron a Harrodsburg durante la noche.

CONSECUENCIAS

La derrota de Bragg en Perryville terminó los planes de los Confederados de traer Kentucky a los estados Confederados.

Staat: Kentucky

Befehlshaber der US:
Generalmajor Don Carlos Buell
Armee der US: Armee des Ohio
Truppenstärke: 39,721
Verluste:
Gefallen: 845
Verwundet: 2,851
Gefangengenommen oder vermißt: 515

Befehlshaber der CS:
General Braxton Bragg
Armee der CS: Armee des Mississippi
Truppenstärke: 16,000
Verluste:
Gefallen: 510
Verwundet: 2,635
Gefangengenommen oder vermißt: 251

KOMMENTAR

Die Schlacht bei Perryville brachte am 8. Oktober 1862 ein Ende zu der am 14. August bei General Braxton Bragg begonnenen Invasion von Kentucky. Die Armee von Generalmajor Buell setzte Bragg behutsam durch den Staat nach. Am 2. Oktober teilte Buell seine Armee in vier Teile - drei Kolonnen gingen südostwärts, während die vierte Kolonne sich ostwärts wendete, und damit die Provisionische Regierung der Konföderation, die ihren Sitz in Frankfort hatte, bedrohte. Die Hitze und der Staub erschwerten den Marsch der Unionsoldaten über das dürre Land.

Am Ende der Woche befahl Buell seinen Kolonnen, sich westlich von Perryville zu konzentrieren, in der Hoffnung, Wasser zu finden. Da General Bragg der Ansicht war, daß der eigentliche Angriff bei Frankfort stattfinden würde, hatte er nur 16,000 Truppen bei Perryville. Am Morgen des 8. Oktober stand nur eine Unionkolonne - unter dem Kommando von Brigadegeneral Gilbert - vor Perryville. Bis 12.00 Uhr Mittags war Gilbert unter stetigem Feuer. Die Ankunft, um 12.00 Uhr, von Generalmajor Crittenden's Korps, verlängerte Gilbert's Linie nach rechts. Zur selben Zeit erreichte das Korps von Generalmajor McCook das Schlachtfeld.

General Bragg befahl sofort einen Angriff auf die linke Seite der Unionarmee. Während McCook im Begriff war, die Aufstellung seiner Truppen auf der linken Flanke zu vervollständigen, wurden sie von den vorrückenden Konföderierten angestürmt. Der Ansturm der Südstaatler löste sich bald an der linken Seite, und entlang der Mitte der Unionlinie, in einen verzweifelten Nahkampf auf. Konföderierte entdeckten eine unbewachte Schlucht zwischen den Kommandanturen von Gilbert und McCook, die eine Lücke in der Unionlinie bildete. Die Südstaatler stürzten sich durch diese und zwangen McCook zum Rückfall. Spät am Nachmittag hatte sich die Unionmitte stabilisiert, und die linke Flanke wurde verstärkt. Obwohl McCook etwa zwei Kilometer zurückgedrängt wurde, hielten seine Linien.

Die Dunkelheit endete das Kämpfen. Buell hatte es vor, am nächsten Tag den Kampf wieder aufzunehmen, aber die Konföderierten, angesichts der weit überlegenen Macht, zogen sich während der Nacht nach Harrodsburg zurück.

BEDEUTUNG

Bragg's Niederlage by Perryville setzte dem Konföderationsplan ein Ende, Kentucky in die Konföderation zu bringen.

View of the battlefield on the Union left where Colonel George Webster commanding the Thirty-fourth Brigade was killed.

FREDERICKSBURG
December 13, 1862

State: Virginia

U.S.
Commander:
  Maj. Gen. Ambrose E. Burnside
U.S. Army: Army of the Potomac
  No. of Troops: 120,000
Casualties:
  Killed: 1,300
  Wounded: 9,600
  Captured or missing: 1,800

C.S.
Commander:
  Gen. Robert E. Lee
C.S. Army: Army of Northern Virginia
  No. of Troops: 80,000
Casualties:
  Killed: 600
  Wounded: 4,100
  Captured or missing: 600

Etat: Virginie

Etat-Unis
Commandant:
  Général de division
  Ambrose E. Burnside
Armée: du Potomac
  120 000 soldats
Pertes:
  Tués: 1 300
  Blessés: 9 600
  Prisonniers ou disparus: 1 800

Etats Confédérés
Commadant:
  Général Robert E. Lee

Armée: de Virginie du Nord
  80 000
Pertes:
  Tués: 600
  Blessés: 4 100
  Prisonniers ou disparus: 600

COMMENTS

In November 1862, Maj. Gen. Ambrose Burnside replaced Gen. McClellan as Commander of the Army of the Potomac. Burnside's plan was to move against Richmond by way of Fredericksburg, VA. The Army of the Potomac made a swift march to Falmouth, a town across the Rappahannock River from Fredericksburg, at a time when the Southern army was widely separated. But due to Burnside's incompetence and a delay in getting pontoon bridges, Lee had time to concentrate his army in the Fredericksburg area. Building the bridges was difficult due to Southern sharpshooters firing from the town.

By Dec. 12 the Federals had crossed the river and were in possession of the town with their line extending south to another pontoon crossing. The Confederate line was established on the high ground west of Fredericksburg. Their seven mile line included a strong position west of town where Southern infantry stood in a sunken road behind a stone wall with artillery massed on Marye's Heights above them.

Burnside started the attack at 9:00 a.m. the next morning. Gen. Reynolds, at the southern most crossing, was ordered to attack Jackson's troops at Hamilton's Crossing in the hopes of turning the Confederate right. Despite heavy artillery fire, Gen. Meade's division broke through the Confederate line making a Union victory possible. But no reserves were sent to support Meade or exploit his breakthrough. By mid-afternoon Jackson's reserves had pushed the Federals back and repaired their line.

Around noon, not waiting for news from Reynolds' attack, Burnside ordered Gen. Sumner to attack Marye's Heights. Sumner's men advanced and were violently repulsed. Burnside, unwilling to accept that his plan failed, ordered continued attacks on the Heights. The artillery atop the hill blew holes in the advancing columns as Longstreet's infantry in the sunken road mowed down wave after wave of Federals. The attacks were suicidal as none of the Federals got within twenty yards of the stone wall. Darkness finally ended the slaughter.

Two days later, under cover of darkness and a heavy rain, the Army of the Potomac recrossed the Rappahannock River.

SIGNIFICANCE

Another "On to Richmond" drive was stopped.

Burnside was soon relived of command of the Army of the Potomac.

Morale was lowered in the Union as Lee was victorious again and inflicted heavy casualties.

COMMENTAIRE

En novembre 1862, le général de division Ambrose Burnside remplaça le général McClellan au poste de Commandant de l'armée du Potomac. Burnside décida d'avancer contre Richmond via Fredericksburg, en Virginie. L'armée de Potomac marcha rapidement sur Falmouth, ville située sur l'autre rive de la rivière Rappahannock par rapport à Fredericksburg, au moment où l'armée sudiste était largement divisée. Mais à cause de l'incompétence de Burnside et du délai de l'arrivée des ponts de bateaux, Lee eut le temps de masser son armée dans la région de Fredericksburg. La construction des ponts était rendue difficile par les Sudistes faisant feu depuis la ville.

Le 12 décembre, leur ligne s'étendant au sud jusqu'à un autre pont, les Fédéraux étaient en possession de la ville. La ligne des Confédérés s'était établie sur une hauteur à l'ouest de Fredericksburg. Leur ligne d'une douzaine de km comprenait une position forte à l'ouest de la ville où leur infanterie se trouvait dans un chemin creux derriére un mur de pierre, avec leur artillerie massée au-dessus sur Marye' Heights.

Le matin suivant, à 9 heures, Burnside commença l'attaque. Le général Reynolds, placé au à la traversée sud, reçut l'ordre d'attaquer les troupes de Jackson à Hamilton, dans l'erpoir de deborder la droite condédérie. En dépit des feux de l'artillerie lourde, la division du général Meade traversa la ligne des Confédérés, donnant l'espoir d'une victoire de l'Union. Mais aucun renfort ne fut envoyé Meade pour le soutenir ou pour exploiter sa percée. Dans l'après-midi, les réserves de Jackson avaient repoussé les Fédéraux et réparé leur ligne.

Vers midi, sans attendre les nouvelles de l'attaque de Reynolds, Burnside donna au général Sumner l'ordre d'attaquer Marye's Heights. Les hommes de Sumner avancèrent et furent violemment repoussés. Refusant de reconnaitre son échec, Burnside donna l'ordre de continuer l'offensive sur les Heights. Du haut de la colline, l'artillerie trouait les colonnes d'infanterie pendant que Longstreet avançait dans le chemin creux, et fauchait des vagues de Fédéraux. Ces attaques étaient suicidaires: aucun Fédéral n'arrivait vivant à 20 m du mur de pierre. La nuit mit fin au massacre.

Deux jours plus tard, sous un ciel sombre et une pluie dense, l'armée du Potomac retraversa la rivière Rappahannock.

CONSEQUENCES

Une autre tentative de prendre Richmond était enrayée.

Burnside fut bientôt déchargé de la responsabilité de l'armée du Potomac.

Le moral de l'Union était abaissé tandis que Lee avait gagné une autre bataille et infligé de lourdes pertes aux Fédéraux.

Important Landmarks

Marye's Heights
The "Sunken Road"
Willis's Hill
Lansdown Valley
Lee's Hill
Howison Hill
Hamilton's Crossing
Prospect Hill
Canal Ditch
Stafford Heights
Rappahannock River
Franklin's Crossing

Important Buildings

Brompton/Marye Mansion
Stevens House
Innis House
Chatham/"Lacy House"
Bernard House
Phillips House

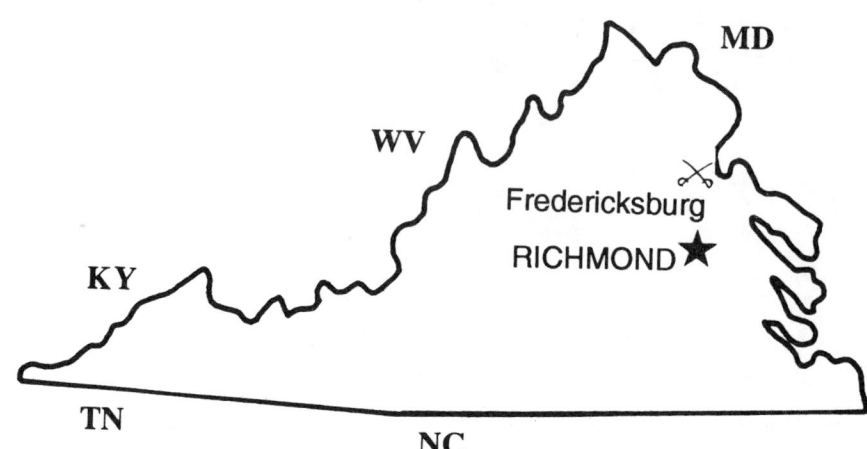

Estado: Virginia

U.S.

Comandante:
 Maj. Gen. Ambrose E. Burnside
U.S. Ejército: Army of the Potomac

No. de tropas: 120,000
Pérdidas:
 Muertos: 1,300
 Heridos: 9,600
 Capturados o ausentes: 1,800

C.S.

Comandante:
 Gen. Robert E. Lee
C.S. Ejército: Army of Northern Virginia

No. de tropas: 80,000
Pérdidas:
 Muertos: 600
 Heridos: 4,100
 Capturados o ausentes: 600

COMENTARIO

En noviembre de 1862 el General Ambrose Burnside reemplazó al General McClellan como comandante del Army of the Potomac. El plan de Burnside era moverse contra Richmond, Virginia por Fredericksburg. El Army of the Potomac hizo una marcha rápida a Falmouth, un pueblo al otro lado del río Rappahannock de Fredericksburg, en una época cuando el ejército Confederado estaba separado. Pero por la incompetencia de Burnside y una demora en conseguir los puentes de pontones, Lee tuvo tiempo para concentrar su ejército en el área de Fredericksburg. Construir los puentes fue difícil debidoa los buenos tiradores Confederados que tiraban desde el pueblo.

El día 12 de diciembre los Federales ya habían cruzado el río y tenían posesión del pueblo, su línea extendiéndose al sur a otro paso de pontones. La línea Confederada se estableció en la tierra alta al oeste de Fredericksburg. Su línea de siete millas incluía una posición fuerte al oeste del pueblo donde la infantería sureña estaba en un camino hundido detrás de una pared de piedras con artillería juntada en Marye's Heighs encima de ellos.

Burnside comenzó el ataque a las 9 de la mañana del 13. El General Reynolds, al paso más sureño, fue mandado atacar a las tropas de Jackson en Hamilton's Crossing con la esperanza de flanquear la derecha Confederada. Aunque el fuego de la artillería era fuerte, la división del General Meade pasó por la línea Confederada, haciendo posible una victoria para la Unión. Pero ninguna reserva se mandó para apoyar a Meade o explotar su éxito. Por la mediatarde las reservas de Jackson habían empujado a los Federales y reparado su línea.

Alrededor de las doce, no esperando noticias del ataque de Reynolds, Burnside ordenó a Sumner que atacara Marye's Heights. Los hombres de Sumner avanzaron y fueron violentamente repulsados. Burnside, no aceptando que su plan había fracasado, siguió con ataques repetidos contra Marye's Heights. La artillería encima abría agujeros grandes en las columnas que avanzaban mientras la infantería de Longstreet en el camino hundido hacía caer ola tras ola de Federales. Los asaltos fueron suicidas porque ningún hombre llegó dentro de 20 metros de la pared. La oscuridad terminó la matanza.

Dos días después, bajo una manta de oscuridad y una lluvia fuerte, el Army of the Potomac recruzó el Rappahannock.

CONSECUENCIAS

Otra avanzada para Richmond fue parada.

Burnside se removió como comandante del Army of the Potomac.

La moral estaba muy baja en el Norte porque Lee tuvo otra victoria e infligió muchas pérdidas.

Staat: Virginia

Befehlshaber der US:
 Generalmajor Ambrose E. Burnside
Armee der US: Armee des Potomac
 Truppenstärke: 120,000
Verluste:
 Gefallen: 1,300
 Verwundet: 9,600
 Gefangengenommen oder vermißt: 1,800

Befehlshaber der CS:
 General Robert E. Lee
Armee der CS: Armee von Nordvirginia
 Truppenstärke: 80,000
Verluste:
 Gefallen: 600
 Verwundet: 4,100
 Gefangengenommen oder vermißt: 600

KOMMENTAR

Generalmajor Ambrose Burnside ersetzte im November 1862 General McClellan als Befehlshaber der Armee des Potomac. Burnside's Plan war, über Fredericksburg, im Staat Virginia, auf Richmond vorzustossen. Die Armee des Potomac machte einen Schnellmarsch nach Falmouth, ein Dorf auf der westlichen Seite des Rappahanock Flußes, kurz vor Fredericksburg. Zu dieser Zeit war die Armee des Südens weit verteilt. Burnside's Unfähigkeit, und die Verzögerung der Zufuhr von Pontonbrücken, gab Lee Zeit, seine Armee in der Fredericksburg Umgebung zu konzentrieren. Unter dem Feuer der südstaatlichen Scharfschützen, die aus der Stadt feuerten, war der Zusammenbau der Brücken schwierig.

Beim 12. Dezember hatten die Föderalisten den Fluß überquert und die Stadt besetzt. Ihre Linie erstreckte sich südwärts bis zu einer weiteren Pontonüberquerung. Die Linie der Konföderierten wurde auf der Höhe, westlich von Fredericksburg, aufgestellt. Ihre 11 Kilometer lange Linie umfasste eine starke Stellung westlich der Stadt, wo südstaatliche Infanterie in einer tiefliegenden Straße hinter einer Steinmauer stand, mit der Artillerie auf Maryes Heights über ihnen massiert.

Am nächsten Morgen, um 9.00 Uhr, begann Burnside den Angriff. General Reynolds, der sich an der südlichsten Überquerung befand, erhielt den Befehl, Jackson's Truppen an Hamilton Crossing anzugreifen, in der Hoffnung, die rechte Flanke der Konföderierten dadurch abwenden zu können. Trotz schwerem Artilleriefeuer durchbrach General Meade's Division die Konföderiertenline, und ein Unionsieg erschien möglich. Es wurden aber keine Reserven gesandt, um Meade zu unterstützen, oder seinen Durchbruch auszunützen. Früh am Nachmittag drängten Jackson's Reserven die Föderalisten zurück und verbesserten ihre Line.

Ohne auf Nachricht über Reynolds Angriff zu warten, befahl Burnside General Sumner, bereits am Mittag Maryes Heights anzugreifen. Sumner's Truppen rückten vor, wurden aber heftig zurückgeschlagen. Burnside, der sich mit der Scheiterung seines Planes nicht abfinden konnte, befahl weitere Angriffe auf die Höhe. Die Artillerie auf der Hohe riss Lücken in die vorrückenden Kolonnen, während Longstreet's Infanterie, die in der tiefliegenden Straße ihre Stellung hatte, eine Föderisterwelle nach der anderen abmähte. Die Angriffe waren glatter Selbstmord, denn keine Föderalisten konnten näher als 60 Meter an die Steinmauer kommen. Enldich setzte die Dunkelheit dem Gemetzel ein Ende.

Zwei Tage später, im Schutze der Dunkelheit und starkem Regen, überquerte die Armee des Potomac wieder den Rappahanock Fluß.

BEDEUTUNG

Noch eine weitere "Auf nach Richmond" Offensive wurde aufgehalten.

Man enthob Burnside des Oberbefehls der Armee des Potomac.

Die Union war entmutigt über einen weiteren Sieg für Lee und die schweren Verluste ihrer Armee.

The town of Fredericksburg from the east side of the Rappahannock River. Marye's Heights rise in the background.

State: Mississippi

U.S.

Commander:
  Maj. Gen. William T. Sherman
U.S. Army: 13th Army Corps
  (Sherman's right wing)
  No. of Troops: 31,000
Casualties:
  Killed: 213
  Wounded: 1,016
  Captured or missing: 561

C.S.

Commander:
  Lt. Gen. John C. Pemberton
C.S. Army: Provisional Division of
  Stephen D. Lee
  No. of Troops: 14,000
Casualties:
  Killed: 58
  Wounded: 119
  Captured or missing: 10

COMMENTS

General Grant's first attempt to capture Vicksburg, a Confederate stronghold on the Mississippi River, called for a two pronged attack by separate wings of the army, one headed by himself and the other by Gen. William T. Sherman.

Sherman's "Expeditionary Force" boarded transports at Memphis, headed down the Mississippi, then up the Yazoo River just north of Vicksburg. There they disembarked and were supposed to take control of the bluffs that were the key to the city to their south. Grant's part in the campaign was to preoccupy Southern troops in north Mississippi so the bluffs north of Vicksburg couldn't be reinforced. On Dec. 20 Grant's supply base at Holly Springs was destroyed by raiding cavalry under Gen. Earl Van Dorn. Grant was forced to withdraw; Sherman was now on his own.

On Dec. 26 Sherman landed his forces. The next day, after shelling the Confederate positions, the Federals advanced through swamps until they ran into a series of lakes and bayous in front of the Confederate defenses. There they found only five narrow approaches to the bluffs. All these, however, were well covered by Confederate infantry and artillery. The next day, Brig. Gen. Steele attempted an attack. He crossed at Blake's Levee only to be turned back by abatis and cannon fire. Gen. Sherman then ordered Brig. Gen. George W. Morgan to prepare an attack aimed at the center of the Confederate defenses. At noon on Dec. 29, nine regiments charged toward the foot of the Walnut Hills overlooking Chickasaw Bayou. Exposed to a withering fire, they forged their way over the abatis and through the mucky, tangled marshes. The Confederates had an easy time picking off the helpless Federals. With a yell, the Northerners rushed toward the defenses, but were met by a storm of shells, canister, and minie balls. The Federal attack was firmly repulsed.

On Jan. 2 Sherman learned that the Southerners had been reinforced and withdrew from the Yazoo River.

SIGNIFICANCE

The Confederates spoiled Grant's first attempt at gaining control of the Mississippi River by capturing Vicksburg and cutting the Confederacy in two.

Etat: Mississipi

Etat-Unis

Commandant:
  Général de Division William T. Sherman
Armée: 13éme Corps d'Armée
  (aile droite de Sherman)
  31 000 soldats
Pertes:
  Tués: 213
  Blessés: 1 016
  Prisonniers ou disparus: 561

Etats Confédérés

Commandant:
  Lieutenant Général John C. Pemberton
Armée: Division Provisoire
  14 000 soldats

Pertes:
  Tués: 58
  Blessés: 119
  Prisonniers ou disparus: 10

COMMENTAIRE

Pour essayer de prendre Vicksburg, place forte des Confédérés sur le Mississipi, Grant dut commencer par une double attaque par deux ailes de l'armée, l'une sous ses propres ordres, l'autre commandée par le général William T. Sherman.

La "force expéditionnaire" de Sherman prit la route à Memphis, descendit le Mississipi puis remonta la rivière Yazoo jusqu'au nord de Vicksburg. Là, ils débarquèrent et devaient se poster sur les falaises pour dominer la ville située au sud. Le travail de Grant était de distraire les troupes sudistes au nord du Mississipi; ainsi, les falaises du nord de Vicksburg ne pouvaient recevoir de renforts. Le 20 décembre, la réserve d'approvisionnement de Grant à Holly Springs fut détruite par un raid de cavalerie dirigé par le général Earl Van Dorn. Grant dut se replier; maintenant, Sherman était seul.

Le 26 décembre Sherman débarqua ses forces. Le jour suivant, après avoir bombardé les positions des Confédérés, les Fédéraux traversèrent des marécages pour se retrouver devant un réseau de lacs et de ruisseaux les séparant des défenses des Confédérés. Pour atteindre les falaises, il n'y avait que cinq étroites approches possibles, et elles étaient peuplées de l'infanterie et de l'artillerie confédérées. Le jour suivant, le brigadier général Steele tenta l'attaque. Il traversa à Blake's Levee mais il fut aussitôt repoussé par des abattis et les feux des canons. Le général Sherman commanda alors au brigadier général George W. Morgan de pérparer une attaque visant au centre des défenses des Confédérés. A midi, le 29 décembre, neuf régiments chargèrent au pied de Walnut Hills qui surplombaient Chickasaw Bayou. Exposés aux foudres des canons, ils s'ouvrirent une voie enjambant les abattis, à travers l'enchevêtrement des marais. Il fut facile pour les Confédérés de tirant sus les Fédéraux épuisés. Avec un cri, les Nordistes se précipitèrent sur leurs défenses, mais firent face à une tempête de boulets et de mitraille. L'attaque des Fédéraux fut fermement repoussée.

Le 2 janvier, Sherman apprit que les Sudistes avaient reçu des renforts venus de Yazoo River.

CONSEQUENCE

Les Confédérés avaient enrayé la première tentative de Grant de prendre le contrôle de la du Mississipi en prenant Vicksburg et en coupant en deux la Confédération.

Important Landmarks
Mississippi River
Yazoo River
Chickasaw Bayou
Walnut Hills
McNutt Lake
County Road
Thompson's Lake
The Mound
Corduroy Road

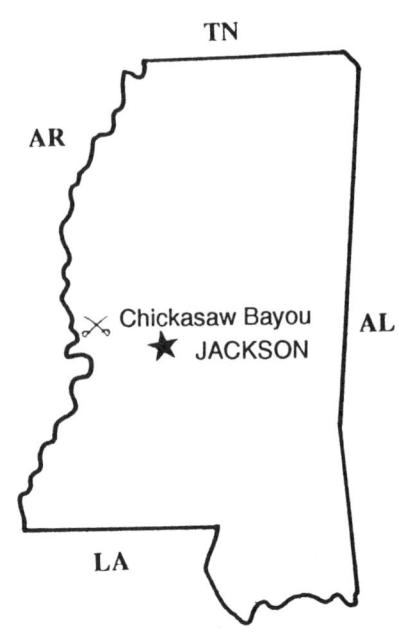

U.S.	C.S.
Comandante:	Comandante:
Maj. Gen. William T. Sherman	Lt. Gen. John C. Pemberton
U.S. Ejército: 13th Army Corps	C.S. Ejército: Provisional División de
(Sherman's right wing)	Stephen D. Lee
No. de tropas: 31,000	No. de tropas: 14,000
Pérdidas:	Pérdidas:
Muertos: 213	Muertos: 58
Heridos: 1,016	Heridos: 119
Capturados o ausentes: 561	Capturados o ausentes: 10

COMENTARIO

El primer intento del General Grant para capturar Vicksburg, una fortaleza Confederada en el río Mississippi, pidió un ataque de dos partes por dos alas distintas de su ejército, una bajo él mismo y la otra bajo el General William T. Sherman.

La fuerza expedicionaria de Sherman embarcó en Memphis, bajó el Mississippi, y subió el río Yazoo al norte de Vicksburg. Allí desembarcó y hubo de tomar control de los precipicios que eran la llave a la ciudad al sur. La parte de Grant en la campaña preocupaba a las tropas Confederadas en la parte norteña de Mississippi para que los precipicios al norte de Vicksburg no se pudieran reforzar. El 20 de diciembre la base de provisiones de Grant en Holly Springs fue destruída por la caballería del General Earl Van Dorn. Grant tuvo que retirarse; Sherman, ahora, estaba solo.

El 26 de diciembre Grant desembarcó su fuerza. El próximo día, después de bombardear las posiciones Confederadas, los Federales avanzaron por marismas hasta encontrarse en una serie de lagos y pantanos en frente de las defensas Confederadas. Allí encontraron sólamente cinco accesos estrechos a los precipicios. Todos estos, sin embargo, estaban bien guardados por artillería e infantería Confederada. El próximo día el General Steele intentó un asalto. Cruzó en Blake's Levee sólo para estar repulsado por tala y cañones. El general Sherman, entonces, mandó al General George W. Morgan que preparara un ataque dirigido al centro de las defensas Confederadas. Al mediodía el 29 de diciembre, nueve regimientos asaltaron el pie de las colinas Walnut que miraban a Chickasaw Bayou. Expuestos a un fuego fuerte, ellos hicieron camino por encima de la tala y pasaron por las marismas enredadas y asquerosas. Los Confederados fácilmente repulsaron a los Federales. Con un grito los norteños corrieron hacia las defensas, pero se encontraron con una tormenta de bombas, canister, y balas. El ataque Federal se repulsó fírmemente.

El 2 de enero Sherman comprendió que los Confederados habían sido reforzado y los yanquis se retiraron del río Yazoo.

CONSECUENCIAS

Los Confederados arruinaron el primer intento de Grant para ganar control del río Mississippi capturando Vicksburg y dividiendo los estados Confederados en dos partes.

Befehlshaber der US:	Befehlshaber der CS:
Generalmajor William T. Sherman	Generalleutnant John C. Pemberton
Armee der US: 13. Armeekorps	Armee der CS: Provisionale Division
(Shermans rechter Flügel)	von Stephen D. Lee
Truppenstärke: 31,000	Truppenstärke: 14,000
Verluste	Verluste
Gefallen: 213	Gefallen: 58
Verwundet: 1 016	Verwundet: 119
Gefangengenommen oder	Gefangengenommen oder
vermißt: 561	vermißt: 10

KOMMENTAR

General Grant's erster Versuch, die Stadt Vicksburg, ein Stützpunkt der Konföderierten, zu erobern, erforderte einen Angriff mit zwei Spitzen. Getrennte Flügel seiner Armee sollten diese Angriffe führen, einer unter seinem eigenen Befehl, der andere unter General William T. Sherman.

Sherman's Expeditionskorps ging an Bord der Truppentransporte in Memphis, folgtem dem Mississippi flußabwärts, dann nördlich auf dem Yazoo, bis zu einem Punkt etwas nördlich von Vicksburg.

Sherman's Truppen verließen die Transporte an diesem Punkt, mit der Aufgabe, Kontrolle über die Steilküste, die den Schlüssel zur Stadt in südlicher Richtung hielt, zu erzielen. Grant's Aufgabe in der Kampagne bestand darin, die südstaatlichen Truppen in Nordmississippi völlig in Anspruch zu nehmen, und sie damit zu hindern, die Steilküste nördlich von Vicksburg weiter verstärken zu können. Am 20. Dezember überfiel die Kavallerie, unter General Earl Van Dorn, Grant's Versorgungslager bei Holly Springs und zerstörte es. Grant wurde gezwungen, zurückzuziehen - Sherman war jetzt auf sich selbst angewiesen.

Am 25. Dezember landete Sherman seine Streitkräfte. Nachdem die Föderalisten am folgenden Tag die Stellungen der Konföderierten zuerst beschossen, rückten sie sich durch Sümpfe vor, bis sie auf eine Reihe von Seen und sumpfigen Flußarmen vor den Verteidigungsanlagen der Konföderierten stiessen. Dort fanden sie nur fünf enge Zugänge, die auf die Steilküste führten. Alle fünf waren allerdings von der Infanterie und Artillerie der Konföderierten gut gedeckt. Am folgenden Tag versuchte Brigadegeneral Steele, einen Angriff zu machen. Er überquerte das Wasser am Blakes Levee, wurde aber wegen Baumbarrieren und Kanonenfeuer zurückgewiesen. General Sherman befahl Brigadegeneral George W. Morgan, einen Angriff auf die Mitte der Verteidigung der Konföderierten vorzübereiten. Am 29. Dezember stürmten neun Regimente, um 12.00 Uhr mittags, gegen den Fuß der Walnut Hills, die einen Überblick über die Chickasaw Bayou erforderten. Unter vernichtendem Feuer brachen die Truppen Bahn, über Baumbarrieren und durch die matschigen, verhedderten Sümpfe. Für die Konföderierten war es ein Spiel, die hilflosen Föderalisten abzuknallen. Mit einem wilden Schrei stürzten sich die Südstaatler auf die Verteidigungslinien, wo ein Hagel von Granaten, Kartätschen und Kugeln sie empfang. Der Föderalistenangriff wurde hart zurückgeschlagen.

Als Sherman am 2. Januar lernte, daß die Südstaatler verstärkt worden waren, zog er sich vom Yazoo Fluß zurück.

BEDEUTUNG

Die Konföderierten vereitelten Grant's ersten Versuch, den Mississippi Fluß, durch Eroberung von Vicksburg, unter ihre Kontrolle zu gewinnen, und damit die Spaltung der Konföderierten zu erzielen.

Scene of Sherman's defeat at Chickasaw Bayou.

Maj. Gen. William T. Sherman

Lt. Gen. John C. Pemberton

State: Tennessee

U.S.	C.S.
Commander:	Commander:
Maj. Gen. William S. Rosecrans	Gen. Braxton Bragg
U.S. Army: Army of the Cumberland	C.S. Army: Army of Tennessee
No. of Troops: 43,400	No. of Troops: 37,712
Casualties:	Casualties:
Killed: 1,630	Killed: 1,236
Wounded: 7,397	Wounded: 7,766
Captured or missing: 3,673	Captured or missing: 868

COMMENTS

The town of Murfreesboro, Tennessee, with Stones River to the west became the center of activity during December 1862, as Bragg positioned his troops there to block any attempt by the Union army at Nashville to move into the lower south.

General Rosecrans led the Union army out of Nashville on Dec. 26. By the 30th the two armies faced each other along Stones River. The opposing commanders formulated similar battle plans for the next day; both planned to attack the right wing of their enemy.

As the morning of Dec. 31 arrived, the Confederates struck first. Their vicious attack drove the Union right and part of the center back to the Nashville Pike. Stubborn fighting by Generals Thomas and Sheridan was the only thing that averted a Union disaster. Meanwhile, the units assigned to the Union attack were rushing back to form the new defensive line on high ground near the pike and embankment of the Nashville and Chattanooga railroad. The Confederates rushed out of the trees toward the new Union line, but were met by withering fire from the fresh troops. In desperate fighting, rifle butts and bayonets were used to repel the Southern charges. After suffering heavy losses the Southern infantrymen fell back.

January 1 followed without any fighting as Bragg expected Rosecrans to retreat. However, after dark a Union division under Col. Beatty crossed Stones River and was posted on a ridge that commanded the Confederate right. The Federals stayed there until the late afternoon of Jan. 2 when General Breckinridge was ordered to assault their position. The attack succeeded and, after dislodging the Federals, the Southerners chased them back across the river.

When the Federals realized the perilous position of Col. Beatty's division they massed 57 cannon across the river from him. As soon as his soldiers recrossed the river, artillery chief Maj. John Mendenhall opened fire on the Confederates who had pursued Beatty to the banks of the river. The cannons, firing more than 100 rounds a minute, erased the Southern attack as 1800 soldiers fell dead and wounded in a matter of minutes. Fresh Union troops charged back across the river and, by nightfall, had driven Breckinridge back to his original position.

On Jan. 3 the Confederates withdrew toward Tullahoma and the Federals occupied Murfreesboro on the 4th.

SIGNIFICANCE

The victory at Murfreesboro was the first step in the Union plan for cutting the Confederacy east of the Mississippi River in two. The Northern armies could now aim for Chattanooga and then the lower south.

Etat: Tennessee

Etats-Unis	Etats Confédérés
Commandant:	Commandant:
Général de Division Wm. Rosecrans	Général Braxton Bragg
Armée: de Cumberland	Armée: du Tennessee
43 400 soldats	37 712 soldats
Pertes:	Pertes:
Tués: 1 630	Tués: 1 236
Blessés: 7 397	Blessés: 7 766
Prisonniers ou disparus: 3 673	Prisonniers ou disparus: 868

COMMENTAIRE

A l'ouest de Stones River, la ville de Murfreesboro, dans le Tennessee, devint le centre des activités en décembre 1862, tandis que Bragg y mettait ses troupes en position pour bloquer toute tentative de l'armée unioniste à Nashville d'occuper le bas sud.

Le 26 décembre, le général Rosecrans émergeait de Nashville avec son armée. Le 30, les deux armées étaient face à face le long de Stones River. Les commandants préparaient des plans de bataille similaires pour le jour suivant: chacun voulait attaquer l'aile droite de l'ennemi.

Le matin du 31 décembre, les Confédérés attaquèrent les premiers. Leur assaut enragé repoussa la droite et une partie du centre de l'armée de l'Union jusqu'à la route de Nashville. L'union fut sauvée du désastre par les luttes acharnées des généraux Thomas et Sheridan. Pendant ce temps, les troupes offensives de l'Union revenaient prestement pour former une nouvelle ligne de défense sur des hauteurs près de la route et des quais de Nashville et de la voie ferrée de Chattanooga. Les Confédérés surgirent des arbres pour se précipiter sur la ligne de l'Union, et reçurent les foudres des canons des nouvelles troupes. Dans une lutte désespéré, crosses de fusils et baionnettes furent utilisées pour repousser les charges des Sudistes. Après de lourdes pertes, l'infanterie sudiste se replia.

Le 1er janvier, tandis que Bragg comptait sur la retraite de Rosecrans, aucune bataille n'eut lieu. Cependant, après la tombée de la nuit, la division unioniste du colonel Beatty traversa Stones River et se plaça sur une hauteur qui surplombait l'aile droite des Confédérés. Les Fédéraux y restèrent jusqu'à l'après-midi du 2 janvier où le général Breckinridge reçut l'ordre d'assillir leur position. L'attaque réussit, et après avoir délogé les Fédéraux, les Sudistes les poursuivirent jusqu'à ce qu'ils retraversent la rivière.

Quand les Fédéraux s'aperçurent de la position de péril de la division de Beatty, ils rassemblèrent 57 canons en face de lui, de l'autre coté de la rivière. Dès que ses soldats eurent retraversé la rivière, le chef d'artillerie major John Mendenhall ouvrit le feu sur les Confédérés qui les poursuivaient. Tirant plus de 100 coups par minute les canons nettoyèrent l'armée sudiste: en quelques instants, 1 800 soldats tombèrent morts ou blessés. De nouvelles troupes unionistes chargèrent à nouveau, retraversant la rivière. A la tombée du jour, Breckinridge était revenu à sa position initiale.

Le 3 janvier, les Confédérés se retirèrent vers Tullahoma et le 4 les Fédéraux occupèrent Murfreesboro.

CONSEQUENCES

La victoire à Murfreesboro était la première étape, dans le plan de l'Union, de couper en deux la Confédération à l'est du Mississipi. Les armées nordistes pouvaient maintenant diriger leurs efforts sur Chattanooga, puis avancer au sud.

Important Landmarks

Stones River
Nashville Pike
The Cedars
Franklin Road
Wilkinson Pike
Round Forest
"Hell's Half Acre"
McFadden' Ford
Wayne's Hill
Hazen Monument

Important Buildings

Smith House
Cowan House
Harding House
Rosecran's HQ
Gresham House
Hord House

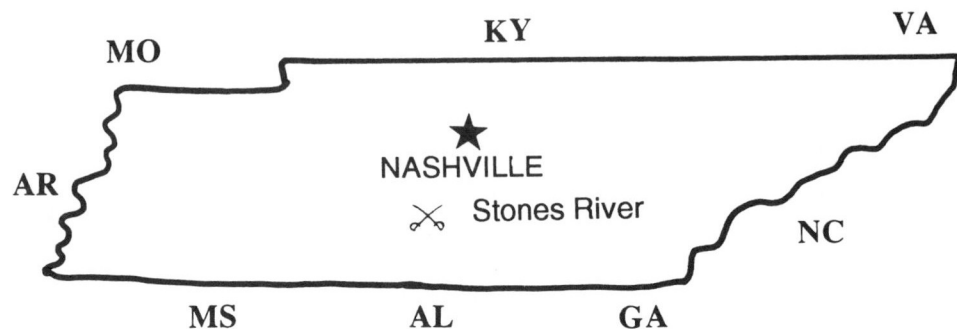

Estado: Tennessee

U.S.	C.S.
Comandante:	**Comandante:**
Maj. Gen. Wm. S. Rosecrans	Gen. Braxton Bragg
U.S. Ejército: Army of the Cumberland	C.S. Ejército: Army of Tennessee
No. de tropas: 43,400	No. de tropas: 37,712
Pérdidas:	Pérdidas:
Muertos: 1,630	Muertos: 1,236
Heridos: 7,397	Heridos: 7,766
Capturados o ausentes: 3,673	Capturados o ausentes: 868

COMENTARIO

El pueblo de Murfreesboro, Tennessee, con el río Stones al oeste, llegó a ser el centro de actividad durante diciembre de 1862 porque Bragg posicionó sus tropas allí para bloquear cualquier intento por el ejército Federal en Nashville para moverse al sur bajo.

El General Rosecrans llevó al ejército Federal fuera de Nashville el 26 de diciembre. El día 30 los dos ejércitos se enfrentaban uno al otro por el río Stones. Los comandantes opuestos formularon planes parecidos para la batalla el próximo día; los dos planearon atacar el ala derecha del enemigo.

Cuando llegó la mañana del 31 de diciembre, los Confederados abrieron la batalla. Su ataque furioso empujó la derecha y una parte del centro Federal hasta Nashville Pike. La lucha obstinada de los Generales Thomas y Sherman fue la única cosa que evitó un desastre para la Unión. Mientras tanto, las unidades asignadas al ataque Federal se daban prisa para formar una línea defensiva nueva en tierra alta cerca del pike (carretera) y terraplén del ferrocarril de Nashville y Chattanooga. Los Confederados avanzaron desde los árboles hacia la línea Federal nueva, con un fuego dañoso de tropas frescas. En una lucha desesperada, bayonetas y rifles usados como batones se usaron para repulsar los ataques de los Confederados. Despúes de sufrir muchas pérdidas, la infantería sureña se retiró.

El 1 de enero siguió sin batalla porque Bragg esperaba que se retirara Rosecrans. Sin embargo, al oscurecer una división Federal bajo el Col. Beatty cruzó el río Stones y se situó en una elevación que controlaba la derecha Confederada. Los Federales se quedaron allí hasta tarde por la tarde del día 2 cuando el General Breckinridge fue mandado atacar su posición. El asalto tuvo éxito y, después de desalojar a los Federales, los sureños los persiguieron através del río.

Cuando los Federales se dieron cuenta de la posición peligrosa en que estaba la división de Beatty, juntaron 57 cañones al otro lado del río de él. En cuanto los soldados recruzaron el río, los cañones abrieron fuego a los Confederados que habían perseguido a Beatty a las orillas del río. Los cañones, disparando más de cien rondas por minuto, borraron el ataque sureño. 1800 soldados cayeron muertos o heridos dentro de pocos minutos. Tropas Federales frescas atacaron el otro lado del río de nuevo y cuando llegó la noche, ellos habían empujado a Breckinridge a su posición original.

El 3 de enero los Confederados se retiraron hacia Tullahoma y los Federales ocuparon Murfreesboro el día 4.

CONSECUENCIAS

La victoria en Murfreesboro fue el primer paso en cortar la Confederación al este del Mississippi en dos partes. Los ejércitos norteños ahora podían dirigirse para Chattanooga y el sur bajo.

Staat: Tennessee

Befehlshaber der US:	Befehlshaber der CS:
Generalmajor William S. Rosecrans	General Braxton Bragg
Armee der US: 13. Armee des Cumberland	Armee der CS: Armee von Tennessee
Truppenstärke: 43,300	Truppenstärke: 37,712
Verluste	Verluste
Gefallen: 1,630	Gefallen: 1,236
Verwundet: 7,397	Verwundet: 7,766
Gefangengenommen oder vermißt: 3,673	Gefangengenommen oder vermißt: 868

KOMMENTAR

Die Stadt Murfreesboro, im Staat Tennessee, mit dem Stones River im Westen, wurde im Dezember 1862 der Mittelpunkt der Aktionen. Bragg bezog dort Stellung, um jeden Versuch der Unionarmee zu blockieren, sich von Nashville in den tieferen Süden zu ziehen.

Am 26. Dezember führte General Rosecrans die Unionarmee aus Nashville. Am 30. standen sich beide Armeen entlang Stones River gegenüber. Die gegnerischen Befehlshaber entwarfen für den folgenden Tag ähnliche Kampfstrategien - beide planten den rechten Flügel ihres Feindes anzugreifen.

Als der Morgen des 31. Dezembers dämmerte, unternahmen die Konföderierten den ersten Schlag. Ihr brutaler Angriff trieb die rechte Flanke der Union, und einen Teil ihrer Mitte, bis auf die Nashville Pike zurück. General Thomas' und Sheridan's zäher Kampf verhinderte eine unvermeidliche Katastrophe. Inzwischen raschten die Einheiten, die dem Unionangriff zugeteilt waren, zurück, um auf der Höhe, nahe der Landstraße, und am Bahndamm der Nashville-und-Chattanooga Eisenbahn, eine neue Abwehrlinie aufzustellen. Die Konföderierten stürzten aus den Bäumen auf die neue Unionlinie heraus, wo sie dem vernichtenden Feuer der frischen Truppen begegneten. Im verzweifelten Gefecht benutzten die Unionsoldaten Gewehrkolben und Bajonette, um den Ansturm der Konföderierten zurückzuschlagen. Die Konföderierte Infanterie fiel zurück, nachdem sie schwere Verluste erlitten hatte.

Der erste Januar folgte ohne Kampf, denn Bragg erwartete Rosecrans' Rückzug. Jedoch, nach Einbruch der Dunkelheit überquerte eine Uniondivision, unter Oberst Beatty, Stones River und nahm Stellung auf einem Hügelrücken, der die rechte Flanke der Konföderierten beherrschte. Die Föderalisten besetzten diese Stellung bis Spätnachmittag des 2. Januar, als General Breckinridge den Befehl erhielt, ihre Stellung anzugreifen. Der erfolgreiche Angriff der Konföderierten drängte die Unionarmee zurück und verfolgte sie über den Fluß.

Mittlerweile, als die Föderalisten die bedrohliche Stellung von Beatty's Division erkannten, massierten sie 57 Kanonen gegenüber seiner Stellung, auf der anderen Seite des Flußes. Sobald Beatty's Soldaten den Fluß wieder überquert hatten, öffnete der Artillerieführer, Major John Mendenhall, Feuer auf die Konföderierten, die Beatty bis ans Ufer verfolgt hatten. Die Kanonen, die mehr als 100 Schuß pro Minute abfeuerten, eradierten den Konföderierten Angriff innerhalb weniger Minuten, als 1,800 Soldaten entweder verwundet, oder tot, fielen. Frische Uniontruppen drängten sich noch einmal über den Fluß, und beim Einbruch der Nacht hatten sie Breckinridge in seine ursprüngliche Stellung zurückgetrieben.

Am 3. Januar zogen sich die Konföderierten nach Tullahoma zurück. Am 4. Januar besetzten die Föderalisten Murfreesboro.

BEDEUTUNG

Der Sieg bei Murfreesboro war der erste Schritt im Plan der Union, die Konföderierten östlich des Mississippi in zwei Teile zu schneiden. Die Armeen der Union konnten nun ihr Ziel auf Chattanooga richten, und dann auf den tieferen Süden.

Scene of the fighting of Palmer's and Rousseau's Divisions. On the left is the railroad, in the center the Nashville Pike, and in the right distance are The Cedars.

State: Arkansas

U.S.
Commander:
  Maj. Gen. John A. McClernand
U.S. Army: Army of the Mississippi
  No. of Troops: 30,000 + Navy
  Gunboats
Casualties:
  Killed: 134
  Wounded: 898
  Captured or missing: 29

C.S.
Commander:
  Brig. Gen. Thomas J. Churchill
C.S. Army: Garrison of Fort Hindman
  No. of Troops: 5,000

Casualties:
  Killed: 60
  Wounded: 75
  Captured or missing: 4,791

COMMENTS

Fort Hindman at Arkansas Post, Arkansas, was one of the strongest forts in the Confederacy. Located on a hill overlooking the Arkansas River and with its land-side protected by trenches, it was easily defended against land and river assaults by its 5,000 man garrison. The garrison was divided into three brigades. One brigade under Col. Dunnington was in the fort while the remaining two, commanded by Gen. Churchill, manned the trenches.

In the early days of 1863 General McClernand, commander of the Union Army of the Mississippi, and Lt. Porter's Naval forces planned an expedition against the fort.

By Jan. 10, 32,000 Federal troops, three ironclads, and six gunboats had landed a few miles downriver from the fort. Later that day, while the Army was marching toward the fort, the ships moved up river and shelled the fort for a few hours.

At noon the next day McClernand's troops were finally in position. By 1:00 p.m. Porter's ships moved up and again began bombarding the fort. After three hours, all but one cannon in Fort Hindman had been silenced. The Federal infantry, however, was having little success. The Confederates repulsed every attack the Northerners had made upon their trenches. But around 4:30 p.m., after the heavy naval bombardment, white flags started popping up along the Confederate line. A formal surrender soon followed.

SIGNIFICANCE

McClernand captured 5,000 prisoners, large amounts of supplies and guns.

This victory raised Northern spirits at a time when Federals forces had been unsuccessful on several battlefields.

Etat: Arkansas

Etats-Unis
Commandant:
  Général de Division John A. McClernand
Armée: de Mississipi
  30 000 soldats + canonnières
Pertes:
  Tués: 134
  Blessés: 898
  Prisonniers ou disparus: 29

Etats Confédérés
Commandant:
  Général de Division Thomas J. Churchill
Armée: Garnison de Fort Hindman
  5 000 soldats
Pertes:
  Tués: 60
  Blessés: 75
  Prisonniers ou disparus: 4 791

COMMENTAIRE

Fort Hindman à Arkansas Post, en Arkansas, était un des forts les plus robustes de la Confédération. Situé sur une colline dominant la rivière de l'Arkansas, ses rives protégées par des tranchées, il était en bonne posture de défense contre les assauts arrivant de la terre ou de la rivière avec les 5 000 hommes de sa garnison. Celle-ci était divisée en trois brigades; l'une, commandée par le colonel Dunnington était au fort; les deux autres, sous les ordres du général Churchill, emplissaient les tranchées.

Dans les premiers jours de 1863, le général McClernand, le commandant de l'armée unioniste du Mississipi, et le lieutenant Porter des Forces Navales préparèrent une expédition contre le fort.

Le 10 janvier, 32 000 troupes féféraux, des cuirassées, et six canonnières s'étaient postés sur la rivière à quelques kilomètres du fort. Plus tard ce jour-là, tandis que l'armée marchait vers le fort, les bateaux remontèrent la rivière et attaquèrent le fort à coups de boulets pendant près de deux heures.

A midi, le jour suivant, les troupes de McClernand étaient finalement en position. Vers 1 heure, les bateaux de Porter avancèrent et recommencèrent à bombarder le fort. Au bout de trois heures, tous les canons, sauf un, du Fort Hindman, avaient été réduits au silence. L'infanterie fédérale avait remporté quelques petites victoires. Mais les Confédérés repoussèrent chaque attaque des Nordistes dans leurs tranchées. Pourtant, vers 16h30, après un lourd bombardement naval, les lignes des Confédérés firent flotter les drapeaux blancs. Bientôt, ce fut la reddition officielle.

CONSEQUENCES

McClernand prit 5 000 prisonniers et de grandes quantités d'approvisionnement et de fusils.

Cette victoire remonta le moral des Nordistes à un monument où les forces fédérales avaient perdu plusieurs batailles.

Important Landmarks
Arkansas River

Important Buildings
Fort Hindman

Estado: Arkansas

U.S.	C.S.
Comandante:	Comandante:
Maj. Gen. John A. McClernand	Brig. Gen. Thomas J. Churchill
U.S. Ejército: Army of the Mississippi	C.S. Ejército: Garrison of Fort
No. de tropas: 30,000 + barcos	Hindman
armados	No. de tropas: 5,000
Pérdidas:	Pérdidas:
Muertos: 134	Muertos: 60
Heridos: 898	Heridos: 75
Capturados o ausentes: 29	Capturados o ausentes: 4,791

COMENTARIO

El fuerte Hindman en Arkansas Post, Arkansas, era uno de los fuertes más fuertes en la Confederación. Situado en una colina mirando al río Arkansas y con su lado terrenal protegido por trincheras, se defendía fácilmente contra asaltos de tierra o río por su guarnición de 5,000 hombres. La guarnición estaba dividida en tres brigadas. Una brigada bajo el Col. Dunnington estaba en el fuerte mientras las otras dos, bajo el General Churchill, estaban en las trincheras.

En los días tempranos de 1863 el General McClernand, comandante de Army of the Mississippi Federal, y las fuerzas de la armada bajo Lt. Porter, planearon una expedición contra el fuerte.

El día 10 de enero 32,000 tropas Federales, 3 barcos acorazados y 6 barcos armados se habían situado unas millas bajo el río del fuerte. Más tarde durante el día, mientras el ejército marchaba hacia el fuerte, los barcos se movieron por el río y bombardearon el fuerte por un par de horas.

Al mediadía el próximo día las tropas de McClernand ya estaban en posición. A la una los barcos avanzaron otra vez y empezaron a bombardear el fuerte de nuevo. Después de tres horas todos los cañones menos uno en Fort Hindman estaban callados. La infantería Federal, sin embargo, tuvo poco éxito. Los Confederados habían repulsado todos los ataques que se habían hecho contra sus trincheras. Pero alrededor de las 4:30, después del bombardeo fuerte hecho por la armada, banderas blancas comenzaron a mostrarse en la línea Confederada. Una rendición formal siguió un poco después.

CONSECUENCIAS

McClernand capturó 5,000 prisioneros, muchas armas y otras provisiones.

Esta victoria levantó el espíritu norteño en una época en que las fuerzas Federales habían tenido poco éxito en varios campos de batalla.

Staat: Arkansas

Befehlshaber der US:	Befehlshaber der CS:
Generalmajor John A. McClernand	Brigadegeneral Thomas J. Churchill
Armee der US: Armee des Mississippi	Armee der CS: Garnison des Fort
Truppenstärke: 30,000 +	Hindman
Kanonenboote der Marine	Truppenstärke: 5,000
Verluste:	Verluste:
Gefallen: 134	Gefallen: 60
Verwundet: 898	Verwundet: 75
Gefangengenommen oder	Gefangengenommen oder
vermißt: 29	vermißt: 4,791

KOMMENTAR

Fort Hindman bei Arkansas Post, im Staat Arkansas, war eines der stärksten Forte in der Konföderation. Mit seiner Lage auf einem Hügel, mit Überblick auf den Arkansas Fluß, und seine Landseite von Schützengräben verstärkt, konnte die Garnison von 5,000 Mann das Fort leicht gegen Angriffe, über Land und Fluß, verteidigen. Die Garnison war in drei Brigaden aufgeteilt. Eine Brigade unter Oberst Dunnington war im Fort, während die beiden anderen, unter General Churchill, die Schützengräben besetzten.

Während der ersten Tage des Jahres 1863, planten General McClernand, Befehlshaber der Unionarmee des Mississippi, und die Marine, unter Leutnant Porter, eine Expedition gegen das Fort.

Am 10 Januar landeten 32,000 Föderalisten, drei Panzerschiffe, und sechs Kanonenboote, einige Kilometer flußabwärts vom Fort. Später an Tag fuhren die Schiffe flußaufwärts und beschoßen das Fort für einige Stunden, während sich die Armee auf den Marsch nach dem Fort begab.

Am folgenden Tag, um 12.00 Uhr, waren McClernand's Truppen endlich in Stellung. Um 13.00 Uhr waren Porter's Schiffe ebenso wieder in Stelling und begannen, das Fort zu bombardieren. Nach drei Stunden hatten sie alle Kanonen auf Fort Hindman, mit der Ausnahme von einer, zum Schweigen gebracht. Bis zu dieser Zeit hatte die Föderalisteninfanterie wenig Erfolg. Die Konföderierten schlugen alle Angriffe gegen ihre Schützengräben zurück. Nachdem, ungefähr um 16.30 Uhr, die schwere Bombardierung zu Ende kam, tauchten nach und nach, entlang der Konföderiertenlinie, weiße Fahnen auf. Eine offizielle Kapitulation folgte in Kürze.

BEDEUTUNG

McClernand nahm 5,000 Truppen gefangen und eroberte große Mengen von Provianten und Gewehren.

Dieser Sieg kam zu einer Zeit, in der die Streitkräfte des Nordens auf mehreren Schlachtfeldern keinen Erfolg hatten. Der Sieg brachte große Aufmunterung für die Föderalisten.

Maj. Gen. John A. McClernand

Brig. Gen. Thomas J. Churchill

State: Virginia		Etat: Virginie	
U.S.	**C.S.**	**Etats-Unis**	**Etats Confédérés**
Commander:	Commander:	Commandant:	Commandant:
Maj. Gen. Joseph Hooker	Gen. Robert E. Lee	Général de Division Joseph Hooker	Général Robert E. Lee
U.S. Army: Army of the Potomac	C.S. Army: Army of Northern Virginia	Armée: du Potomac	Armée: de Virginie du Nord
No. of Troops: 130,000	No. of Troops: 60,000	130 000 soldats	60 000 soldats
Casualties:	Casualties:	Pertes:	Pertes:
Killed: 1,600	Killed: 1,700	Tués: 1 600	Tués: 1 700
Wounded: 9,800	Wounded: 9,100	Blessés: 9 800	Blessés: 9 100
Captured or missing: 5,900	Captured or missing: 2,000	Prisonniers ou disparus: 5 900	Prisonniers ou disparus: 2 000

COMMENTS

The new commander of the Army of the Potomac, Joseph Hooker, came up with a brilliant plan to attack Lee at Fredericksburg. Sedgwick with 40,000 men, built bridges and threatened to cross as Burnside had done in December 1862. Meanwhile, Hooker with 75,000 men marched upriver and headed toward Fredericksburg from the west, threatening Lee's rear. Instead of retreating, Lee left 10,000 men at Fredericksburg to face Sedgwick and marched the rest of his troops westward to stop Hooker.

The battle began on May 1st when troops led by Jackson opposed Hooker's advance on the Orange Turnpike and Orange Plank Road. Fighting flared along the line and Hooker, who admitted that he "lost his nerve," withdrew to a defensive position around Chancellorsville crossroads. With Hooker on the defensive, Lee quickly took control of the battle. That night Lee and Jackson planned a daring flank march. On May 2nd, Jackson with 32,000 men, marched 12 miles to get in position to attack the exposed Federal right flank. By late afternoon Jackson was ready. His initial advance was so swift that the surprised XI Corps was unable to resist. A complete rout followed and the whole right of the Union line dissolved. Darkness and tangled Confederate commands ended Jackson's advance. While reconnoitering along the lines that night Jackson was struck 3 times by a volley fired by his own men.

On May 3rd Lee pressed the Federals again. With 50 cannon massed on the high ground at Hazel Grove, the Southerners forced Hooker back to an intrenched position covering U.S. Ford.

By this time Lee learned that General Sedgwick finally made a move. Sedgwick had pushed through the outnumbered defenders at Fredericksburg and was heading for Lee's rear. Leaving 25,000 men to watch Hooker, the remainder of his army moved fast and checked Sedgwick's column at Salem Church. On May 3rd heavy fighting raged around the church. The next day Sedgwick's flank and rear became threatened by General Early. The Federals held out until dark and then withdrew across the river during the night. Hooker's command retired across the river the following night.

SIGNIFICANCE

Lee lost his most able field commander—Jackson died of pneumonia eight days after he was shot.

Lee and most of his army began to believe that they were invincible—this eventually led to disaster at Gettysburg.

COMMENTAIRE

Le nouveau commandant de l'armée du Potomac, Joseph Hooker, avait un plan brillant pour attaquer Lee à Fredericksburg. Sedgwick, avec 40 000 hommes, bâtit des ponts et menaça de traverser comme Burnside l'avait fait en décembre 1862. Pendent ce temps, avec 75 000 hommes, Hooker marchait en amont de la rivière, depuis l'ouest, vers Fredericksburg. Ainsi, il menaçait les arrières de Lee. Au lieu de battre en retraite, Lee laissa 10 000 hommes à Fredericksburg pour faire face à Segwick et dirigea le reste de ses troupes vers l'ouest pour arrêter Hooker.

La bataille commença le 1er mai quand les troupes de Jackson s'opposèrent à l'avance de Hooker sur la route à péage d'Orange et sur l'Orange Plank Road. La lutte fit rage et Hooker, admettant qu'il "a perdu son sang froid," se retira dans une position de défense près de l'intersection de Chancellorsville. Hooker étant sur la défensive, Lee prit rapidement la situation en main. Cette nuit-là, Lee et Jackson eurent l'idée d'une marche audacieuse pour prendre l'ennemi de flanc. Le 2 mai, avec 32 000 hommes, Jackson fit près de 18 kilomètres pour se mettre en position d'attaquer le flanc droit exposé de l'armée fédérale. En fin d'après midi, Jackson était prêt. Sa première avance fut si rapide que le corps d'armée fédéral XI, pris par surprise, ne put résister. Une déroute complète s'ensuivit: tout l'aile droite de l'Union fut défaite. La nuit et la confusion des ordres des Confédérés mirent fin à l'avance de Jackson. Cette nuit-là, pendant qu'il était en reconnaissance dans ses lignes, Jackson fut frappé trois fois par une volée de balles de ses propres hommes.

Le 3 mai, Lee fit encore pression sur les Fédéraux. Avec 50 canons massés sur la hauteur de Hazel Grove, les Sudistes forcèrent Hooker à retourner à ses tranchées protégeant U. S. Ford.

A ce moment, Lee apprit que le général Sedgwick avait avancé. Sedgwick s'était frayé un passage parmi les défenseurs en surnombre à Fredericksburg, et marchait sur l'arrière-garde de Lee. Lee laissa 25 000 hommes pour surveiller Hooker, et le reste de son armée avança rapidement et arrêta la colonne de Sedgwick à Salem Churh. Le 3 mai, une furieuse bataille eut lieu autour de l'église. Le jour suivant, le flanc et les arrières de Sedgwick furent menacés par le général Early. Les Fédéraux résistèrent jusqu'à la nuit, puis se retirèrent de l'autre côté de la rivière. Hooker se retira la nuit suivante.

CONSEQUENCES

Lee perdit son meilleur commandant, Jackson, qui mourut d'une pneumonie huit jours après ses blessures.

Lee et l'ensemble de son armée commencèrent à se croire invincibles, ce qui devait amener le désastre de Gettysburg.

Important Landmarks

Fairview
Mineral Springs Road
Hazel Grove
Ely's Ford Road
Orange Turnpike
Bank's Ford
Orange Plank Road
Bullock Road
Unfinished Railroad
Rappahannock River
United States Ford

Important Buildings

Salem Church
Talley House
Chancellor House
Dowdall's Tavern
Wilderness Church
Catharine Furnace

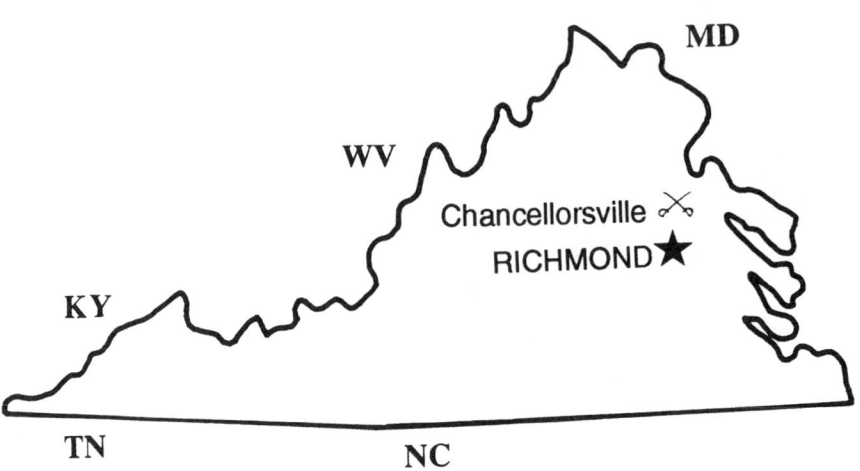

Estado: Virginia

	U.S.		C.S.
Comandante:		Comandante:	
Maj. Gen. Joseph Hooker		Gen. Robert E. Lee	
U.S. Ejército: Army of the Potomac		C.S. Ejército: Army of Northern Virginia	
No. de tropas: 130,000		No. de tropas: 60,000	
Pérdidas:		Pérdidas:	
Muertos: 1,600		Muertos: 1,700	
Heridos: 9,800		Heridos: 9,100	
Capturados o ausentes: 5,900		Capturados o ausentes: 2,000	

COMMENTARIO

El comandante nuevo del Army of the Potomac, Joseph Hooker, inventó un plan brillante para atacar a Lee en Fredericksburg. Sedgwick, con 40,000 hombres, construyó puentes y pensó en cruzar como Burnside había hecho en diciembre de 1862. Mientras tanto, Hooker, con 75,000 soldados marchó río arriba y se dirigió a Fredericksburg desde el oeste, amenazando la retaguardia de Lee. En vez de retirarse, Lee dejó 10,000 hombres en Fredericksburg para enfrentarse con Sedgwick y marchó al resto de sus tropas para el oeste para parar a Hooker.

La batalla comenzó el 1 de mayo cuando las tropas bajo Jackson se opusieron al avance de Hooker en Orange Turnpike y Orange Plank Road. La pelea creció por toda la línea y Hooker, quien admitió que había perdido los nervios, se retiró a una posición defensiva nueva cerca de los cruces del camino cerca de Chancellorsville. Con Hooker en la defensa, Lee rápidamente tomó control de la batalla. Aquella noche Lee y Jackson planearon una marcha de flanco atrevida. El 2 de mayo Jackson, con 32,000 soldados, marchó 12 millas para ponerse en posición para atacar el flanco derecho Federal que estaba expuesto. Durante la tarde Jackson preparó todo y sus tropas estaban listas. Su primer avance fue tan rápido que el cuerpo XI, complétamente sorprendido, no pudo resistir. Una rota completa siguió y toda la derecha de la línea Federal se disolvió. La oscuridad y comandancias Confederadas enredadas terminaron el avance de Jackson. Mientras Jackson hacía un reconocimiento por las líneas aquella noche, él recibió tres balas disparadas por sus propios hombres.

El 3 de mayo Lee atacó de nuevo. Con 50 cañones juntados en la tierra alta de Hazel Grove, los sureños empujaron a Hooker a una posición atrincherada que protegía U.S. Ford.

En esta hora Lee se dio cuenta que Sedgwick había hecho un movimiento. Sedgwick había avanzado por los pocos defensores de Fredericksburg e iba para la retaguardia de Lee. Dejando 25,000 soldados para vigilar a Hooker, el resto del ejército de Lee se movió rápidamente y paró la columna de Sedgwick en la iglesia Salem. El tres de mayo una pelea violenta ocurrió alrededor de la iglesia. El próximo día el flanco y la retaguardia de Sedgwick fueron amenazados por el General Jubal Early. Los Federales se mantuvieron hasta el oscurecer y entonces se retiraron através del río por la noche. La comandancia de Hooker siguió la noche siguiente.

CONSECUENCIAS

Lee perdió su comandante más capaz-Jackson se murió de pulmonía ocho días después de recibir sus heridas.

Lee y su ejército empezaron a creerse invincibles. Esto evéntualmente causó el desastre en Gettysburg.

Staat: Virginia

Befehlshaber der US:	Befehlshaber der CS:
Generalmajor Joseph Hooker	General Robert E. Lee
Armee der US: Armee des Potomac	Armee der US: Armee von Nordvirginia
Truppenstärke: 130,000	Truppenstärke: 60,000
Verluste	Verluste
Gefallen: 1,600	Gefallen: 1,700
Verwundet: 9,800	Verwundet: 9,100
Gefangengenommen oder vermißt: 5,900	Gefangengenommen oder vermißt: 2,000

KOMMENTAR

Der neue Befehlshaber der Armee des Potomac, Generalmajor Joseph Hooker, dachte einen glänzenden Plan aus, Lee bei Fredericksburg anzugreifen. Mit 40,000 Mann baute Sedgwick Brücken und drohte, den Rappahannock zu überqueren, gerade so wie Burnside im Dezember 1862 getan hatte. Mit seinen 75,000 Soldaten marschierte Hooker inzwischen flußaufwärts, und rückte von westlicher Richtung auf Fredericksburg. Dies bedrohte Lee im Rücken. Anstatt zurückzuziehen, ließ Lee 10,000 Truppen bei Fredericksburg zurück, zum Widerstand gegen Sedgwick, während der andere Teil der Truppen westwärts marschierte, um Hooker aufzuhalten.

Die Schlacht begann am 1. Mai, als Truppen, unter Jackson, sich Hooker's Vormarsch auf der Orange Turnpike und Orange Plank Road entgegenstellten. Entlang der Linie flammte das Kämpfen auf, und Hooker, der zugab, daß er seine Nerven verlor, zog sich in eine Defensivstellung, in der Nähe von Chancellorsville Crossing zurück. Mit Hooker in der Defensive, Lee übernahm blitzschnell die Kontrolle der Schlacht. In der Nacht planten Lee und Jackson einen dreisten Flankenmarsch. Am 2. Mai marschierte Jackson, mit 32,000 Mann, 19 Kilometer, um eine Stellung zu beziehen, die es ihm ermöglichte, die ungeschützte rechte Flanke der Föderalisten angreifen zu können. Am Spätnachmittag war Jackson bereit. Sein erster Vorstoss kam mit einer Schnelle, die dem überraschten XI. Korps keine Abwehr erlaubte. Das XI. Korps war in voller Flucht, was die Auflösung der ganzen rechten Flanke der Unionlinie mit sich brachte. Die Dunkelheit, und unklare Befehle der Konföderierten, trugen zum Ende von Jackson's Vormarsch bei. Während Jackson in der Nacht entlang der Linien erkundete, wurde er dreimal von Salven seiner eigenen Truppen getroffen.

Am 3. Mai drängte Lee wieder gegen die Föderalisten. Mit 50 Kanonen, massiert auf der Höhe bei Hazel Grove, zwangen die Konföderierten Hooker auf eine verschanzte Stellung zurück, die das US Ford deckte.

Inzwischen lernte Lee, daß General Sedgwick sich endlich in Bewegung gesetzt hatte. Sedgwick war durch die zahlenmäßig unterlegenen Verteidiger bei Fredericksburg durchgedrungen, und marschierte gegen Lee's Rücken. Lee überließ 25,000 Truppen die Wache auf Hooker. Er selbst zog sich mit dem Überrest seiner Armee auf Schnellmarsch, um Sedgwick's Kolonne bei Salem Church aufzuhalten. Am 3. Mai tobte der Kampf um die Kirche. Am nächsten Tag wurden Sedgwick's Flanke und Rücken durch Early in Gefahr gesetzt. Die Föderalisten hielten bis zum Einbruch der Dunkelheit aus, und zogen sich dann während der Nacht über den Fluß zurück.

BEDEUTUNG

Lee verlor seinen fähigsten Befehlshaber, Jackson, acht Tage nachdem er verwundet wurde, starb er an Lungenentzündung.

Lee, und der größte Teil seiner Armee, bekamen immer mehr der Überzeugung, daß sie unbesiegbar waren. Dies führte am Ende zur Katastrophe in der Schlacht von Gettysburg.

The Chancellor House lent its name to the battlefield. Destroyed by Confederate artillery fire, part of the house was rebuilt after the war.

State: Mississippi

U.S.	C.S.
Commander:	Commander:
Maj. Gen. U.S. Grant	Lt. Gen. John Pemberton
U.S. Army: Army of the Tennessee	C.S. Army: Army of Vicksburg
No. of Troops: 32,000	No. of Troops: 23,000
Casualties:	Casualties:
Killed: 410	Killed: 381
Wounded: 1,844	Wounded: 1,018
Captured or missing: 187	Captured or missing: 2,441

COMMENTS

Early on the morning of May 16, 1863, General Grant received news that Confederate forces were at Edwards Station preparing to march east. He immediately ordered his columns forward. Moving westward from Bolton and Raymond, Union soldiers slogged over muddy roads in three parallel columns. About 7 a.m. the southernmost column made contact with Confederate pickets and the battle of Champion Hill, the bloodiest and most decisive action of the Vicksburg Campaign, began.

Lt. Gen. John C. Pemberton, the Confederate commander, quickly deployed his three divisions with Gen. Carter Stevenson on the left, Gen. John Bowen in the center, and Gen. William Loring on the right. The Confederate battleline, three miles in length, ran from southwest to northeast along the military crest of a ridge overlooking Jackson Creek. The crest of Champion Hill, on the left of the line, was picketed as a security measure. Pemberton's position was suited for defense and was especially formidable against attacks via the Middle and Raymond Roads. The Confederate commander, however, was unaware that a strong Union column was pushing down the Jackson Road toward his unprotected left flank. If unchecked, the Union force would capture Edwards and cut the Confederates off from their base of operations—Vicksburg. To counter this threat, Pemberton shifted troops to the endangered area but to no avail.

At 10:30 Grant launched an attack on Stevenson's Confederates. Union troops surged into the heavy musket and artillery fire pushing the Confederates from the hill. The Southerners under Bowen counterattacked and in the vicious fighting that ensued Champion Hill and crossroads changed hands several times.

Finally by 5:00 p.m. the Confederates were retreating from the battlefield, leaving 27 cannon and hundreds of prisoners. In the retreat Gen. Loring's division was cut off from the rest of the army. Eventually, Loring was able to join Gen. Joseph E. Johnston's army in Jackson.

SIGNIFICANCE

The most severe contest of the Vicksburg Campaign.

Pemberton slowed Grant's progress only slightly and he lost valuable men and guns with which to later man the Vicksburg defenses.

Etat: Mississipi

Etats-Unis	Etats Confédérés
Commandant:	Commandant:
Major Général U. S. Grant	Lieutenant Général John Pemberton
Armée: du Tennessee	Armée: de Vicksburg
32 000 soldats	23 000 soldats
Pertes:	Pertes:
Tués: 410	Tués: 381
Blessés: 1 844	Blessés: 1 018
Prisonniers ou disparus: 187	Prisonniers ou disparus: 2 441

COMMENTAIRE

A l'aube du 16 mars 1863, le général Grant fut informé que les forces des Confédérés préparaient une marche en direction est depuis Edwards Station. Il envoya immédiatement ses colonnes en avant. Sur des routes boueuses, les soldats de l'Union avançaient en trois colonnes parallèles vers l'ouest, depuis Bolton et Raymond. Vers 7 heures, la colonne sud se heurta aux piquets des Confédérés, et la bataille de Champion Hill commença. Ce fut la bataille la plus sanglante et la plus décisive de la campagne de Vicksburg.

Le lieutenant général John C. Pemberton, commandant des Confédérés, déploya rapidement ses trois divisions: le général Carter Stevenson à gauche, le général Bowen au centre, et le général William Loring à droite. La ligne de bataille des Confédérés, d'environ cinq kilomètres, s'étalait en direction sud-ouest nord-est le long d'une crête dominant Jackson Creek. La crête de Champion Hill, à gauche de la ligne, avait des piquets installés par mesure de sécurité. La position de Pemberton était calculée pour la défensive, particulièrement forte contre toute attaque venant des routes Middle et Raymond. Le commandant des Confédérés ignorait cependant qu'une puissante colonne de l'Union se pressait sur Jackson Road, son flanc gauche non protégé. S'il n'y prenait pas garde, cette force de l'Union allait prendre Edwards et couper les Confédérés de leur base d'opérations: Vicksburg. Alerté de cette menace, Pemberton plaça inutilement des troupes pour renforcer la région vulnérable.

A 10h30, Grant lança l'attaque sur les Confédérés de Stevenson. Les troupes de l'Union surgirent dans les feux des mousquets et de l'artillerie délogeant les Confédérés de la colline. Les Sudistes aux ordres de Bowen contre-attaquèrent. Dans la bataille brutale qui fit rage à Champion Hill, les armées ennemies changèrent plusieurs fois de rôles.

Finalement, vers 17 heures, les Confédérés abandonnaient le champ de bataille, laissant 27 canons et des centaines de prisonniers. Dans la retraite, la division du général Loring fut coupée du reste de l'armée. Plus tard, Loring réussit à rejoindre l'armée du général Johnston à Jackson.

CONSEQUENCES

Ce fut le combat le plus rigoureux de la campagne de Vicksburg.

Pemberton ralentit à peine les progrès de Grant, et il perdit beaucoup de bons soldats et de fusils qui devaient assurer la défense de Vicksburg.

Important Landmarks
Champion Hill
Baker's Creek
Jackson Creek
Jackson Road
Middle Road
Southern R.R. of Miss.
Raymond Road
Ratliff Plantation

Important Buildings
Champion House (No longer standing)
Roberts House (No longer standing)
Coker House

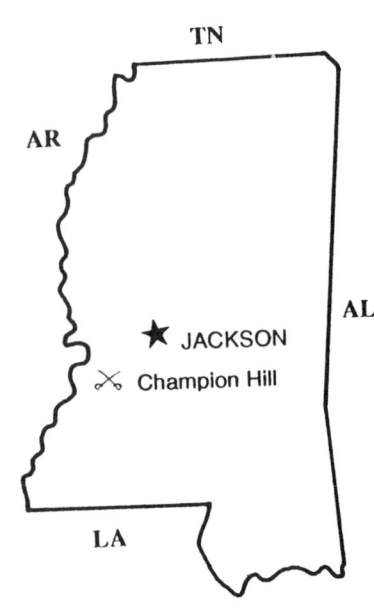

Estado: Mississippi

U.S.	C.S.
Comandante:	Comandante:
Maj. Gen. U.S. Grant	Lt. Gen. John Pemberton
U.S. Ejército: Army of the Tennessee	C.S. Ejército: Army of Vicksburg
No. de tropas: 32,000	No. de tropas: 23,000
Pérdidas:	Pérdidas:
Muertos: 410	Muertos: 381
Heridos: 1,844	Heridos: 1,018
Capturados o ausentes: 187	Capturados o ausentes: 2,441

COMENTARIO

Temprano por la mañana del 16 de mayo de 1863, el General Grant recibió noticias que las fuerzas Confederadas estaban en Edwards Station preparándose para marchar al este. Inmédiatamente Grant ordenó sus columnas al avance. Moviéndose al oeste desde Bolton y Raymond, los soldados Federales avanzaron por caminos llenos de barro en tres columnas parelelas. Alrededor de las 7 de la mañana la columna más al sur hizo contacto con piquetes Confederados y la batalla de Champion Hill, la acción más sangrienta y decesiva de la campaña de Vicksburg, comenzó.

El Lt. General John C. Pemberton, el comandante Confederado, rápidamente desplegó sus tres divisiones con el General Carter Stevenson en la izquierda, el General John Bowen en el centro, y el General William Loring en la derecha. La línea de batalla Confederada, tres millas en longitud, iba desde el sudoeste hasta el noreste por la cresta militar de una elevación que miraba a Jackson Creek. La cima de Champion Hill, en la izquierda de la línea, tenía piquetes como método de seguridad. La posición de Pemberton era muy buena para la defensa y especiálmente formidable contra los ataques de los caminos Middle y Raymond. El comandante Confederado, sin embargo, no sabía que una columna fuerte de Federales estaba llegando por el Jackson Road hacia su flanco izquierdo no protegido. Si no se parara, esta fuerza Federal capturaría Edwards y cortaría a los Confederados de su base de operaciones - Vicksburg. Para defenderse contra esta amenaza, Pemberton mudó tropas a este área de peligro, pero esto no ayudó.

A las 10:30 Grant lanzó un ataque contra los Confederados de Stevenson. Las tropas Federales surgieron al fuego de balas y bombas empujando a los Rebeldes de la colina. Los sureños bajo Bowen contraatacaron y en una pelea violenta Champion Hill y los crucecaminos cambiaron de mano varias veces.

Finalmente a las 5 los Confederados se retiraban del campo de batalla, dejando 27 cañones y cientos de prisioneros. Durante la retirada la división del General Loring se separó del resto del ejército. Eventuálmente, Loring pudo juntarse con el ejército del General Joseph E. Johnston en Jackson.

CONSECUENCIAS

Fue la contienda más severa de la campaña de Vicksburg.

Pemberton retardó el progreso de Grant sólamente un poco y perdió hombres y armas valiosos los que podría haber usado en la defensa de Vicksburg.

Staat: Mississippi

Befehlshaber der US:	Befehlshaber der CS:
Generalmajor U.S. Grant	Generalleutnant John Pemberton
Armee der US: Armee von Tennessee	Armee der CS: Vicksburger Armee
Truppenstärke: 32,000	Truppenstärke: 23,000
Verluste:	Verluste:
Gefallen: 410	Gefallen: 381
Verwundet: 1,844	Verwundet: 1,018
Gerfangengenommen oder vermißt: 187	Gefangengenommen oder vermißt: 2,441

KOMMENTAR

Am 16. Mai 1863, vor Tagesanbruch, wurde General Grant benachrichtigt, daß Konföderierte Streitkräfte bei Edwards Station waren, und sich vorbereiteten, ostwärts zu marschieren. Grant befahl seine Kolonnen zum sofortigen Aufbruch. Die Unionsoldaten schleppten sich, von Bolton und Raymond, über schlammigen Wegen westwärts. Um etwa 7.00 Uhr kam die südlichste Kolonne mit Konföderierten Vorposten in Kontakt, und die Schlacht am Champion Hill begann — die blutigste und entscheidendste Aktion im Vicksburger Feldzug.

Generalleutnant John C. Pemberton, Befehlshaber der Konföderierten, stelle seine drei Divisionen schnell auf: General Carter Stevenson links, General John Bowen Mitte, und General William Loring rechts. Die fünf Kilometer lange Konföderierte Angriffslinie lief vom Südwesten nach Nordosten, an einer Linie unterhalb des Hügelkammes entlang (military crest), mit Überblick auf Jackson Creek. Auf dem Kamm von Champion Hill waren Vorposten aus Sicherheitsgründen aufgestellt. Pemberton's Stellung eignete sich gut für die Verteidigung, insbesondere gegen Angriffe vom Middle Road und Raymond Road. Dem Befehlshaber der Konföderierten war es nicht bewußt, daß eine starke Unionkolonne sich auf Jackson Road gegen seine unbeschützte linke Flanke drängte. Sollte es nicht möglich sein, diese Uniontruppen aufzuhalten, würde es ihnen gelingen, Edwards Station zu erobern, und dadurch die Konföderierten von ihrer Operationsbasis, Vicksburg, abzuschneiden. Um dieser Gefahr entgegenzuwirken, versetzte Pemberton seine Truppen an die gefährdete Stellung, aber ohne Erfolg.

Um 10.30 Uhr ging Grant zum Angriff gegen Stevenson's Konföderierte über. Uniontruppen fluteten ins schwere Musketen-und Artilleriefeuer und warfen die Konföderierten vom Hügel. Aber die Konföderierten, unter Bowen, schlugen zurück, und im nachfolgenden brutalen Kampf, wechselten Champion Hill und Crossroads mehrmals den Besitzer.

Endlich, um 17.00 Uhr, begannen die Konföderierten ihren Rückzug vom Schlachtfeld. Sie ließen 27 Kanonen und Hunderte von Gefangenen zurück. Beim Rückzug wurde General Loring's Division vom Rest der Armee abgeschnitten. Später konnte sich Loring der Armee von General Joseph E. Johnston in Jackson anschließen.

BEDEUTUNG

Dies war der härteste Kampf in der Vicksburger Kampagne.

Pemberton verlangsamte Grant's Vorrücken nur wenig und verlor wertvolle Truppen und Gewehre, die er zur Verteidigung Vicksburg's hätte einsetzen können.

The Federal attack on Pemberton's lines.

State: Mississippi

U.S.
Commander: Maj. Gen. U.S. Grant
U.S. Army: Army of the Tennessee
No. of Troops by end of siege:
77,000
Casualties:
Killed: 800
Wounded: 3,900
Captured or missing: 200

C.S.
Commander: Lt. Gen. John Pemberton
C.S. Army: Garrison
No. of Troops: 32,000
Casualties:
Killed: 900
Wounded: 2,500
Captured or missing: 200
Surrendered: 29,491

Etat: Mississipi

Etats-Unis
Commandant:
  Général de Division U. S. Grant

Armée: du Tennessee
  77 000 soldats à la fin du siège
Pertes:
  Tués: 800
  Blessés: 3 900
  Prisonniers ou disparus: 200

Etats Confédérés
Commandant:
  Lieutenant Général John
  Pemberton
Armée: Garnison
  32 000 soldats
Pertes:
  Tués: 900
  Blessés: 2 500
  Prisonniers ou disparus: 29 491

COMMENTS

By May 18 Grant's army was nearing Vicksburg after successfully positioning itself between Pemberton and Johnston.

Sherman moved north of Vicksburg taking the hills overlooking the Yazoo River. Possession of these hills assured Grant's reinforcement and supply from the North. McPherson and McClernand's columns were approaching from the east.

The Federals now faced a very strong line of trenches and forts surrounding the Confederate city. Inside these works was Lt. General John Pemberton and 32,000 Confederate soldiers. Pemberton planned to hold Vicksburg until Johnston could raise reinforcements and attack Grant from the rear.

By noon on the 19th all of Grant's force had reached the field. Grant wasted no time, deciding to attack immediately before Pemberton had time to post his defenses strongly. Sherman, who arrived first, was the only one prepared for an attack. At 1:00 p.m. the Federals charged. They made it as far as the walls of a Confederate fort but, unable to force a breakthrough, were eventually repulsed, losing 1,000 men. Despite these losses, Grant wasn't willing to resort to a siege and ordered another assault for 10:00 a.m. on May 22.

The Federals attacked along a 3 mile section of the Confederate works containing six forts. The Union infantrymen were mowed down as the rushed toward the strong defenses. A few Federals got into one fort, but they were soon shot down as the Southerners counterattacked. The Federal attack was crushed by Pemberton's men. The 4 hour attack cost Grant another 3,000 men.

By May 25 Grant realized that he couldn't take Vicksburg by storm and began siege operations. The city of Vicksburg was shelled around the clock by Union army and naval batteries. Meanwhile sniping and hand grenades took their toll in the trenches. But sickness and hunger were the biggest problems in the Confederate city. By July 3 Pemberton realized he had no choice but to surrender. On July 4th the Federals entered Vicksburg.

SIGNIFICANCE

The fall of Vicksburg together with Lee's defeat at Gettysburg the day before, seemed to mark the turning point in the war.

Except for Port Hudson, LA, the Federals now controlled the Mississippi River.

COMMENTAIRE

Le 18 mai, l'armée de Grant s'approchait de Vicksburg après s'être mise en bonne position entre Pemberton et Johnston.

Sherman avança au nord de Vicksburg et prit les collines dominant la rivière Yazoo. Pour Grant, cette position assurait approvisionnement et renforts venus du nord. Les colonnes de McPherson et de McClernand venaient de l'est.

Les Fédéraux faisaient face à une forte ligne de tranchées et de forts entourant la ville confédérée. A l'intérieur se trouvait le lieutenant général Pemberton avec 32 000 soldats. Celui-ci pensait tenir Vicksburg jusqu'à ce que Johnston puisse envoyer des renforts et attaquer Grant à l'arrière.

Le 1 à midi, toutes ses forces ayant atteint le champ de bataille, Grant ne perdit pas une minute. Il décida d'attaquer immédiatement, avant que Pemberton ait le temps de poster solidement ses défenses. Sherman, arrivé le premier, était le seul prêt à l'attaque. À 2 heures, les Fédéraux chargèrent. Ils atteignirent le mur d'un fort confédéré, mais ils furent repoussés et perdirent 1 000 hommes. En dépit de ces pertes, Grant ne voulut pas assiéger la ville, et le 22 mai à 10 heures, il ordonna une nouvelle attaque.

Les Fédéraux attaquèrent le long de cinq kilomètres de ligne confédérée contenant six forts. L'infanterie de l'Union fut fauchée dès qu'elle se précipita sur les défenses. Les quelques Fédéraux qui pénétrèrent dans le fort furent fusillés dans la contre-attaque des Sudistes. L'attaque fédérale fut écrasée par les hommes de Pemberton. Elle dura quatre heures et coûta 3 000 hommes de plus à Grant.

Le 25 mai, Grant comprit qu'il ne pourrait pas prendre ainsiVicksburg et il entreprit de l'assiéger. La ville fut bombardée de boulets pendant 24 heures par l'armée unioniste et les batteries navales. Pendant ce temps, l'ennemi était canardé et grenadé dans les tranchées. Mais la maladie et la faim étaient les problèmes les plus graves de la ville confédérée. Le 3 juillet, Pemberton comprit qu'il n'avait pas le choix: il fallait se rendre. Le 4 juillet, les Fédéraux entrèrent à Vicksburg.

CONSEQUENCES

La chute de Vicksburg et la défaite de Lee à Gettysburg le jour précédent semblent avoir marqué un tournant décisif dans la guerre.

Si l'on excepte Port Hudson, en Louisiane, les Fédéraux étaient maintenant victorieux sur le Mississipi.

Important Landmarks
Mississippi River
Graveyard Road
Fort Hill
Second Texas Lunette
Fort Garrott
Jackson Road
Battery De Galyer
Stockade Redan
The Great Redoubt
Railroad Redoubt
South Fort
Hall's Ferry Road
Third Louisiania Redan
Battery Selfridge
Baldwin Ferry Road
Southern R.R. of Miss.
Battery Benton

Important Buildings
Shirley House
Rock House
Candon Hearth
Warren County Court House
Willis-Cowan House
Anchuca
Cedar Grove
Riddle House
Balfour House
McRaven

Estado: Mississippi

U.S.	C.S.
Comandante:	Comandante:
Maj. Gen. U.S. Grant	Lt. Gen. John Pemberton
U.S. Ejército: Army of the Tennessee	C.S. Ejército: Army Garrison
No. de tropas al final del asedio:	No. de tropas: 32,000
77,000	Pérdidas:
Pérdidas:	Muertos: 900
Muertos: 800	Heridos: 2,500
Heridos: 3,900	Capturados o ausentes: 200
Capturados o ausentes: 200	Rendidos: 29,491

COMENTARIO

El 18 de mayo el ejército de Grant ya se acercaba a Vicksburg después de situarse entre Pemberton y Johnston.

Sherman se mudó al norte de Vicksburg tomando las colinas que miraban al río Yazoo. La posesión de estas colinas aseguró a Grant que podían llegar sus refuerzos y provisiones del norte. Las columnas de McPherson y McClernand se acercaban del este.

Ahora los Federales se enfrentaban con una línea muy fuerte de trincheras y fuertes que rodeaban la ciudad Confederada. Dentro de estas fortificaciones estaba el General John Pemberton con 32,000 soldados. Pemberton pensaba mantener Vicksburg hasta que Johnston pudiera levantar refuerzos y atacar a Grant en la espalda.

Al mediodía el día 19 toda la fuerza de Grant había llegado al campo. Grant no desperdició tiempo, decidiendo atacar inmediátamente antes de que Pemberton tuviera tiempo para poner sus defensas más fuertes. Sherman, quien llegó primero, era el único preparado para un ataque. A las dos de la tarde los Federales atacaron. Llegaron hasta las paredes del fuerte Confederado, pero no pudiendo forzar un agujero en las defensas, eventuálmente fueron repulsados perdiendo 1,000 hombres. A pesar de estas pérdidas, Grant no quería acudir a un asedio y mandó otro ataque para las 10 de la mañana el 22.

Los Federales atacaron por tres millas la posición Confederada que contenía 6 fuertes. La infantería de la Unión se caía rápidamente mientras asaltaba las defensas fuertes. Unos pocos Federales entraron en un fuerte pero también fueron disparados porque los Rebeldes contraatacaron. El ataque Federal fue aplastado por los soldados de Pemberton. Este ataque de cuatro oras le costó a Grant otros 3,000 soldados.

El 25 de mayo Grant se dio cuenta de que no podía tomar la ciudad de Vicksburg de sorpresa y empezó las operaciones de siteo. La ciudad de Vicksburg estaba protegida continuamente por la armada de la unión y las baterías navales. Mientras tanto granadas de mano tomó todos sus puestos en las trincheras. Pero en la ciudad Confederada la hambre y las enfermedades eran los problemas más graves. El 3 de julio Pemberton se dio cuenta de que no podía hacer otra cosa excepto rendirse. El 4 de julio los Federales entraron en Vicksburg.

CONSECUENCIAS

La caída de Vicksburg junto con la derrota de Lee en Gettysburg el día antes pareció marcar el punto de cambio en la guerra.

Excepto por Port Hudson en Louisiana, los Federales tenían control del río Mississippi.

Staat: Mississippi

Befehlshaber der US:	Befehlshaber der CS:
Generalmajor U.S. Grant	Generalleutnant John Pemberton
Armee der US: Armee von Tennessee	Armee der CS: Garnison
Truppenstärke: (am Ende der Belagerung) 77,000	Truppenstärke: 32,000
Verluste:	Verluste:
Gefallen: 800	Gefallen: 900
Verwundet: 3,900	Verwundet: 2,500
Gerfangengenommen oder vermißt: 200	Gefangengenommen oder vermißt: 200
	Kapituliert: 29,491

KOMMENTAR

Am 18. März näherte sich Grant's Armee Vicksburg, nachdem es Grant gelungen war, sich zwischen Pemberton und Johnston zu stellen.

Sherman zog nördlich von Vicksburg und eroberte die Hügel, die den Yazoo Fluß überblicken. Der Besitz dieser Hügel versicherte Grant die Zufuhr von verstärkungen und Provianten ansdem Norden. Die kolonnen von McPherson und McClernand näherten sich vom Osten.

Die Föderalisten sahen sich jetzt gegenüber einer stark befestigten Konföderiertenstadt, umgeben von Schützengräben und Forten. Innerhalb dieser Befestigungen waren Generalleutnant John Pemberton und 31,000 Konföderationsoldaten. Pemberton plante, Vicksburg zu halten, bis Johnston Verstärkungen aufbringen konnte, um Grant im Rücken anzugreifen.

Beim Mittag des 19. hatten alle Streifkräfte Grant's das Feld erreicht. Grant verlor keine Zeit. Er entschloß sich, sofort anzugreifen, ehe Pemberton völlig abwehrbereit war. Sherman, der zuerst ankam, war der einzige, der zum Angriff bereit war. Um 14.00 Uhr griffen die Föderalisten an. Sie drangen bis an die Mauern eines Konföderierten Forts vor, aber ein Durchbruch scheiterte und sie wurden am Ende zurückgeschlagen, mit einem Verlust von 1,000 Mann. Trotz dieser Verluste war Grant nicht willig, eine Belagerung anzuwenden, und am 22. Mai, um 10.00 Uhr, befahl er nochmals einen Angriff.

Die Föderalisten stürmten gegen eine fünf Kilometer lange Strecke der Konföderierten Befestigungen, die sechs Forte enthielten. Die Unioninfanterie wurde abgemäht, als sie sich auf die starken Verteidigungsanlagen stürzten. Einige Föderalisten drangen in ein Fort ein, wurden aber kurz danach, in einem nachfolgenden Konföderierten Gegenangriff, niedergeschoßen. Pemberton's Truppen schlugen den Föderalistenangriff nieder. Der vierstündige Kampf kostete Grant weitere 3,000 Mann.

Grant sah ein, daß er Vicksburg durch einen Angriff nicht erobern konnte, und am 25. Mai begann er mit der Belagerung. Die Stadt Vicksburg wurde Tag und Nacht von Armee-und-Marinebatterien beschoßen. Handgranaten und Heckenschützen forderten weitere Opfer in den Schützengräben. Die größten Probleme in der Konföderiertenstadt aber waren Krankheit und Hunger. Am 3. Juli sah Pemberton ein, daß er keine andere Wahl als die der Kapitulation hatte. Am 4. Juli marschierten die Föderalisten in Vicksburg ein.

BEDEUTUNG

Die Eroberung von Vicksburg, zusammen mit der Niederlage von Lee bei Gettysburg am vorigen Tage, erschien als der Wendepunkt im Krieg.

Mit Ausnahme von Port Hudson, im Staat Louisiana, kontrollierten die Föderalisten jetzt den ganzen Mississippi Fluß.

The Shirley House or "white house" was used as headquarters by the 45th Illinois. Federal bombproofs in the foreground protected the troops from enemy artillery fire.

State: Louisiana

U.S.

Commander:
Maj. Gen. Nathaniel P. Banks
U.S. Army: Army of the Gulf
No. of Troops: 20,000
Casualties:
Killed: 708
Wounded: 3,336
Captured or missing: 319

C.S.

Commander:
Maj. Gen. Franklin Gardner
C.S. Army: Garrison
No. of Troops: 6,500
Casualties:
Killed: 176
Wounded: 447
Captured or missing: 6,400

COMMENTS

The section of the Mississippi River between Vicksburg and Port Hudson (about 110 miles) was all that remained in control of the Confederacy by March 1863. The capture of the Confederate stronghold at Port Hudson was a critical part of the Union plan to divide the Confederacy along the Mississippi.

On March 14 Admiral Farragut bombarded the Confederate batteries during his passage up the river toward Vicksburg. During this engagement the USS Mississippi was lost. At that time it was decided that an assault by land would be needed to capture the works, and General Banks' Army of the Gulf was assigned to the task. Banks advanced on Port Hudson and, by May 23, had encircled the Confederate position.

At dawn on the 27th the battle opened as planned with a joint Army-Navy bombardment of the Confederate lines. But uncoordinated attacks by the infantry allowed the Southerners to hold on.

On June 13 Banks planned another assault. All day the Confederates were shelled by the Union army and Navy. The next day, at 4:00 p.m., an entire Union division moved across the rugged terrain toward a big fort in the center of the defenses, but their comrades were unable to exploit the breakthrough. The Confederates repulsed this attack and all that followed. The Federals continued the attacks all morning, but with decreasing intensity. After the attacks had failed, Banks decided to conduct a siege of Port Hudson, hoping to starve the Confederate army out of its stronghold.

On July 7, after 46 days of siege, Banks planned another assault, but it was postponed due to bad weather. The next day news of the surrender of Vicksburg reached the Union camps. The Confederate commander, believing the news was planted to induce his surrender, was given proof and formally surrendered on July 9.

SIGNIFICANCE

The Union now controlled the Mississippi River, cutting the Confederacy in half.

The South lost thousands of troops as prisoners at a time when manpower was virtually impossible to replace.

Etat: Louisiane

Etats-Unis

Commandant:
Général de Division Nathaniel P. Banks
Armée: du Gulfe
20 000 soldats
Pertes:
Tués: 708
Blessés: 3 336
Prisonniers ou disparus: 319

Etats Confédérés

Commandant:
Général de Division Franklin Gardner
Armée: Garnison
6 500 soldats
Pertes:
Tués: 176
Blessés: 447
Prisonniers ou disparus: 6 400

COMMENTAIRE

En mars 1863, la partie du Mississipi entre Vicksburg et Port Hudson, environ 180 kilometres, était tout ce qui restait sous le contrôl de la Confédératión.

Le 1 mars, l'amiral Farragut bombarda les batteries confédérées tandis qu'il passait en amont de la rivière en se dirigeant sur Vicksburg. Avec la perte de l'USS Mississipi. L'Union décida de capturer hommes et bateaux par un assaut lancé de la terre, et l'armée du Golfe du général Banks fut chargée de cette mission. Banks avança sur Port Hudson, et le 23 mai, il avait encerclé les Confédérés.

A l'aube du 27 la bataille commença comme prévue; la marine et l'armée bombardèrent les lignes confédérés. Mais l'incohérence des attaques de l'infanterie permirent aux Sudistes de résister.

Le 13 juin, Banks prépara un autre assaut. Les Confédérés reçurent les boulets de l'armée et de la marine pendant toute la journée. Le jour suivant, toute une division unioniste avança sur le terrain accidenté jusqu'à un énorme fort au centre des lignes confédérées. Arrivant au fort depuis toutes les directions, les soldats de l'Union percèrent les défenses. Mais leurs camarades ne purent exploiter la brèche. Les Confédérés repoussèrent cette attaque et les suivantes. Les Fédéraux continuèrent leurs attaques toute la matinée, mais perdirent peu à peu leur ferveur. Après l'échec, Banks décida de mettre le siège sur Port Hudson, espérant que la faim aurait raison des Confédérés.

Le 7 juillet, après 46 jours de siège, Banks organisa un autre assaut, mais il dut le remettre à cause du mauvais temps. Pendant les jours suivants, l'Union apprit la reddition de Vicksburg. Le commandant des Confédérés, croyant d'abord que ces nouvelles étaient inventées pour le décourager, en reçut la preuve irréfutable, et se rendit à son tour le 9 juillet.

CONSEQUENCES

L'Union maitrisait maintenant tout le Mississipi, coupant en deux la Confédération.

Le Sud perdit des milliers de soldats devenus prisonniers à un moment où les pertes étaient impossibles à remplacer.

Important Landmarks

Mississippi River
Sandy Creek
Foster Creek
Fort Babcock
Artillery Ridge
Slaughter's Field
Jackson Road
Citadel
Miss. Redoubt
Bennett's Redoubt
Ala./Ark. Redoubt
Commissary Hill
Fort Desperate

Important Buildings

Frame House-Port Hudson
White House
Slaughter's House
Troth's House

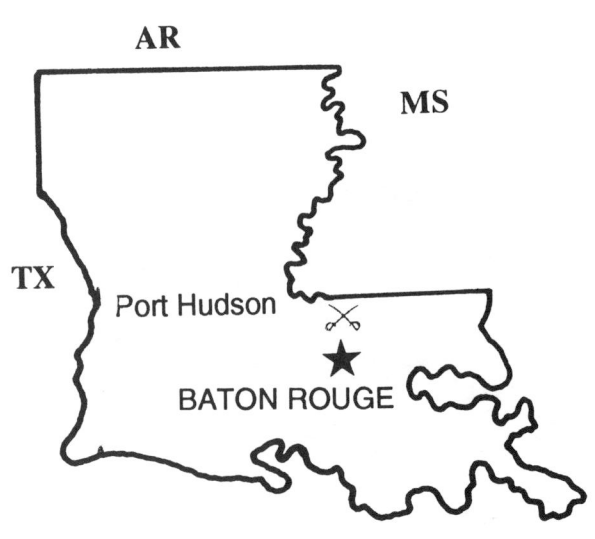

Estado: Louisiana

U.S.

Comandante:
 Maj. Gen. Nathaniel P. Banks
U.S. Ejército: Army of the Gulf
 No. de tropas: 20,000
Pérdidas:
 Muertos: 708
 Heridos: 3,336
 Capturados o ausentes: 319

C.S.

Comandante:
 Maj. Gen. Franklin Gardner
U.S. Ejército: Garrison
 No. de tropas: 6,500
Pérdidas:
 Muertos: 176
 Heridos: 447
 Capturados o ausentes: 6,400

COMENTARIO

La sección del río Mississippi entre Vicksburg y Port Hudson (110 millas) era todo lo que quedaba en control de la Confederación en marzo de 1863. La captura de la fortaleza en Port Hudson era una parte critica del plan Federal para dividir la Confederación por el Mississippi.

El 14 de marzo el Admiral Farragut bombardeó las baterías Confederadas durante su paso río arriba hacia Vicksburg. Durante esta pelea el USS Mississippi se perdió. En ese momento se decidió que un asalto de tierra sería necesario para capturar la fortaleza, y el Army of the Gulf del General Banks recibió el quehacer. Banks avanzó a Port Hudson, y el día 23 de marzo, ya había rodeado la posición Confederada.

Al alba del 27 la batalla abrió fuego como se había pensado con un bombardeo del ejército y la armada a las líneas Confederadas. Pero los ataques mal coordinados por la infantería dejaron que los sureños mantuvieran su posición.

El 13 de junio Banks planeó otro asalto. Por todo el día los Confederados fueron bombardeados por el ejército y la armada. El próximo día, a las 4, una división Federal entera se movió a través de la tierra rugosa hacia un fuerte grande en el centro de la línea Confederada. Los Federales llegaron hasta el fuerte y abrieron una brecha en las defensas, pero sus compañeros no pudieron explotar la abertura. Los Confederados repulsaron este ataque y todos los demás. Los Federales continuaron los ataques por toda la mañana, pero con menos intensidad. Después de que los ataques fracasaron, Banks decidió hacer un asedio a Port Hudson, con la esperanza de que la fortaleza confederada se rindiera por hambre.

El 7 de julio, después de 46 días de asedio, Banks planeó otro asalto, pero se pospuso por mal tiempo. El próximo día las noticias de la rendición de Vicksburg llegó a los Federales. El comandante Confederado, creyendo que las noticias habían sido inventadas para inducir su rendición, recibió la prueba y se rindió formálmente el 9 de julio.

CONSECUENCIAS

La Unión ahora controlaba todo el río Mississippi, cortando la Confederación en dos partes.

El Sur perdió miles de tropas como prisioneros en una época en que era imposible reemplazarlas.

Staat: Louisiana

Befehlshaber der US:
 Generalmajor Nathaniel P. Banks
Armee der US: Armee des Golfs
 Truppenstärke: 20,000
Verluste:
 Gefallen: 708
 Verwundet: 3,336
 Gerfangengenommen oder
 vermißt: 319

Befehlshaber der CS:
 Generalmajor Franklin Gardner
Armee der CS: Garnison
 Truppenstärke: 6,500
Verluste:
 Gefallen: 176
 Verwundet: 447
 Gefangengenommen oder
 vermißt: 6,400

KOMMENTAR

Die Strecke des Mississippi, zwischen Vicksburg und Port Hudson — etwa 176 Kilometer — umfaßte, was sich seit Anfang März 1863 noch in der Gewalt der Konföderierten befand. Die Eroberung des Konföderationstützpunktes Port Hudson war ein kritischer Teil der Unionstrategie, die Konföderation am Mississippi Fluß zu teilen.

Am 14. März beschoß Admiral Farragut die Batterien der Konföderierten auf seinem Weg flußaufwärts nach Vicksburg. Während dieses Gefechts sank die USS Mississippi. Zur gleichen Zeit kam der Norden zur Überzeugung, daß ein Angriff auf die Befestigungen bei Land die einzige Möglichkeit war, sie erobern zu können. Diese Aufgabe wurde der Armee des Golfs, unter General Banks, zugestellt. Banks rückte auf Port Hudson vor und, am 23. Mai war die Umfassung der Konföderierten Stellung geschloßen.

Wie geplant, eröffnete er am 27., bei Tagesanbruch, den Kampf. Die Armee und Marine bombardierten gemeinsam die Linien der Konföderierten, aber unkoordinierte Angriffe der Infanterie ermöglichte es den Konföderierten, festzuhalten.

Banks plante einen weiteren Angriff für den 13. Juni. Den ganzen Tag beschoßen seine Armee und Marine die Konföderierten. Um 16.00 Uhr, am folgenden Tage, zog eine volle Uniondivision über das rauhe Terrain gegen ein großes Fort, das in der Mitte der Konföderiertenlinie stand. Die Uniontruppen fluteten auf das Fort und durchbrachen die Befestigung, aber ihre Kameraden konnten den Durchbruch nicht ausnützen. Die Konföderierten schlugen diesen Sturm, und alle folgenden, zurück. Die Föderalisten wiederholten ihre Angriffe über den ganzen Morgen, aber mit verminderter Intensität. Angesichts der Scheiterung der Angriffe, entschloß sich Banks, eine Belagerung von Port Hudson durchzuführen, in der Hoffnung, die Konföderationsarmee, durch Aushungern, aus ihrem Stützpunkt zu zwingen.

Nach 46 Tagen der Belagerung, plante Banks am 7. Juli einen weiteren Angriff, aber dieser wurde, infolge schlechten Wetters, verschoben. Am nächsten Tag erreichte die Nachricht von Vicksburgs Kapitulation das Unionlager. Der Befehlshaber der Konföderierten glaubte, die Nachricht wäre manipuliert, um seine Kapitulation herbeizuführen. Nachdem ihm aber der Beweis vorgelegt wurde, ergab er sich offiziell am 9. Juli.

BEDEUTUNG

Die Union kontrollierte jetzt den Mississippi, was die Konföderation in zwei Teile schnitt.

Der Süden verlor tausende von Truppen in die Gefangenschaft, zu einer Zeit, in der es unmöglich war, sie zu ersetzen.

Confederate artillery position at Port Hudson overlooking the Mississippi River.

State: Pennsylvania

U.S.

Commander:
Maj. Gen. George G. Meade
U.S. Army: Army of the Potomac
No. of Troops: 93,693

Casualties:
Killed: 3,149
Wounded: 14,501
Captured or missing: 5,157

C.S.

Commander:
Gen. Robert E. Lee
C.S. Army: Army of Northern Virginia
No. of Troops: 70,136

Casualties:
Killed: 4,559
Wounded: 12,355
Captured or missing: 5,643

COMMENTS

This battle was the climax of Lee's second northern invasion and it started on the morning of July 1 when Confederate infantry attacked Union cavalry west of the town. Buford's dismounted troopers repulsed several Confederate attacks while waiting for infantry support. Around 10 a.m. Reynolds' I Corps arrived to relieve Buford. Later, Howard's XI Corps extended the Union line north of the town, but Confederate reinforcements also reached the battlefield. The whole Federal line was soon engaged in desperate fighting. Taking heavy losses, Howard's men broke and ran into town. By 4 p.m. the I Corps also retreated toward Gettysburg.

A new Union position was anchored at both ends by hills; Cemetery and Culp's Hills to the north, and Big and Little Round Top to the south. The Confederate attacks of July 2 were planned with these goals in mind and by 4 p.m. Longstreet launched his attack aimed at the Union left. The Confederates hit Sickles' III Corps which had moved forward, out of line, to an exposed position. Longstreet drove the Federals in heavy fighting through the Peach Orchard, the Wheatfield and Devil's Den. But, the V Corps defenders stopped repeated attacks on the rocky slopes of Little Round Top. Late in the day Lee struck the Union right on Cemetery and Culp's Hills. The bloody fighting ended after dark when Union reserves finally repulsed the attackers.

At dawn on July 3, the fighting in the Culp's Hill area was resumed, however, by noon the Confederates withdrew across Rock Creek. Lee now prepared for a great assault on the Union center. At 1 p.m. 140 cannons opened fire on the Federal line. The bombardment ended after two hours and then 12,000 men marched out of the woods on Seminary Ridge. In a storm of canister and musket balls they hit the Union line. The center was breached, but the exhausted attackers could not hold their ground. The survivors of "Pickett's Charge" streamed back to their original positions. Simultaneously, a three hour cavalry fight progressed east of Gettysburg, but "Jeb" Stuart was stalemated by Gregg's Union forces and the battle was over. On the afternoon of July 4 Lee began his retreat back to Virginia.

SIGNIFICANCE

Lee's second invasion of the North was stopped.
The South could never replace the manpower lost at Gettysburg.
Together with Vicksburg, the "High Water" mark of the Confederacy.

Etat: Pennsylvanie

Etats-Unis

Commandant:
Général de Division George G. Meade
Armée: du Potomac
93 693 soldats
Pertes:
Tués: 3 149
Blessés: 14 501
Prisonniers ou disparus: 5 157

Etats Confédérés

Commandant:
Général Robert E. Lee
Armée: de Virginie du Nord
70 136 soldats
Pertes:
Tués: 4 559
Blessés: 12 355
Prisonniers ou disparus: 5 643

COMMENTAIRE

Cette bataille fut l'apogée de la seconde invasion du Nord par Lee. Elle commença le 1er juillet quand l'infanterie de la Confédération attaqua la cavalerie de l'Union à l'ouest de la ville. Les cavaliers démontés de Buford repoussèrent plusieurs attaques confédérées en attendant le soutien de l'infanterie. Vers 10 heures le premier corps d'armée de Reynolds arriva pour prendre la relève de Buford. Plus tard, le sixième corps d'armée d'Howard allongea la ligne de l'Union jusqu'au nord de la ville, mais les renforts des Confédérés atteignirent le champ de bataille aussi. Toute la ligne fédérale fut bientôt engagée dans une lutte acharnée. Ayant Souffert de lourdes pertes, les hommes d'Howard coururent à la ville. A 16 heures, le premier corps s'était aussi retiré vers Gettysburg.

L'Union installa une nouvelle position à chaque extrémité des collines: Cemetery et Culp's Hill au nord, Big et Little Round Top au Sud. Les attaques des Confédérés du 2 juillet tinrent compte de la situation; à 16 heures, Longstreet lança son attaque visant la gauche de l'Union. Les Confédérés frappèrent le troisième corps d'armée commandé par Sickles qui s'était exposé en dehors de la ligne. Longstreet engagea les Fédéraux dans une dure bataille à travers le Peach Orchard, le Wheatfield et Devil's Den. Mais le corps dut cesser les attaques sur les pentes rocheuses de Little Round Top. Plus tard dans la journée, Lee frappa la droite de l'Union sur les collines de Cemetery et Culp. La lutte sanglante ne cessa qu'après la tombée de la nuit où les réserves de l'Union repoussèrent finalement les assaillants.

A l'aube du 3 juillet, la lutte reprit dans la région de Culp's Hill; à midi, les Confédérés se retirèrent sur l'autre rive de Rock Creek. Lee préparait alors un grand assaut contre le centre de l'Union. A 13 heures, 140 canons firent feu sur la ligne fédérale. Le bombardement s'arrêta au bout de deux heures et 12 000 hommes sortirent des bois de Seminary Ridge. La ligne de l'Union reçut une tempête de balles de mousquets et de mitraille. Le centre fut percé, mais les attaquants ne pouvaient y rester. Les survivants de "Pickett's Charge" revinrent en masse à leur position initiale. Simultanément, une lutte de cavalerie avait fait rage pendant trois heures à l'est de Gettysburg. Mais "Jeb" Stuart fut paralysé par les forces unionistes de Gregg et la bataille prit fin. D'après midi du 4 juillet, Lee reprit la route pour la Virginie.

CONSEQUENCES

L'Union avait enrayé la deuxième invasion du Nord par Lee.
Le Sud ne pourrait jamais remplacer les pertes humaines de Gettysburg.
Avec Vicksburg, Gettysburg fut la "maré haute" de la Confédération.

Important Landmarks

Cemetery Hill
Big Round Top
Spangler's Spring
Devil's Den
Oak Ridge
Chambersburg Pike
Little Round Top
Wheatfield
Barlow Knoll
Cemetery Ridge
Peach Orchard
Emmitsburg Road
Seminary Ridge
McPherson Ridge
Valley of Death
Culp's Hill

Important Buildings

Evergreen Cemetery Gateway
Pennsylvania Hall — College
"Old Dorm" — Seminary
Thompson Home
Trostle Farm
Codori Farm
Bryan Farm
Wentz House
McPherson Farm
Rummel Farm
Leister House
Sherfy House

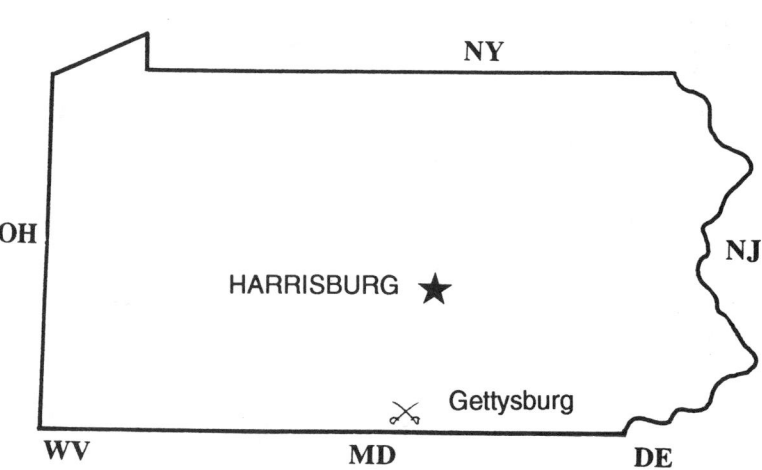

Estado: Pennsylvania

U.S.	C.S.
Comandante:	Comandante:
Maj. Gen. George G. Meade	Gen. Robert E. Lee
C.S. Ejército: Army of the Potomac	C.S. Ejército: Army of Northern Virginia
No. de tropas: 93,693	No. de tropas: 70,136
Pérdidas:	Pérdidas:
Muertos: 3,149	Muertos: 4,559
Heridos: 14,501	Heridos: 12,355
Capturados o ausentes: 5,157	Capturados o ausentes: 5,643

COMENTARIO

Esta batalla fue el clímax de la segunda invasión norteña de Lee y empezó por la mañana del 1 de julio cuando la infantería Confederada atacó la caballería Federal al oeste del pueblo. Las tropas desmontadas de Buford repulsaron varios ataques Confederados mientras esperaban el apoyo de su propia infantería. Cerca de las 10 de la mañana el cuerpo I de Reynolds llegó para relevar a Buford. Luego, el cuerpo XI de Howard extendió la línea Federal al norte del pueblo, pero refuerzos Confederados llegaron también al campo de batalla. La línea Federal entera trabó una lucha desesperada. Tomando muchas pérdidas, las tropas de Howard cayeron y se fueron hacia el pueblo. A las 4 de la tarde el cuerpo I ya se había retirado al pueblo.

Una posición Federal nueva fue hecha y tenía las colinas grandes en las extremidades. Las colinas Cemetery Hill y Culp's Hill al norte, y Big y Little Round Top al sur. Los ataques Confederados para el 2 de julio se planearon con estas metas en mente y a las 4 de la tarde Longstreet lanzó su ataque dirigido a la izquierda Federal. Los Confederados se enfrentaron con el cuerpo III de Sickles, el cuál había avanzado, fuera de la línea principal, a una posición muy expuesta. Longstreet empujó a los Federales en un lucha violenta en un frutal de melocotones (Peach Orchard), un campo de trigo (Wheatfield) y Devil's Den. Pero, tropas del cuerpo V pararon los ataques repetidos en las cuestas rocosas de Little Round Top. Más tarde en el día Lee golpeó la derecha Federal en las colinas Cemetery y Culp. La pelea sangrienta terminó después de oscurecer cuando reservas Federales finálmente repulsaron a los atacadores.

Al amanecer el día 3, la lucha recomenzó en el área de Culp's Hill, sin embargo, a las 12, los Confederados se retiraron a través de Rock Creek. Lee ahora se preparó para un asalto grande al centro Federal. A la 1 de la tarde 140 cañones abrieron fuego a la línea Federal. El bombardeo acabó después de dos horas y entonces 12,000 hombres marcharon fuera del bosque en Seminary Ridge. En una tormenta de canister y balas ellos golpearon la línea Federal. Abrieron una brecha, pero los atacadores, complétamente cansados, no pudieron mantener su tierra. Los sobrevivientes de "Pickett's Charge" se fueron a sus posiciones originales. Simultáneamente, una lucha de caballería de tres horas progresaba al este de Gettysburg, pero "Jeb" Stuart fue estancado por las fuerzas Federales de Gregg y la batalla terminó. Por la tarde del día 4 Lee empezó su retirada a Virginia.

CONSECUENCIAS

La segunda invasión del norte por Lee parada.

El Sur nunca pudo reemplazar los hombres perdidos en Gettysburg.

Junto con Vicksburg, el "High Water Mark" de la Confederación.

Staat: Pennsylvania

Befehlshaber der US:	Befehlshaber der CS:
Generalmajor George G. Meade	General Robert E. Lee
Armee der US: Armee des Potomacs	Armee der CS: Armee von Nord-virginia
Truppenstärke: 93,693	Truppenstärke: 70,136
Verluste:	Verluste:
Gefallen: 3,149	Gefallen: 4,559
Verwundet: 14,501	Verwundet: 12,355
Gefangengenommen oder vermißt: 5,157	Gefangengenommen oder vermißt: 5,643

KOMMENTAR

Diese Schlacht war der Höhepunkt von Lee's zweiter Invasion des Nordens. Sie begann am Morgen des 1. Juli, als Konföderationinfanteristen Unionkvalleristen westlich der Stadt angriffen. Buford's abgestiegene Kavalleristen schlugen mehrere Konföderiertenangriffe zurück, während sie auf Unterstützung von der Infanterie warteten. Um 10.00 Uhr kam Reynold's I Korps, um Buford abzulösen. Später verlängerte Howard's XI Korps die Unionlinie nördlich der Stadt, jedoch Verstärkungen von Konföderierten hatten nun auch das Schlachtfeld erreicht. Bald nahm die ganze Föderalistenlinie an dem verzweifelten Kampf teil. Howard's Truppen erlitten schwere Verluste, brachen, und rannten in die Stadt. Um 16.00 Uhr zog sich das I Korps ebenfalls nach Gettysburg zurück.

Eine neue Unionstellung wurde an beiden Enden durch Hügel verankert. Cemetery Hill und Culp's Hill im Norden — Big Round Top und Little Round Top im Süden. Mit diesen Zielen im Sinne, wurden die Konföderiertenangriffe für den 2. Juli geplant. Um 16.00 Uhr ging Longstreet zum Angriff gegen die linke Seite der Union über. Die Konföderierten schlugen Sickle's III Korps, das sich aus der Linie nach vorn, in eine ungeschützte Stellung gezogen hatte. In schwerem Kampf trieb Longstreet die Föderalisten durch die Peach Orchard, das Wheatfield, und die Devil's Den. Aber das V Korps wehrte wiederholte Angriffe auf die felsigen Hänge des Little Round Top ab. Spät am Tag griff Lee die rechte Seite der Union auf Cemetery Hill und Culp's Hill an. Das blutige Gefecht endete nach Einbruch der Dunkelheit, als Unionreservisten endlich die Angreifer zurückschlugen.

Bei Tagesanbruch, am 3. Juli, wurde der Kampf in der Gegend von Culp's Hill wieder aufgenommen, aber gegen Mittag zogen sich die konföderierten über Rock Creek zurück. Lee bereitete sich nun auf einen großen Angriff gegen den Mittelabschnitt der Union vor. Um 13.00 Uhr öffneten 140 Kanonen Feuer auf die Föderalistenlinie. Nach zwei Stunden endete das Bombardement — 12,000 Mann marschierten aus dem Wald auf Seminary Ridge. In einem Hagel von Kartätschen und Musketenkugeln stürmten sie gegen die Unionlinie. Sie durchbrachen die Mitte, aber die erschöpften Angreifer konnten sich nicht behaupten. Die Überlebenden von Pickett's Charge strömten nach ihren ursprünglichen Stellungen zurück. Gleichzeitig war ein dreistündiger Kavalleriekampf östlich von Gettysburg im Gange, aber Gregg's Unionkräfte setzten "Jeb" Stuart matt, und der Kampf endete. In der Nacht des 4. Juli trat Lee seinen Rückzug nach Virginia an.

BEDEUTUNG

Lee's zweite Invasion des Nordens wurde aufgehalten.

Der Süden konnte nie die Streitkräfte ersetzen, die in Gettysburg verloren waren.

Zusammen mit Vicksburg war Gettysburg die "Hochwasserstandsmarke" der Konföderation.

Dead Confederate soldier moved to a "sharpshooter's" position in Devil's Den.

Fourscore and seven years ago our fathers brought forth upon this continent, a new nation, conceived in Liberty, and dedicated to the proposition that all men are created equal.

Now, we are engaged in a great civil war, testing whether that nation, or any nation so conceived, and so dedicated, can long endure. We are met on a great battlefield of that war. We have come to dedicate a portion of it as a final resting place for those who here gave their lives that that nation might live. It is altogether fitting and proper that we should do this.

But in a larger sense we cannot dedicate, we cannot consecrate, we cannot hallow this ground. The brave men, living and dead, who struggled here have consecrated it far above our poor power to add or detract. The world will little note, nor long remember what we say here, but it can never forget what they did here. It is for us the living, rather, to be dedicated here to the unfinished work which they have, thus far, so nobly carried on. It is rather for us to be here dedicated to the great task remaining before us—that from these honored dead we take increased devotion to that cause for which they gave the last full measure of devotion—that we here highly resolve that these dead shall not have died in vain—that this nation, under God, shall have a new birth of freedom—and that this government of the people, by the people, for the people, shall not perish from the earth.

ABRAHAM LINCOLN

DISCOURS PRONONCE A LA DEDICATION

DU CIMETIÈRE À GETTYSBURG

Il y a quatre-vingt sept ans, nos pères ont, sur ce continent, mis au monde une nouvelle nation, conçue en liberté et vouée à cette idée que tous les hommes naissent égaux.

Aujourd'hui nous sommes engagés dans une grande guerre civile, pour déterminer si cette nation — ou toute autre nation ainsi conçue et dédiée — peut durer. Nous nous rencontrons sur un grand champ de bataille de cette guerre. Nous nous rencontrons pour en consacrer une parcelle, comme suprême champ de repos, à ceux qui ont donné leur vie pour que la nation puisse vivre. Il est convenable, il est juste que nous le fassions.

Mais en un sens plus large, nous ne pouvons pas consacrer, nous ne pouvons pas dédier, nous ne pouvons pas sanctifier cette terre. Tous les héros, vivants et morts, qui ont lutté ici, l'ont consacrée de manière si haute que nous n'avons plus le pouvoir d'y rien ajouter, ni d'en rien enlever. Le monde remarquera peu ce que nous disons ici et il ne s'en souviendra guère, mais il n'oubliera jamais ce que des braves ont fait en ce lieu. C'est plutôt à nous, les vivants, d'être voués à la tâche encore inachevée qu'ils ont jusqu'ici si noblement accomplie. C'est plutôt à nous d'être dédiés à la grande tâche qui nous reste — afin que ces morts vénérés nous inspirent un dévouement accru pour la cause qui leur a fait combler la mesure du dévouement — afin que nous soyons fermement résolus à ce que ces morts ne soient pas morts en vain; afin que cette nation, devant Dieu, renaisse à la liberté — et afin que le gouvernement du peuple, par le peuple, pour le peuple, ne soit pas effacé de cette terre.

ABRAHAM LINCOLN.

PALABRAS PRONUNCIADAS AL DEDICAR

EL CEMENTERIO DE GETTYSBURG

Ochenta y siete años ha, nuestros padres crearon en este continente una nueva nación, concebida bajo el signo de la libertad y consagrada al principio de que todos los hombres nacen iguales.

Estamos ahora envueltos en una vasta guerra civil que pone a prueba la idea de que esa nación, o cualquier otra así concebida y consagrada, pueda por largo tiempo subsistir. Nos hemos reunido en la escena de una de las grandes batallas de esa guerra. Hemos acudido para dedicar parte del campo de batalla a que sirva de última morada de quienes dieron sus vidas para que la nación viviese. Es enteramente justo y propio que obremos de este modo.

Con todo, a decir verdad, mal podríamos dedicar, ni consagrar, ni glorificar este campo. Los valientes, vivos aún o muertos ya, que aquí combatieron, lo han consagrado muy por encima de nuestros escasos poderes. El mundo apenas si advertirá o recordará lo que aquí se diga, mas no podrá olvidar jamás lo que aquí hicieron aquéllos. A los vivos nos corresponde, ante todo, dedicarnos a completar la obra que tan noblemente adelantaron los que aquí combatieron. Más bien, nos corresponde a nosotros dedicarnos a la ingente tarea que nos aguarda: que esos muertos venerados inspiren en nosotros una mayor devoción a la causa por la cual dieron ellos la postrera suma de su fé; que aquí solemnemente proclamemos que estos muertos no habrán muerto en vano; que esta nación, bajo la guía de Dios, vea renacer la libertad, y que el gobierno del pueblo, por el pueblo y para el pueblo no desaparezca de la faz de la tierra.

ABRAHAM LINCOLN.

ANSPRACHE, GEHALTEN BEI DER EINWEIHUNG DES FRIEDHOFS ZU GETTYSBURG

Dreizehn Jahre noch und es wird ein Jahrhundert vergangen sein, seit unsere Väter auf diesem Kontinent eine neue Nation gründeten, welche der Freiheit ihr Dasein verdankt und welche auf den Grundsatz vereidigt ist, dass alle Menschen als Gleiche erschaffen wurden.

Mit dem grossen Bürgerkrieg, den wir jetzt führen, machen wir die Probe darauf, ob diese Nation oder irgendeine Nation, welche so begründet und so vereidigt ist, lange leben kann. Wir haben uns auf einem grossen Schlachtfeld dieses Krieges versammelt. Wir sind hierher gekommen, um einen Teil dieses Feldes denjenigen als letzte Ruhestatt zu weihen, die an diesem Ort ihr Leben liessen, damit die Nation leben könne. Es ist nichts als recht und billig, dass wir dies tun.

In einem höheren Sinn aber können wir dieses Stück Erde weder weihen noch heiligen. Die tapferen Männer, die hier kämpften, haben es geweiht und geheiligt, und zwar weit über unsere armseligen Kräfte, zu mehren oder zu mindern, was sie getan. Die Welt wird kaum bemerken und gewiss nicht lange im Gedächtnis bewahren, was wir hier sagen, aber unvergesslich wird für alle Zeiten sein, was jene hier vollbrachten. Eher also sollten wir selber, die Überlebenden, hier der grossen unvollendeten Arbeit geweiht werden, welche diejenigen, welche kämpften, so edelmütig bis zu diesem Punkt vorwärts getrieben haben. Es ist also an uns, uns selber der grossen Aufgabe zu weihen, die noch vor uns liegt; von diesen in Ehren Gestorbenen die stets wachsende Kraft der Hingabe an das Ziel zu erben, dem sie in der Fülle ihrer äussersten Hingabe dienten; zu geloben, dass der Tod dieser Toten nicht vergeblich sein darf; dass diese Nation mit Gottes Hilfe von neuem die Freiheit aus sich hervorbringt, und diejenige Staatsform, in welcher das Volk allein durch das Volk zum besten des Volkes herrscht, nicht von der Erde verschwindet.

ABRAHAM LINCOLN.

一八六三年十一月十九日

エイブラハム・リンカーン
（高木八尺・斎藤光訳）

ゲティスバーグ國有墓地の奉献式場で述べた演説

八十七年前、われわれの父祖たちは、自由の精神にはぐくまれ、すべての人は平等につくられているという信条に献げられた、新しい国家を、この大陸に打ち建てました。

現在われわれは一大国内戦争のさなかにあり、これによりこの国家が、あるいはまた、このような精神にはぐくまれ、このように献げられたあらゆる国家が、永続できるか否かの試錬を受けているわけであります。われわれはこの戦争の一大激戦の地で相い会しています。われわれはこの国家が永らえるようにと、ここでその生命を投げ出した人々の、最後の安息の場所として、この戦場の一部を献げるために来たのであります。われわれが、このことをするのはまことに適当であり、また適切であります。

しかし、更に大きな意味において、われわれは、この土地を献げることはできません・聖別することもできません・生き残っている者と戦死した者とを問わず、ここで戦った勇敢な人々こそ、この場所を聖め献げたのでありまして、われわれの微力をもってしては、それに寸毫の増減も企てがたいのであります。世界はさして注意を払わないでありましょう、また永く記憶することもないでしょう、しかし彼らがここでなしたことは、決して忘れられることはないのであります。ここで戦った人々が、これまでかくも立派にすすめて来た未完の大事業に、ここで身を捧げるべきは、むしろ生きているわれわれ自身であります——それは、これらの名誉の戦死者が最後の全力を尽して身命を捧げた、偉大な主義に対して、われわれが一層の献身を決意するため、これら戦死者の死をむだに終らしめないように、われらがここで堅く決心するため、神のもとに、この国家をして、新しく自由の誕生をなさしめるため、そして人民の、人民による、人民のための、政治を地上から絶滅させないため、であります。

State: Georgia

U.S.

Commander:
Maj. Gen. Wm. Rosecrans
U.S. Army: Army of the Cumberland
No. of Troops: 57,000
Casualties:
Killed: 1,656
Wounded: 9,749
Captured or missing: 4,774

C.S.

Commander:
Gen. Braxton Bragg
C.S. Army: Army of Tennessee
No. of Troops: 49,000
Casualties:
Killed: 2,312
Wounded: 14,674
Captured or missing: 1,468

Etat: Georgie

Etats-Unis

Commandant:
Général de Division Wm.
Rosecrans
Armée: du Cumberland
57 000 soldats
Pertes:
Tués: 1 656
Blessés: 9 749
Prisonniers ou disparus: 4 774

Etats Confédérés

Commandant:
Général Braxton Bragg
Armée: du Tennessee
49 000 soldats
Pertes:
Tués: 2 312
Blessés: 14 674
Prisonniers ou disparus: 1 468

COMMENTS

Union General Rosecrans' Army of the Cumberland was widely separated as it marched through the southern countryside. General Bragg meanwhile was constantly receiving reinforcements and made several attempts at attacking the Federal columns individually but with little success.

On Sept. 13 General Rosecrans ordered his separate commands to concentrate at Lee and Gordon's Mill on the Chickamauga Creek. General Bragg marched his army to the Chickamauga and crossed north of Lee and Gordon's Mill. He hoped to block the road to Chattanooga and crush the Union left. This would allow the Confederates to re-occupy Chattanooga and possibly destroy the Army of the Cumberland before it retreated into Tennessee.

On the morning of the 19th the fighting began as planned. Bragg's army started hammering away at the Union left. In dense woods the two armies attacked and counter-attacked during the deadly day-long struggle. Although the Federals took a beating, neither side made any gains.

The next day Bragg's Confederates continued their vicious assaults on the Union left. Around 10 a.m. Rosecrans was told there was a gap in his line. (There was no gap, but because of the thick woods in this area, the Federal troops were not visible.) Rosecrans ordered General Wood to move his men from the right to fill the imaginary hole. Where Wood's men were located moments before, Generals Longstreet's troops surged through. Rosecrans and about half of the Union army were swept back and fled.

General Thomas, now in command, repositioned some of his remaining men along Snodgrass Hill to meet Longstreet's advance from the south. Longstreet unleased a series of savage assaults on the hill only to be repulsed every time. When darkness finally brought an end to the bloody fighting, General Thomas' lines were still intact earning him the nickname "Rock of Chickamauga." Thomas withdrew during the night and by Sept. 21st the whole Union army was back in Chattanooga.

SIGNIFICANCE

This victory gave the Confederacy some hope after the defeats at Gettysburg and Vicksburg.

Confederate losses were very high, depleting Bragg's ranks for the coming fight at Chattanooga.

COMMENTAIRE

L'armée unioniste du Cumberland aux ordres du général Rosecrans était très égrenée durant sa marche à travers la campagne. Pendant ce temps, le général Bragg recevait des renforts et essaya plusieurs fois d'attaquer les colonnes fédérales isolées mais sans grand succès.

Le 13 septembre, le général Rosecrans donna ordre à ses troupes séparées de se concentrer sur Lee et Gordon's Mill sur Chickamauga Creek. Le général Bragg arriva à la Chickamauga avec son armée et traversa au nord de Lee et Gordon's Mill. Il espérait barrer la route de Chattanooga et écraser la gauche de l'Union. Ceci devait permettre aux Confédérés de réoccuper Chattanooga et si possible de détruire l'armée du Cumberland avant sa retraite dans le Tennessee.

Le matin du 19, la bataille commença comme prévue. L'armée de Bragg se mit à frapper la gauche de l'Union. Les deux armées s'affrontèrent en attaques et contre-attaques dans les bois épais. La lutte dura le jour entier. Si les Fédéraux reçurent de nombreux coups, rien ne fut gagné d'aucun côté.

Le jour suivant, les Confédérés, avec Bragg, continuèrent leurs assauts furieux contre la gauche de l'Union. Vers 10 heures, Rosecrans fut informé qu'il y avait une trouée dans sa ligne. (Il n'y avait pas de trouée, mais l'épaisseur des bois rendait les Fédéraux invisibles.) Rosecrans donna ordre au général Wood de déplacer ses hommes sur la droite pour remplir le trou inexistant. Les troupes de Longstreet se précipitèrent à l'endroit laissé vide par le mouvement de Wood. Rosecrans et une grande partie de l'Union furent balayés.

Le général fédéral qui commande maintenant, le général Thomas, remit en position ce qui restait des troupes le long de Snodgrass Hill pour faire face à l'avance de Longstreet depuis le sud. Longstreet se livra à une série d'attaques sauvages sur la colline, et fut à chaque fois repoussé. Quand la nuit fit cesser la lutte, les lignes du général Thomas restaient intactes, ce qui lui valut le surnom de "Rock of Chickamauga." Thomas se retira pendant la nuit, et le 21 septembre toute l'armée de l'Union était revenue à Chattanooga.

CONSEQUENCES

Cette victoire de la Confédération lui redonna espoir après les défaites de Vicksburg et de Gettysburg.

Cependant, les pertes des Confédérés étaient assez sérieuses pour affaiblir les rangs de Bragg dans la bataille suivante à Chattanooga.

Important Landmarks

Poe Road
Lafayette Road
Snodgrass Hill
Viniard Field
Chickamauga Creek
Bloody Pond

Important Buildings

Snodgrass Cabin
Gordon-Lee House
Brotherton House
Lee and Gordon's Mill

Estado: Georgia

U.S.	C.S.
Comandante:	Comandante:
Maj. Gen. Wm. Rosecrans	Gen. Braxton Bragg
U.S. Ejército: Army of the Cumberland	U.S. Ejército: Army of Tennessee
No de tropas: 57,000	No de tropas: 49,000
Pérdidas:	Pérdidas:
Muertos: 1,656	Muertos: 2,312
Heridos: 9,749	Heridos: 14,674
Capturados o ausentes: 4,774	Capturados o ausentes: 1,468

COMENTARIO

La Armada de Cumberland del General Rosecrans estaba muy serperada mientras marchaba por el campo sureño. El General Bragg, mientras tanto, constántemente recibía refuerzos y hizo varios intentos de atacar las columnas Federales individuálmente, pero sin éxito.

El 13 de septiembre Rosecrans mandó que sus comandancias seperadas se concentraran en Lee y Gordon's Mill en Chickamauga Creek. El General Bragg marchó a su ejército a Chickamauga y cruzó al norte de Lee y Gordon's Mill. El esperaba bloquear la carreterra a Chattanooga y aplastar la izquierda Federal. Esto dejaría que los Confederados reocuparan Chattanooga y posíblemente destruiría la Armada de Cumberland antes de que se retirara a Tennessee.

El día 19 por la mañana la lucha empezó como estaba planeada. El ejército de Bragg empezó por atacar a la izquierda Federal. En una selva densa los ejércitos se atacaron y se contraatacaron en un esfuerzo mortal que duró por todo el día. Aunque los Federales perdieron mucho, ningún lado ganó ninguna ventaja.

El próximo día los Confederados siguieron con sus asaltos violentos contra la izquierda Federal. Alrededor de las 10 de la mañana se dijo a Rosecrans que había una abertura en su línea. (No había ninguna, pero por la densidad de la selva en esta área, las tropas Federales no estaban visibles.) Rosecrans ordenó al General Wood que mudara a sus hombres de la derecha para llenar el agujero imaginario. Por donde los hombres de Wood habían estado hacía pocos minutos, las tropas de Longstreet pasaron. Rosecrans y la mitad de su ejército fueron empujados y huyeron.

El General Thomas, ahora el comandante, reposicionó a algunos de los hombres que quedaban en Snodgrass Hill para parar el avance de Longstreet que venía desde el sur. Longstreet lanzó una serie de asaltos salvajes en esta colina pero cada vez sus tropas fueron repulsadas. Cuando por fin la oscuridad terminó la pelea sangrienta, las líneas de Thomas todavía estaban en su posición, lo que le ganó a Thomas el apodo de "Rock of Chickamauga." Thomas se retiró durante la noche y en el 21 de septiembre todo el ejército ya estaba en Chattanooga.

CONSECUENCIAS

Esta victoria dio un poco de esperanza a los Confederados después de sus derrotas en Gettysburg y Vicksburg.

Las pérdidas Confederadas fueron muchas, vaciando las filas de Bragg para la batalla que venía en Chattanooga.

Staat: Georgia

Befehlshaber der US:	Befehlshaber der CS:
Generalmajor William Rosecrans	General Braxton Bragg
Armee der US: Armee des Cumberland	Armee der CS: Armee von Tennessee
Truppenstärke: 57,000	Truppenstärke: 49,000
Verluste:	Verluste:
Gefallen: 1,656	Gefallen: 2,312
Verwundet: 9,749	Verwundet: 14,674
Gefangengenommen oder	Gefangengenommen oder
vermißt: 5,774	vermißt: 1,468

KOMMENTAR

Die Armee des Cumberland, unter Uniongeneral Rosecrans, marschierte, weit ausgedehnt, durch das südstaatliche Land. Während dieser Zeit bekam General Bragg laufend Verstärkungstruppen, aber seine wiederholten Versuche, die Föderalistenkolonnen einzeln anzugreifen, brachten wenig Erfolg.

Am 13. September befahl General Rosecrans jedem seiner Kommandanten, sich bei Lee und Gordon's Mill am Chickamauga Creek zu konzentrieren. General Bragg marschierte seine Armee an den Chickamauga und überquerte ihn nördlich von Lee und Gordon's Mill. Es war Bragg's Hoffnung, die Landstraße nach Chattanooga zu blockieren, und die linke Flanke der Union niederzuschlagen. Dies würde den Konföderierten die Möglichkeit geben, Chattanooga wieder zu besetzen, und möglicherweise die Armee des Cumberland zu vernichten, ehe diese sich in den Staat Tennessee zurückziehen konnte.

Am Morgen des 19. begann der Kampf wie geplant. Bragg's Armee begann, auf die linke Flanke der Union einzuhämmern. Im dichten Wald trugen beide Armeen Angriffe und Gegenangriffe vor, während der tödliche Kampf den ganzen Tag raste. Obwohl die Föderalisten tüchtig verprügelt wurden, war weder die eine, noch die andere Seite erfolgreich.

Am folgenden Tag setzten Bragg's Konföderierte ihre brutalen Stürme auf die linke Seite der Union fort. Man teilte Rosecrans mit, daß eine Lücke in seiner Linie sprang. Keine Lücke war entstanden, jedoch wegen des dicken Waldes in dieser Gegend waren die Nordtruppen nicht sichtbar. Rosecrans befahl General Wood, seine Truppen von der rechten Seite abzuziehen, um die scheinbare Lücke zu füllen. Wo Wood's Truppen sich nur wenige Augenblicke vorher befanden, fluteten jetzt General Longstreet's Truppen durch. Rosecrans, und ungefähr die Hälfte der Unionarmee wurden zurückgetrieben und flohen.

Der jetzige Befehlshaber, General Thomas, verlegte einige seiner übriggebliebenen Truppen an Snodgrass Hill, um Longstreet's Vorrücken aus dem Süden entgegenzustehen. Longstreet entfesselte eine Reihe von brutalen Stürmen auf den Hügel, aber er wurde jedesmal zurückgeschlagen. Als die Dunkelheit dem blutigen Gefecht endlich ein Ende machte, waren die Linien von General Thomas immer noch intakt, wodurch er sich den Spitznamen "Rock of Chickamauga" verdiente. Während der Nacht trat Thomas den Rückzug an, und am 21. September war die ganze Unionarmee zurück in Chattanooga.

BEDEUTUNG

Nach Niederlagen bei Gettysburg und Vicksburg gab dieser Sieg der Konföderierten ihnen Hoffnung.

Die Verluste der Konföderierten waren sehr hoch, und das brachte eine Verringerung von Bragg's Truppen für den bevorstehenden Kampf bei Chattanooga.

Lee & Gordon's Mill on Chickamauga Creek near the Union right on the first day.

State: Tennessee		Etat: Tennessee	
U.S.	**C.S.**	**Etats-Unis**	**Etats Confédérés**
Commander: Maj. Gen. U.S. Grant	Commander: Gen. Braxton Bragg	Commandant:	Commandant:
U.S. Army: Armies of the Cumberland, Tennessee, and Potomac	C.S. Army: Army of Tennessee	Général de Division U. S. Grant	Général Braxton Bragg
No. of Troops: 60,000	No. of Troops: 44,000	Armée: du Cumberland, du Tennessee et du Potomac	Armée: du Tennessee
		60 000 soldats	44 000 soldats
Casualties:	Casualties:	Pertes:	Pertes:
Killed: 687	Killed: 361	Tués: 687	Tués: 361
Wounded: 4,346	Wounded: 2,160	Blessés: 4 346	Blessés: 2 160
Captured or missing: 349	Captured or missing: 4,146	Prisonniers ou disparus: 349	Prisonniers ou disparus: 4 146

COMMENTS

Following its defeat at Chickamauga, the Union army retreated to Chattanooga where it was besieged by Bragg's Confederates. By October 30th, after a month long siege, supply lines were reopened and the Union Army of the Cumberland was reinforced. With Grant directing the revitalized army, plans were soon in the works for lifting the siege and attacking the Confederates who held fortified positions along Missionary Ridge and Lookout Mountain.

On November 23rd the only fighting took place when General Thomas moved out from his defenses around the city and drove a light Confederate force from Orchard Knob, a low hill about a mile in front of Missionary Ridge only to find that a wide, deep ravine separated him from the main Confederate works. Meanwhile, south of Chattanooga, Hooker attacked the Confederates at Lookout Mountain. The Federals advanced as far as a plateau, about half way up the mountain when the Confederates were finally able to stop them. By 2 p.m. poor visibility and a shortage of ammunition caused Hooker to halt his advance. Due to the thick fog and mist which shrouded the mountain from observers below this action became known as "The Battle Above the Clouds." During the night the Confederates on Lookout Mountain withdrew to the line on Missionary Ridge.

The next day Grant planned a grand attack. Sherman was to push south along the ridge. Hooker would march to Missionary Ridge and attack the Confederate left, pushing northward. When this had happened Thomas would attack the center. But as morning arrived Grant's plans failed from the start. Sherman repeatedly attacked the heavily fortified Confederate right only to be repulsed every time. Grant, realizing Hooker was delayed and wanting to relieve the pressure on Sherman, ordered Thomas to advance. Four divisions charged toward the ridge. The Federals overwhelmed the Confederate line at the foot of the ridge and pursued them upward. The Southerners were followed so close that their comrades on the crest hesitated to shoot for fear of hitting their own men. This allowed Thomas' men to reach the crest in force and break the Confederate line in several places. Bragg's center fled down the eastern slope and the remainder of his troops withdrew during the night. On the 26th Thomas and Sherman went in pursuit.

SIGNIFICANCE

With Bragg's retreat, most of Tennessee, containing many important rail centers and food-producing regions, was now in Union hands.

Bragg was relieved of command.

Grant was elevated to commander of all U.S. Armies.

COMMENTAIRE

Après sa défaite à Chickamauga, l'armée de l'Union se retira à Chattanooga qui était entouré par les Confédérés de Braggs. Le 30 octobre, les lignes d'approvisionnement étaient à nouveau ouvertes, et l'armée unioniste du Cumberland reçut des renforts. Tandis que Grant dirigeait une armée revivifiée, des plans furent établis pour lever le siège et attaquer les Confédérés qui tenaient de fortes positions le long de Missionary Ridge et Lookout Mountain.

Le 23 novembre, il n'y eut qu'un combat quand le général Thomas sortit de ses défenses et délogea une petite force des Confédérés d'Orchard Knob, basse colline située à moins de 2 km devant Missionary Ridge. Le 2 à 16 heures, Sherman attaqua et saisit l'extrémité nord de Missionary Ridge et se trouva séparé des Confédérés par un large et profond ravin. Cependant, au sud de Chattanooga, Hooker attaqua les Confédérés à Lookout Mountain. Les Fédéraux avancèrent jusqu'à un plateau, environ à mi-chemin de la montagne, quand les Confédérés parvinrent à les arrêter. A 14 heures, la mauvaise visibilité et le manque de munitions obligèrent Hooker à faire halte. A cause du brouillard qui cachait les montagnes des observateurs d'en bas, cet épisode fut appelé "La bataille au-dessus des nuages." Pendant la nuit, les Confédérés de Lookout Mountain se retirèrent sur la ligne de Missionary Ridge.

Le jour suivant, Grant organisa une grande attaque. Sherman devait se concentrer le long du sud de l'arête. Hooker devait marcher sur Missionary Ridge pour attaquer la gauche de la ligne confédérée, poussant vers le nord. Ensuite, Thomas attaquerait le centre. Mais quand vint le matin, tous les plans de Grant furent renversés. Sherman attaquait sans cesse la droite fortifiée des Confédérés et fut toujours repoussé. Grant, comprenant que Hooker était retardé et voulant soutenir Sherman, ordonna à Thomas d'entrer en ligne. Quatre divisions chargèrent. Les Fédéraux submergèrent la ligne des Confédérés au pied de l'arête et les poursuivirent en grimpant. Les Sudistes étaient suivis de si près que leurs camarades sur la crête hésitaient à tirer de peur de tuer leurs propres hommes. Cela permit aux hommes de Thomas d'atteindre en force le sommet et de briser, à plusieurs endroits, la ligne des Confédérés. Le centre de Bragg s'enfuit par les pentes de l'est, et le reste des troupes se retirèrent pendant la nuit. Le 26, Thomas et Sherman les poursuivirent.

CONSEQUENCES

Grâce à la retraite de Bragg, une grande partie du Tennessee, contenante des centres ferroviaíres et des ressources alimentaires, était maintenant aux mains des Fédéraux.

Bragg perdit le commandement.

Grant fut élevé au grade de général-en-chef des Armées des Etats-Unis.

Important Landmarks
Tunnel Hill
Orchard Knob
Western & Atlantic R.R.
Missionary Ridge
Lookout Mountain
Tennessee River
Moccasin Point

Important Buildings
Cravens House

A portion of Missionary Ridge in the distance; the Federals attacked across this open ground in full view of the Confederates.

U.S.

Comandante:
 Maj. Gen. U.S. Grant
U.S. Ejército: Armies of the
 Cumberland, Tennessee, y
 Potomac
No. de tropas: 60,000
Pérdidas:
 Muertos: 687
 Heridos: 4,346
 Capturados o ausentes: 349

C.S.

Comandante:
 Gen. Braxton Bragg
C.S. Ejército: Army of Tennessee
No. de tropas: 44,000
Pérdidas:
 Muertos: 361
 Heridos: 2,160
 Capturados o ausentes: 4,146

COMENTARIO

Después de su derrota en Chickamauga, el ejército Federal se retiró a Chatta-nooga donde fue asediado por los Confederados de Braxton Bragg. El 30 de octubre, después de un mes de asedio, las líneas de provisiones ya estaban abiertas y el Army of the Cumberland fue reforzado. Con Grant dirigiendo el ejército revitalizado, planes se hicieron para levantar el asedio y atacar a los Confederados quienes mantenían posiciones fortificadas en Missionary Ridge y Lookout Mountain.

El 23 de noviembre la única lucha sucedió cuando el General Thomas salió de sus defensas alrededor de la ciudad y empujó una fuerza Confederada ligera de Orchard Knob, una colina baja más o menos a una milla en frente de Missionary Ridge. El 24 a las 4 de la tarde Sherman atacó y cogió la parte norteña de Missionary Ridge solo para descubrir que un barranco hondo y ancho le seperaba de las posiciones Confederadas principales. Mientras tanto, al sur de Chattanooga, Hooker atacó a los Confederados en Lookout Mountain. Los Federales avanzaron hasta una meseta que estaba a la mitad de la montaña cuando los Confederados finálmente pudieron pararlos. A las 2 de la tarde la visibilidad pobre y la falta de municiones causaron que Hooker dejara su avance. Por la niebla densa y la llovizna que envolvían la montaña de los observadores de abajo, esta acción llegó a tener el nombre de "The Battle Above the Clouds" (La Batalla encima de las Nubes). Durante la noche los Confederados se retiraron a la línea en Missionary Ridge.

Al próximo día Grant planeó un ataque grande. Sherman habría de ser empujado al sur por el terraplén. Hooker marcharía a Missionary Ridge para atacar la izquierda Confederada, empujando al norte. Cuando esto ya hubiera pasado, Thomas atacaría el centro. Pero cuando llegó la mañana los planes fracasaron desde el principio. Sherman repetídamente atacó la derecha Confederada bien fortificada y fue repulsado cada vez. Grant, dándose cuenta de que Hooker se retrasaba y deseando remediar la presión en Sherman, mandó que Thomas avanzara. Cuatro divisiones asaltaron el terraplén. Los Federales oprimieron a los Confederados en el pie del terraplén y los persiguieron hacia arriba. Los sureños estaban perseguidos desde tan cerca que sus compañeros encima vacilaban en disparar por el miedo de matar a sus propios amigos. Esto dejó que la fuerza de Thomas llegara a la cima bien intacta y que ellos cortaran la línea Confederada en varios sitios. El centro de Bragg huyó por la cuesta oriental y los que quedaban se retiraron durante la noche. El día 26 Thomas y Sherman salieron para perseguirlos.

SIGINIFICACION

Con la retirada de Bragg, la mayor parte de Tennessee, que contenía muchos centros de ferrocarriles y regiones que producían comida, estaba en las manos de la Unión.

Bragg se relevó de la comandancia.
Grant se elevó a Comandante de todos los ejércitos Federales.

Staat: Tennessee

Befehlshaber der US:
 Generalmajor U.S. Grant
Armee der US: Die Armeen des
 Cumberlands, Tennessees und
 Potomacs
Truppenstärke: 60,000
Verluste:
 Gefallen: 687
 Verwundet: 4,346
 Gefangengenommen oder
 vermißt: 349

Befehlshaber der CS:
 General Braxton Bragg
Armee der CS: Armee von Tennessee
 Truppenstärke: 44,000

Verluste:
 Gefallen: 361
 Verwundet: 2,160
 Gefangengenommen oder
 vermißt: 4,146

KOMMENTAR

Nach ihrer Niederlage bei Chickamauga zog sich die Unionarmee nach Chattanooga zurück. Dort kam sie unter Belagerung bei Bragg's Konföderierten. Nach einer 30-tägigen Belagerung wurden die Versorgungslinien am 30. Oktober wieder geöffnet, und die Unionarmee des Cumberlands wurde verstärkt. Mit der neubelebten Armee unter der Führung von Grant waren Pläne bald im Gang, die Belagerung aufzuheben, und die Konföderierten anzugreifen, welche die befestigten Anlagen auf Missionary Ridge und Lookout Mountain hielten.

Der einzige Kampf fand am 23. November statt, als General Thomas aus seinen Verteidigungsanlagen um die Stadt zog und eine leichte Konföderierte Streitkraft vom Orchard Knob trieb, ein niedriger Hügel etwa anderthalb Kilometer vor Missionary Ridge. Am 24. griff Sherman um 16.00 Uhr das Nordende der Missionary Ridge an und eroberte die Stellung. Erst dann entdeckte er, daß eine tiefe, breite Schlucht ihn von den Hauptbefestigungen der Konföderierten trennte. Inzwischen hatte Hooker südlich von Chattanooga die Konföderierten auf Lookout Mountain angegriffen. Die Föderalisten rückten sich bis auf ein Plateau vor, ungefähr auf halber Höhe des Berges, wo die Konföderierten endlich imstande waren, sie aufzuhalten. Es war 14.00 Uhr — schlechte Sicht und Munitionsknappheit zwangen Hooker, nicht weiter vorzurücken. Wegen des dichten Nebels und der Wolken, die den Berg umhüllten, und dadurch Beobachtungsvermögen vom Tal verhinderte, wurde diese Aktion als "Der Kampf über den Wolken" bekannt. Während der Nacht zogen sich die Konföderierten von Lookout Mountain bis zur Abwehrlinie auf Missionary Ridge zurück.

Grant plante einen großartigen Angriff für den nächsten Tag. Sherman sollte sich südlich am Rücken entlang drängen. Hooker sollte gegen Missionary Ridge marschieren, dort die linke Flanke der Konföderierten angreifen und sich weiter nach Norden drängen. Sollte sich all dies verwirklichen, Thomas würde dann die mitte angreifen. Aber schon als der Morgen dämmerte — bei Tagesbeginn — schlugen Grant's Pläne fehl. Sherman stürmte die schwer befestigte rechte Seite der Konföderierten wiederholt an, wurde aber jedesmal zurückgeschlagen. Grant erkannte, daß Hooker aufgehalten wurde, und um den Druck auf Sherman zu erleichtern, befahl er Thomas vorzurücken. Vier Divisionen stürzten sich auf den Hügelkamm zu. Die Föderalisten überwältigten die Linie der Konföderierten am Fuß des Kammes und verfolgten sie bis auf den Hügel. Sie folgten so dicht hinter den Südstaatlern, daß deren Kameraden auf dem Kamm sich zögerten zu schießen. Dies ermöglichte Thomas' Truppen, den Kamm zu erreichen, und die Konföderiertenlinie an mehreren Stellen zu brechen. Bragg's Mitte der Linie floh den Osthang hinab und der Überrest seiner Truppen zog sich in der Nacht zurück. Am 26. begannen Thomas und Sherman die Verfolgung.

BEDEUTUNG

Durch Bragg's Rückzug fiel der größte Teil von Tennessee mit vielen wichtigen Eisenbahnstützpunkten und Nahrungmittel produzierenden Gebieten in die Hände der Union.

Bragg wurde seines Kommando's enthoben.
Grant wurde zum Oberbefehlshaber aller Armeen der US befördert.

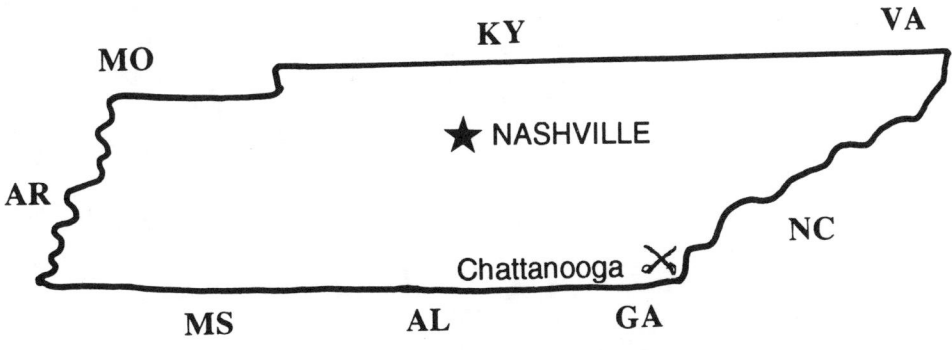

WILDERNESS
May 5-6, 1864

State: Virginia

U.S.	C.S.
Commanders: Lt. Gen. U.S. Grant	Commander: Gen. Robert E. Lee
Maj. Gen. George G. Meade	C.S. Army: Army of Northern
U.S. Army: Army of the Potomac	Virginia
No. of Troops: 100,000	No. of Troops: 60,000
Casualties:	Casualties:
Killed: 2,200	7,500 total killed, wounded, and
Wounded: 12,000	missing
Captured or missing: 3,400	

COMMENTS

The Wilderness Campaign was one part of Grant's master plan of simultaneous pressure on all Southern armies. Unable to reinforce each other, the South's limited manpower supply would soon be exhausted.

On May 4, Meade's Army of the Potomac began crossing the Rapidan River west of Fredericksburg, VA, in an attempt at hitting Lee's right flank. To meet this threat Lee immediately sent Generals Ewell and Hill toward the advancing Federals. The two armies faced each other in an area of dense woods and thickets of scrub pines and laurel known as the Wilderness. On the 5th Meade ordered an attack on the Confederate left. At 1 p.m. Warren's men finally advanced. In desperate fighting amid the underbrush the Federals nearly broke the rebel line, but Warren's delay in launching the attack gave Ewell time to reinforce. A counter-attack pushed the Federals back. Repeated Yankee attacks were repulsed including an attempt by Sedgwick to turn Ewell's left flank.

Meanwhile, at the other end of the field, Hill's Confederates pushed forward until they were stopped by a division of the VI Corps. At 4 p.m., these troops and part of the II Corps charged the advanced Confederate line. Hill's men were waiting for the Federals and easily halted the charge. Another attack, by Hancock, although almost breaking the Confederate line, was also repulsed. Darkness ended the terrible fighting.

On the 6th the fighting resumed early in the morning at the north end of the field. Ewell and Sedgwick spent the day fighting, but with neither making any gains. More serious fighting went on to the south. At 5 a.m. Hancock attacked Hill's Confederates and drove them from the field. Just then, however, Longstreet's Corps arrived. These fresh troops smashed into the advancing Federals and pushed them back. At 11:30 a.m. Longstreet successfully coordinated an attack on Hancock's left flank and front, but while planning to follow up his success he was shot and wounded by his own men. Lee later launched a massive assault on the center of Hancock's line. By 5 p.m., after savage fighting, the Confederates were repulsed with the aid of Union artillery. Darkness again ended the fighting. The next night Grant broke the stalemate by "sidestepping" to the left, attempting to get between Lee and Richmond.

SIGNIFICANCE

The battle was a tactical draw that cost both sides heavy casualties, but Grant was easily able to replace his lost men while Lee could not.

Another one of Lee's ablest Generals, Longstreet, was wounded.

The Union army marched south instead of retreating.

Etat: Virginie

Etats-Unis	Etats Confédérés
Commandants:	Commandant:
Lieutenant Général U.S. Grant	Général Robert E. Lee
Général de Division George G.	
Meade	
Armée: du Potomac	Armée: de Virginie du Nord
100 000 soldats	60 000
Pertes:	Pertes totales:
Tués: 2 200	Tués, blessés et disparus: 7 500
Blessés: 12 000	
Prisonniers ou disparus: 3 400	

COMMENTAIRE

La campagne du Wilderness faisait partie du plan de Grant de faire pression simultanément sur toutes les armées sudistes. Incapable de se donner des renforts, pensait Grant, les armées du Sud succomberaient faute d'hommes.

Le 4 mai, l'armée du Potomac, aux ordres de Meade, se mit à traverser la rivière Rapidan à l'ouest de Fredericksburg, en Virginie. Meade espérait frapper le flanc droit de Lee. Pour faire front, Lee envoya immédiatement les généraux Ewell et Hill à l'encontre des Fédéraux. Les deux armées se firent face dans cette région de forêts denses, de fourrés broussailleux, de pins et de lauriers justement appelée Wilderness. Le 5, Meade donna l'ordre d'attaquer la gauche de la ligne confédérée. A 13 heures, les hommes de Warren avancèrent. En un combat désespéré au milieu des broussailles, les Fédéraux brisèrent presque la ligne des rebelles; mais en prenant trop de temps à lamcer l'attaque, Warren avait donné à Ewell celui de recevoir des renforts. Une contre-attaque repoussa les Fédéraux. Les attaques répétées des Yankees furent neutralisées, en dépit des efforts de Sedgwick de détourner le flanc gauche d'Ewell.

Pendant ce temps, à l'autre extrémité du champ, l'avance des Confédérés menés par Hill fut stoppée par une division du quatrième Corps d'armée. A 16 heures, avec une partie du Corps II, cette division chargea. Mais Hill attendait avec ses hommes qui brisèrent les efforts des Fédéraux. Une autre attaque, dirigée par Hancock, bien que proche de la victoire, fût aussi repoussée par les Confédérés. La nuit mit fin à la terrible bataille.

Tôt le matin du 6 la lutte reprit à l'extrême nord du champ. Ewell et Sedgwick passèrent la journée à se battre, mais sans résultat. Au sud, une autre bataille aboutit; à 5 heures, Hancock attaqua les Confédérés menés par Hill et les poussa hors du champ. A ce moment, cependant, le corps d'armée de Longstreet arriva. Les nouvelles troupes écrasèrent l'avance des Fédéraux et repoussèrent l'adversaire. A 11h30, Longstreet réussit son attaque sur le flanc gauche et le front de Hancock. Mais alors qu'il comptait pousser son soccès plus loin, il fut blessé par ses propres hommes. Plus tard, Lee lança une lourde attaque contre le centre de la ligne de Hancock. A 17 heures, après de sauvages efforts, les Confédérés étaient repoussés grâce à l'aide de l'artillerie unioniste. Une fois de plus, la lutte cessa avec la nuit. La nuit suivante, Grant sortit de l'impasse en s'écartant sur la gauche essayant de se placer entre Lee et Richmond.

CONSEQUENCES

La bataille du Wilderness fut une partie nulle qui coûta de grandes pertes aux deux camps. Mais Grant pouvait aisément remplacer ses hommes perdus tandis que Lee ne le pouvait pas.

Un autre des meilleurs généraux de Lee, Longstreet, fut blessé.

L'armée unioniste s'engagea vers le sud au lieu de battre en retraite.

Important Landmarks
Brock Road
Rapidan River
Orange Plank Road
Germanna Ford
Orange Turnpike

Important Buildings
Wilderness Tavern
Widow Tapp Farm
Lacy House
Chewning Farm

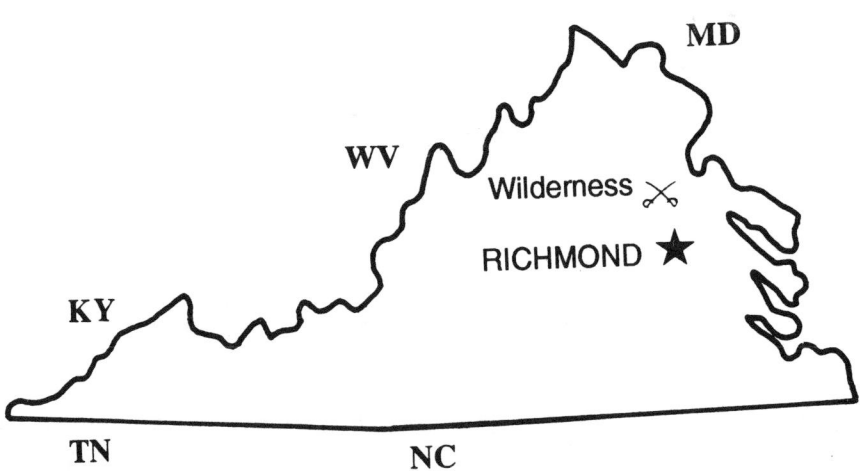

Estado: Virginia

U.S.	C.S.
Comandante:	Comandante:
Lt. Gen. U.S. Grant	Gen. Robert E. Lee
Maj. Gen. George G. Meade	
U.S. Ejército: Army of the Potomac	C.S. Ejército: Army of Northern
No. de tropas: 100,000	Virginia
Pérdidas:	No. de tropas: 60,000
Muertos: 2,200	Pérdidas:
Heridos: 12,000	7,500 en total muertos, heridos y
Capturados o ausentes: 3,400	ausentes

COMENTARIO

La campaña del Wilderness fue una parte de un gran plan de Grant para poner presión simultánea en todos los ejércitos Confederados. Sin poder reforzarse uno al otro, la cantidad limitada de hombres en el sur se consumiría.

El 4 de mayo, el Army of the Potomac de Meade empezó a cruzar el río Rapidan al oeste de Fredericksburg, Va. en un intento de golpear el flanco derecho de Lee. Para enfrentarse con esta amenaza Lee inmediátamente mandó a los Generales Ewell y Hill hacia los Federales que avanzaban. Los dos ejércitos se encontraron cara a cara en un área de selva densa y sotos de pinos y laureles conocido como Wilderness. El 5 Meade ordenó un ataque contra la izquierda Confederada. A la 1 de la tarde los hombres de Warren finálmente avanzaron. En una lucha desesperada entre la maleza los Federales casi rompieron la línea Confederada, pero la tardanza de Warren en lanzar el asalto le dio a Ewell tiempo para reforzarse. Un contraataque empujó a los Federales. Ataques Federales repetidos fueron repulsados incluyendo un intento por Sedgwick de tornar el flanco izquierdo de Ewell.

Mientras tanto, al otro lado del campo, los Confederados de Hill avanzaron hasta estar parados por una división del cuerpo VI. A las 4 de la tarde, estas tropas y una parte del cuerpo II asaltaron la línea avanzada de los Confederados. Las tropas de Hill esperaban este asalto y fácilmente repulsaron el ataque. Otro asalto, por Hancock, aunque casi rompiendo la línea Confederada, fue también repulsado. La oscuridad acabó la pelea terrible.

El día 6 la lucha recomenzó temprano por la mañana al lado norte del campo. Ewell y Sedgwick pasaron el día luchando, pero ninguno ganó nada. Al sur había una pelea más seria. A las 5 de la mañana Hancock atacó a los Confederados de Hill y los empujó del campo. En ese momento, sin embargo, el cuerpo de Longstreet llegó. Estas tropas frescas aplastaron a los Federales y los empujaron para atrás. A las 11:30 de la mañana Longstreet coordinó con éxito un ataque contra el flanco izquierdo de Hancock y contra su frente, pero mientras planeaba explotar su éxito fue disparado y herido por sus propias tropas. Lee luego lanzó un asalto grande contra el centro de la línea de Hancock. A las 5 de la tarde, después de una lucha bárbara, los Confederados ya fueron repulsados con la ayuda de artillería Federal. Otra vez, la oscuridad terminó la batalla. La próxima noche Grant acabó el empate por hacerse a la izquierda, intentando meterse entre Lee y Richmond.

CONSECUENCIAS

La batalla fue un empate táctico que les costó a los dos lados muchísimas pérdidas, pero Grant podía reemplazar fácilmente a sus hombres mientras Lee no pudo.

Otro de los generales más capaces de Lee, Longstreet, fue herido.

El ejército de la Unión marchó para el sur en vez de retirarse.

Staat: Virginia

Befehlshaber der US:	Befehlshaber der CS:
Generalleutnant U.S. Grant	General Robert E. Lee
Generalmajor George G. Meade	
Armee der US: Armee des Potomacs	Armee der CS: Armee von Nord
Truppenstärke: 100,000	virginia
Verluste:	Truppenstärke: 60,000
Gefallen: 2,200	Verluste:
Verwundet: 12,000	Insgesamt 7,500 gefallen,
Gefangengenommen oder	verwundet oder vermißt
vermißt: 3,400	

KOMMENTAR

Die Wildnis Kampagne war ein Teil von Grant's Großstrategie, Druck auf alle Südarmeen gleichzeitig auszuüben. Dies würde eine gegenseitige Verstärkung der Südarmee unmöglich machen und die begrenzte Zahl an Nachschubtruppen bald erschöpfen.

Am 4. Mai begann Meade's Armee des Potomac den Rapidan Fluß westlich von Fredericksburg in Virginia zu überqueren, in einem Versuch, gegen Lee's rechte Flanke zu stoßen. Um dieser Gefahr Widerstand entgegenzusetzen, schickte Lee sofort die Generale Ewell und Hill gegen die vorrückenden Föderalisten. Beide Armeen standen sich in einem Gelände gegenüber, besetzt mit dichtem Wald und Dickichten von Unterholz und Lorbeergebüsch. Dieser Teil der Gegend trägt den Namen "Die Wildnis" (Wilderness). Am 5. befahl Meade einen Angriff auf die linke Flanke der Konföderierten. Um 13.00 Uhr rückten sich Warren's Truppen endlich vor. Während eines verzweifelten Kampfes mitten im dichten Unterholz, gelang es den Föderalisten beinahe die Linie der Rebellen zu brechen. Die Verzögerung von Warren's Angriff gab Ewell Zeit, seine Truppen zu verstärken. Ein Gegenangriff drängte die Föderalisten zurück. Wiederholte Yankee Angriffe, darunter ein Versuch von Sedgwick die linke Flanke von Ewell abzuwenden, wurden zurückgeschlagen.

In der Zwischenzeit drängten sich Hill's Konföderierten auf der anderen Seite des Feldes vor, bis sie von einer Division des 6. Korps aufgehalten wurden. Um 16.00 Uhr stürmten diese Truppen, zusammen mit einem Teil des 2. Korps, die vorgerückte Konföderiertenlinie. Hill's Truppen lagen in Erwartung dieser Föderalisten und hielten ihren Angriff leicht auf. Ein weiterer Angriff, diesmal von Hancock, wurde ebenfalls zurückgeschlagen, obwohl er beinahe durch die Konföderiertenlinie brach. Die Dunkelheit endete das fürchterliche Gefecht.

Am 6. setzte sich das Kämpfen früh am Morgen auf der Nordseite des Feldes wieder fort. Ewell und Sedgwick verbrachten den Tag im Kampf, weder der eine noch der andere mit Erfolg. Ein weitaus ernsthafteres Gefecht trug sich südlich aus. Um 5.00 Uhr ging Hancock gegen Hill's Konföderierte vor und trieb sie vom Feld. Gerade um diese Zeit kam Longstreet's Korps an. Diese frischen Truppen schlugen auf die vorrückende Föderalisten ein und drängten sie zurück. Um 11.30 Uhr koordinierte Longstreet einen erfolgreichen Sturm auf Hancock's Front und linke Flanke. Während er Pläne vervollständigte zur Ausnutzung seines Erfolges, wurde er vom Feuer seiner eigenen Truppen getroffen und verwundet. Später ging Lee zu einem massiven Angriff gegen die Mitte von Hancock's Linie über. Nach einem brutalen Gefecht, unterstützt bei Unionartillerie, wurden die Konföderierten um 17.00 Uhr zurückgeschlagen. Dunkelheit brachte die Schlacht wieder zu Ende. Am nächsten Abend brach Grant das Patt indem er links auswich, in einem Versuch sich zwischen Lee und Richmond stellen zu können.

BEDEUTUNG

Taktisch endete der Kanpf unentschieden und kostete auf beiden Seiten schwere Verluste. Grant konnte seine Verluste leicht ersetzen, Lee dagegen nicht.

Ein weiterer von Lee's fähigsten Generalen, Longstreet, wurde verwundet.

Anstelle eines Rückzuges marschierte die Unionarmee nach Süden.

Confederate trenches and protective works at the edge of the woods in Saunder's Field near the Orange Turnpike.

SPOTSYLVANIA
May 8-21, 1864

State: Virginia

U.S.
Commanders: Lt. Gen. U.S. Grant
Maj. Gen. George G. Meade
U.S. Army: Army of the Potomac
No. of Troops: 110,000
Casualties:
17,500 total killed, wounded, and captured

C.S.
Commander: Gen. Robert E. Lee
C.S. Army: Army of Northern Virginia
No. of Troops: 50,000
Casualties:
10,000 total killed, wounded, and captured

COMMENTS

After the Battle of the Wilderness, both armies raced southeast toward the crossroads town of Spotsylvania Court House. General Anderson's Confederates reached the village first and repulsed the leading Federal units. Both armies rushed their forces into the fighting west of Spotsylvania but the Confederates held their ground. The rest of the night and throughout May 9th the Confederates built very strong earthworks along their line. On the 10th, General Grant attacked these defenses with three corps. The advancing Federals were met by crippling musket and artillery fire and were beaten back with heavy casualties. At 6 p.m. Col. Upton launched another attack. With twelve regiments massed on a narrow front, Upton assaulted the "Mule Shoe" salient in the center of Lee's works. The Federals pierced the vulnerable angle in the Southern lines but didn't have enough troops to exploit the initial breakthrough and were forced back. Encouraged by Upton's partial success Grant planned a similar attack using General Hancock's entire corps. At 4:30 a.m. on May 12th Hancock's men struck the tip of the salient. The Federals broke the line and captured a whole Confederate division of infantrymen. A Southern counterattack soon stalled Hancock's advance. For the next 20 hours the two intermingled forces engaged in some of the war's most vicious hand-to-hand fighting around the salient, soon to be renamed "The Bloody Angle." As the fighting raged Lee built a new line of defenses behind the angle. When they were completed he withdrew to this new stronger line.

On May 18th Grant attacked these works. After suffering huge losses the Federal attackers retired. The next day Lee went on the offensive, his lines swung across the Ny River to attack the Union right. The fighting was severe but the Confederates were repulsed, ending the fighting at Spotsylvania.

On May 21st Grant started to move his army, again sidestepping to the left, hoping to get around the Army of Northern Virginia.

SIGNIFICANCE

Lee, although not really losing any battles, was being forced South toward Richmond.

Lee's losses in killed, wounded, and captured were irreplaceable; his army was slowly disappearing.

Etat: Virginie

Etats-Unis
Commandants:
Lieutenant Général U.S. Grant
Général de Division George G. Meade
Armée: du Potomac
100 000 soldats
Pertes totales:
Tués, blessés et prisonniers: 17 500

Etats Confédérés
Commandant:
Général Robert E. Lee
Armée: de Virginie du Nord
50 000
Pertes totales:
Tués, blessés et disparus: 10 000

COMMENTAIRE

Après la bataille du Wilderness, les deux armées marchèrent en direction sud-est, vers le carrefour de Spotsylvania Court House. Les Confédérés du général Anderson furent les premiers à atteindre le village et repoussèrent les tetes des unités fédérales. Les deux armées jettèrent leurs forces dans la bataille à l'ouest de Spotsylvania, mais les Confédérés gardaient leur avantage. Le reste de la nuit et toute la journée du mai, les Confédérés s'adonnèrent à de grands travaux de terrassement le long de leur ligne. Le 10, le général Grant attaqua les défenses avec trois corps d'armée. L'avance des Fédéraux fut confrontée aux mousquets et aux feux de l'artillerie; souffrant de grandes pertes, les unionistes étaient repoussés. A 6 heures, le colonel Upton lança une autre attaque. Avec douze régiments massés sur un front étroit, Upton assaillit la "Mule Shoe" qui émergeait au centre des travaux en terre de Lee. Les Fédéraux percèrent l'angle vulnérable des lignes sudistes, mais ils n'avaient pas assez d'hommes pour profiter de cette brèche, et ils furent repoussés. Encouragé par le succès partiel d'Upton, Grant prépara une attaque similaire qui emploierait tout le corps d'armée du général Hancock. A 16h30, le 12 mai, les hommes de Hancock frappèrent l'extrémité exposée de la partie saillante. Les Fédéraux brisèrent la ligne et firent prisonnière toute une division de l'infantrie confédérée. Une contre-attaque sudiste bloqua l'advance de Hancock. Pendant les vingt heures qui suivirent, les deux forces emmelées furent aux prises avec un des plus brutales luttes corps à corps sur ce lieu nommé depuis le "Bloody Angle" (angle sanglant). Dans la rage de la bataille, Lee construisit une nouvelle ligne de défense derrière l'angle. Dès qu'elle fut prête, il se replia dessus.

Le 18 mai, Grant attaqua ces constructions. Après avoir subi de lourdes pertes, les Fédéraux se retirèrent. Le jour suivant, Lee reprit l'offensive en lançant ses lignes à travers la rivière Ny pour attaquer la droite de l'Union. La lutte fut dure mais, en repoussant les Confédérés, les Nordistes mirent fin à la bataille de Spotsylvania.

Le 21 mai, Grant commença à faire avancer son armée, s'écartant encore vers la gauche, espérant contouner l'armée de la Virginie de Nord.

CONSEQUENCES

Bien que n'ayant perdu aucune bataille, Lee fut poussé vers le sud de Richmond.

Les pertes de Lee en morts, blessés et prisonniers étaient irremplaçables. Son armée se désagrégeait lentement.

Important Landmarks
Brock Road
Po and Ny Rivers
Bloody Angle
Old Court House Road

Important Buildings
Scott House
McCoull House
Spotsylvania Court House
Landram House
Harrison House
Alsop Farm

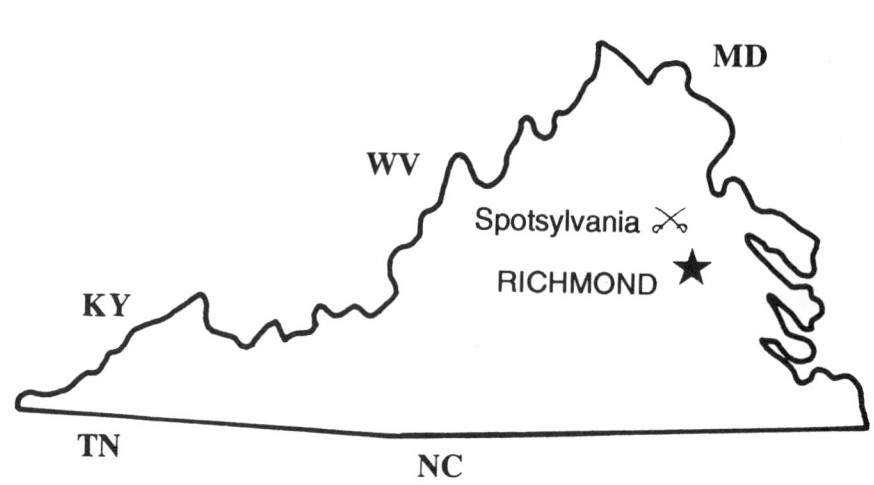

Estado: Virginia

U.S.	C.S.
Comandante:	Comandante:
Lt. Gen. U.S. Grant	Gen. Robert E. Lee
Maj. Gen. George G. Meade	C.S. Ejército: Army of Northern
U.S. Ejército: Army of the Potomac	Virginia
No. de tropas: 110,000	No. de tropas: 50,000
Pérdidas:	Pérdidas:
17,500 total muertos, heridos, y capturados	10,000 total muertos, heridos, y capturados

COMENTARIO

Después de la Batalla del Wilderness, los dos ejércitos corrieron de prisa para el pueblo de crucecaminos de Spotsylvania Court House. Los Confederados del General Anderson llegaron al pueblo primero y repulsaron a las primeras unidades Federales. Ambos ejércitos se arrojaron a la lucha al oeste de Spotsylvania pero los Confederados mantuvieron su posición. Por el resto de la noche y a lo largo del 9 de mayo los Confederados construyeron defensas y trincheras muy fuertes por toda su línea. El 10, el General Grant atacó estas defensas con tres cuerpos de infantería. Lo Federales que avanzaban se encontraron con una tormenta de fuego de rifles y artillería y fueron empujados para atrás con muchas pérdidas. A las 6 de la tarde el Col. Upton lanzó otro ataque. Con doce regimientos juntados en un frente estrecho, Upton asaltó el saliente "Mule Shoe" (Zapato de Mulo) en el centro de las defensas de Lee. Los Federales perforaron el ángulo vulnerable pero no había bastante tropas para explotar la brecha y tuvieron que retirarse. Alentado por el éxito en parte de Upton, Grant planeó otro ataque parecido usando el cuerpo entero del General Hancock. A las 4:30 de la mañana el día 12 los hombres de Hancock golpearon el punto del saliente. Los Federales rompieron la línea y capturaron una división entera de infantería Confederada. Pronto, un contraataque de los sureños paró el avance de Hancock. Por las próximas 20 horas las dos fuerzas entremezcladas participaron en una de las luchas más salvajes de cuerpo a cuerpo alrededor del saliente, que se renombró un poco después "Bloody Angle." Mientras la batalla rabiaba Lee construyó una línea nueva de defensas detrás del ángulo. Cuando se terminaron él retiró a sus tropas a la línea más fuerte.

El 18 de mayo Grant atacó estas trincheras. Después de sufrir pérdidas grandísimas los atacadores Federales se retiraron. El próximo día Lee se puso en la ofensa, sus líneas tornaron a través del río Ny para atacar la derecha Federal. La pelea fue bastante violenta, pero los Confederados fueron repulsados, acabando la batalla de Spotsylvania.

El 21 de mayo Grant empezó a mudar su ejército, otra vez haciéndose a la izquierda, esperando pasar alrededor del Army of Northern Virginia.

CONSECUENCIAS

Lee, aunque reálmente no perdía batallas, fue forzado hacia Richmond.

Las pérdidas de Lee en muertos, heridos, y capturados eran irreemplazables; su ejército, poco a poco, desaparecía.

Staat: Virginia

Befehlshaber der US:	Befehlshaber der CS:
Generalleutnant U.S. Grant	General Robert E. Lee
Generalmajor George G. Meade	Armee der CS: Armee von Nord virginia
Armee der US: Armee des Potomacs	Truppenstärke: 50,000
Truppenstärke: 110,000	Verluste:
Verluste:	10,000
Gefallen: 17,500	Insgesamt gefallen, verwundet oder vermisst
Insgesamt gefallen, verwundet oder vermisst	

KOMMENTAR

Nach der Schlacht in der Wilderness raschten beide Armeen südostwärts gegen eine kleines Dorf an einer Kreuzung — Spotsylvania Court House. General Anderson's Konföderierten erreichten das Dorf zuerst und schlugen die führenden Föderalisteneinheiten zurück. Die Streitkräfte beider Armeen waren sofort im Kampf westlich von Spotsylvania entwickelt, aber die Konföderierten hielten ihre Stellungen. In den Nachtstunden, die den Konföderierten übrigblieben, und durch den ganzen Tag des 9. Mai, bauten sie starke Schanzwerke entlang ihrer Linie. Am 10. griff General Grant mit drei Korps diese Verteidigungsanlage an. Lähmendes Artillerie- und Musketenfeuer begegnete die heranrückenden Föderalisten und sie wurden mit schweren Verlusten zurückgeschlagen. Um 18.00 Uhr ging Oberst Upton zum Angriff über. Zwölf Regimente unter Upton, auf einer engen Front massiert, stürmten "Mule Shoe", ein vorspringender Winkel in der Mitte von Lee's Schanze. Die Föderalisten durchstießen diesen ungeschützten Winkel in der Südlinie, jedoch der Mangel an Truppen verweigerte einen Erfolg dieses ersten Vorstoßes, und sie wurden zurückgetrieben. Ermutigt bei Upton's teilweisem Erfolg, plante Grant einen ähnlichen Angriff, mit General Hancock's vollem Korps. Am 12. Mai griffen Hancock's Truppen um 6.30 Uhr die Mitte der Ausbuchtung an. Die Föderalisten brachen die Linie und nahmen eine ganze Infanteriedivision der Konföderierten gefangen. In Kürze hielt ein Gegenangriff der Südstaatler Hancock's Vormarsch auf. Zwanzig Stunden lang kämpften die ineinandervermischten Armeen in der Gegend um den Linienwinkel. Es war einer der brutalsten Handkämpfe im Bürgerkrieg, der später den Namen "The Bloody Angle" erhielt. Als der Kampf weitertobte, baute Lee hinter den Winkel eine neue Abwehrlinie. Nach ihrer Vollendung zog er sich hinter diese neue, stärkere Linie zurück.

Am 18. Mai griff Grant diese Schanze an. Nach schweren Verlusten zogen sich die Föderalisten zurück. Am folgenden Tag ging Lee auf die Offensive, mit seinen Linien sich über den Ny Fluss abbiegend, um die rechte Seite der Union anzugreifen. Es war ein schwerer Kampf, die Konföderierten wurden zurückgetrieben, und die Schlacht bei Spotsylvania endete.

Am 21. Mai begann Grant, seine Armee nach links abzuziehen, in der Hoffnung, die Armee von Nordvirginia zu umgehen.

BEDEUTUNG

Obwohl Lee keine Schlacht verloren hatte, wurde er allmählich südwärts nach Richmond gedrängt. Grant konnte seine Verluste leicht ersetzen, Lee's Verluste — die Gefallenen, Verwundeten und Gefangenen — waren unersetzlich, langsam verschwand seine Armee.

Dead Confederate soldier on the Alsop Farm killed during the attack on May 19, 1864.

State: Virginia

U.S.

Commander:
  Maj. Gen. Franz Sigel
U.S. Army: Department of West Virginia
No. of troops 8,940
Casualties:
  Killed: 97
  Wounded: 520
  Captured or Missing: 225

C.S.

Commander:
  Maj. Gen. John Breckinridge
C.S. Army: Department of Western Virginia
No. of troops 5,325
Casualties:
  Killed: 43+
  Wounded: 474+
  Captured or Missing: 3

COMMENTS

At the beginning of the Civil War both the Union and Confederate high commands realized the importance of Virginia's Shenandoah Valley. To the Southerners the Valley was the agricultural heart of the Confederacy. It also contained vital rail lines which connected Tennessee and Virginia. Union forces had attempted to capture the region earlier in the war, but Confederate forces by 1864 still controlled most of the area. To win control of the valley Gen. Grant, Union Commander-Chief, ordered Union Gen. Franz Sigel to advance south, coordinating his movement with other Union advances and seize the Valley.

Confederate Gen. Robert E. Lee ordered Gen. Breckinridge to hold the Valley and defeat any Union forces operating there. Breckinridge was given command of units all over the area, including the Virginia Military Institute corp of cadets. Some of these cadets were as young as fifteen.

Gen. Sigel moved south slowly and on May 13, 1864, met a Confederate Cavalry force under Brig. Gen. Imboden. The engagement was sharp and the outnumbered Confederates fell back to a defensive position south of the small town of New Market. By May 15th Breckinridge's men, occupied a high position south and west of town on Shirley's Hill. Sigel's men occupied the town itself and the high ground north of the Bushong Farm.

May 15th was a day of continuous rain and the battle took place in the worst of conditions. Breckinridge had hoped Sigel would attack him but when this did not occur, Breckinridge decided to attack the Union forces at 10:00 A.M. he deployed his two infantry brigades under Generals Echols and Wharton on a line from Shirley's Hill east to Smith Creek. The men were formed in a staggered line so as to deceive Union forces as to the strength of the Confederates. Breckinridge's men moved north off the hill into the town and valley below. The Union forces were driven back and by 12:30 P.M. the town was in Confederate hands. The Southerners pressed forward toward the Union line just north of the Bushong Farm. The line was strong and Breckinridge's men took heavy casualties from Union artillery. The Union soldiers attempted to charge the exhausted Confederates but failed. The VMI cadets were used to reinforce the Confederate line and Sigel's men were driven farther to the north, near Cedar Grove church. The Confederates pursued but an artillery battery checked their advance. Breckinridge tried to regroup his men but by 7:00 P.M. Sigel and his men escaped by crossing the Shenandoah River and destroying the bridge.

SIGNIFICANCE

Held Union forces out of the Shenandoah Valley a little longer.

247 VMI cadets participated in the battle, 10 killed or mortally wounded and 50 wounded.

Sigel's defeat allowed Breckinridge to temporarily reinforce Lee's army.

Etat: Virginie

Etats-Unis

Commandant:
  Général de División Franz Sigel
Armée: Département de la Virginie de l'Ouest
  8 940 soldats
Pertes:
  Tués: 97
  Blessés: 520
  Prisonniers ou disparus: 225

Etats Confédérés

Commandant: Général de División John Breckenridge
Armée: Département de la Virginie de l'Ouest
  5 325 soldats
Pertes:
  Tués: 43+
  Blessés: 474+
  Prisonniers ou disparus: 3

COMMENTAIRE

Dès le commencement de la Guerre Civile les deux adversaires eurent reconnu l'importance de la Vallée du Shenandoah. Pour les sudistes, la vallée etait le coeur agricole de la Confédération. Elle contenaient aussi des lignes ferroviares qui liaient les états de Virginie et du Tennessee. Des forces fédérales avaient essayé d'occuper cette région plus tôt, mais en 1864, les Confédérés en contrôlaient encore la plupart. Pour conquérir la Vallée, le général-en-chef, le général Grant, ordonna au général Sigel d'avancer vers le sud, coordonnant son mouvement avec ceux des autres forces fédérales, et prendre possession de la Vallée.

Les ordres du général confédéré Breckenridge était de tenir la Vallée et de vaincre toute force unioniste y opérante. Le général Breckenridge commandait toutes les unités sudistes de la région, y compris les cadets du Military Institute of Virginia. Quelques-uns de ces cadets n'avaient que quinze ans.

Le général Sigel avança lentement vers le sud, et le 13 mai, rencontra de la cavalrie confédérée sous le général Imboden. L'engagement fut vif. Les confédérés, moins nombreux, se retira dans une position défensive au sud du petit village de New Market. Le 15 mai, les hommes de Breckenridge occupaient Shiley's Hill qui dominait le village au sud et à l'ouest. Sigel prit position dans le village et aux hauteurs du nord de la ferme Bushong.

Il pleuvait sans relâche pendant toute la journée du 15, et la bataille eut lieu sous de pires conditions. Breckenridge avait espéré que Sigel attaquerait le premier, mais quand cela ne se produisit pas, Breckenridge décida à 10 heures du matin d'attaquer les Nordistes. Il déploya ses deux brigades d'infanterie sous les généraux Echols et Wharton sur une ligne depuis Shiley's Hill vers l'est jusqu'a Smith's Creek. Il forma ses lignes d'une façon discontinue pour tromper les fédéraux sur le nombre réel de ses forces. L'attaque des Confédérés se porta dans la vallée en bas et à travers le village. Les fédéraux durent se replier, et vers midi et demi, le village fut aux mains des sudistes. Ils continuèrent d'assaillir la ligne unioniste du nord de la ferme Bushong. Leur ligne fut forte, et leur artillerie fit des ravages dans les rangs confédérés. Les unionistes contre-attaquèrent les sudistes épuisés, mais ce fut un échec. Les Confédérés employèrent les cadets de l'institut comme renforts, et les hommes de Sigel furent poussés vers le nord près de Cedar Creek Church. Les Confédérés se lancèrent à la poursuite, mais leur avance fut arrêtée par une batterie d'artillerie ennemie. Breckenridge essaya de réorganiser ses hommes, mais vers 7 heures Sigel échappa en traversant la rivière Shenanndoah et détruisit le pont.

CONSEQUENCE

Les Confédérés réussirent à exclure les Fédéraux de la Vallée un plus lontemps.

Les Cadets particpèrent à la bataille, ayant perdu 10 tués et 50 blessés ou disparus.

La défaite de Sigel a permis à Breckenridge de renforce l'armée de Lee temporairement.

Important Landmarks

Smith Creek
Bushong Hill
Rude's Hill
Shirley's Hill
New Market
Sigel's Hill
Shenandoah River

Important Buildings

Bushong House
Rice House
St. Matthew's Lutheran Church
Cedar Grove Church
Neff House
Rude House

VMI cadets in action.

Estado: Virginia

U.S.	C.S.
Comandante:	Comandante:
Maj. Gen. Franz Sigel	Maj. Gen. John Breckinridge
U.S. Ejército: Departamento de Virginia del oeste	C.S. Ejército: Departamento de Virginia occidental
No. de tropas: 8,940	No. de tropas: 5,325
Pérdidas:	Pérdidas:
Muertos: 97	Muertos: 43+
Heridos: 520	Heridos: 474+
Capturados o desaparecidos: 225	Capturados o desaparecidos: 3

COMENTARIO

Al principio de la Gerra Civil las comandancias de la Unión y de los Confederados comprendieron la importancia del valle Shenandoah en Virginia. Para los sureños el valle era el corazón agrícola de la Confederación. También contenía vías de ferrocaril que conectaban Tennessee y Virginia. Fuerzas de la Unión habían intentado capturar la región al principio de la de Guerra, pero las fuerzas confederadas cerca de 1864, todavía controlaban la mayor área. Para ganar el control del valle el general Grant, comandante en jefe de la Unión, ordenó al general Franz Sigel de la Unión avanzar hacia el sur, coordinando sus movimientos con otros avances de la Unión y capturar el valle.

El general confederado Robert E. Lee ordenó al general Breckinridge defender el valle y vencer las fuerzas de la Unión operando allí. A Breckinridge fue dado el mando de las unidades de todo el área, incluyendo el cuerpo de cadetes del Instituto Militar de Virginia. Algunos de estos cadetes tenían unos quince años.

El general Sigel se movió hacia el sur lentamente, y el 13 de mayo de 1864 se encontró con una fuerza de la caballería confederada bajo el mando del general de brigada Imboden. El combate fue duro y los confederados menos en número, retrocedieron en una posición defensiva al sur de la pequeña cuidad de New Market. Hacia el 15 de mayo los hombres de Breckinridge ocuparon una posición alta al sur y al oeste de la cuidad en la colina de Shirley. Los hombres de Sigel ocuparon la cuidad y las tierras altas al norte de Bushong Farm.

El quince de mayo fue un día de lluvia continúa y la batalla tomó lugar en las peores condiciones. Breckinridge había esperado que Sigel lo atacara pero cuando esto no ocurrió, Breckinridge decidió atacar las fuerzas de la Unión a las 10 de la mañana. El desplegó sus dos brigadas de infantería bajo los generales Echols y Wharton en una línea desde el este de la colina de Shirley a Smith Creek. Los hombres estaban formados en una línea escalonada de menera que engañara a las fuerzas de la Unión así como para la fuerza de los confederados.

Los hombres de Breckinridge se movieron hacia el norte fuera de la colina hacia la cuidad y el valle abajo. Las fuerzas de la Unión fueron empujadas hacia atrás y a eso de las 12:30 de la tarde la ciudad estaba en manos confederadas. Los sureños avanzaron hacia la Unión justo al norte de Bushong Farm. La línea era fuerte y los hombres de Breckinridge causaron grandes pérdidas a la artillería de la Unión. Los soldados de la Unión intentaron atacar a los cansados confederados pero fallaron. Los cadetes del Instituto Militar de Virginia fueron usados para reforzar la línea confederada y las iglesia Cedar Grove. Los confederados siguieron pero una batería de artillería detuvo su avance. Breckinridge trató de reagrupar a sus hombres, pero a eso de las 7:00 de la noche Sigel y sus hombres escaparon cruzando el río Shenandoah y destruyendo el puente.

CONSECUENCIAS

Se mantuvo las fuerza de la Unión fuera del Valle de Shenandoah por un poco más de tiempo.

247 cadetes del Instituto Militar de Virginia participaron en la batalla, 10 muertos o mortalmente heridos y 50 heridos.

La derrota de Sigel permitió a Breckinridge reforzar la armada de Lee temporalmente.

Staat: Virginia

Befehlshaber der US:	Befehlshaber der CS:
Generalmajor Franz Sigel	Generalmajor John Breckinridge
Armee der US:	Armee der CS: Armee von Western Virginia
Armee von Westvirginia	
Truppenstärke: 8,940	Truppenstärke: 5,335
Verluste:	Verluste:
Gefallen: 97	Gefallen: 43+
Verwundet: 520	Verwundet: 474+
Gefangengenommen oder vermißt: 225	Gefangengenommen oder vermißt: 3

KOMMENTAR

Zu Beginn des Zivilkrieges erkannten die Befehlshaber beider Armeen - Union und Konföderation - die bedeutsame Wichtigkeit des Virginia Shenandoah Tales. Für die Südstaaten war das Tal der landwirtschaftliche Kern der Konföderation. Ebenso lagen dort lebenswichtige Eisenbahnlinien, welche Tennessee und Virginia verbanden. Zu Beginn des Krieges hatten Unionstreitkräfte versucht, dieses Gebiet zu erobern, aber um 1864 knotrollierten Konföderierte Streitkräfte immer noch den größten Teil des Gebietes. Um Kontrolle über das Tal zu gewinnen, gab Genexal Grant, Hauptbefehlshaber der Unionarmee, Union General Franz Sigel den Befehl, in Zusammenarbeit mit anderen Unionstreitkräften, sich dem Süden zuzuwenden, um das Tal zu erobern.

General Robert E. Lee befahl General Breckinridge die im Tal operierenden Unionstreitkräfte zu vernichten, und das Tal zu halten. Breckinridge wurde das Kommando über alle Einheiten in diesem Gebiet, einbegriffen das Korps der Kadetten des Virginia Military Institutes (VMI), übergeben. Einige der Kadetten waren nicht mehr als 15 Jahre alt.

General Sigel bewegte sich langsam südlich. Am 13. März 1864 traf er auf eine Konföderierte Kavallerie Streitkraft unter Brigadiergeneral Imboden. Das Gefecht war heftig und die zahlenmäßig unterlegenen Konföderierten fielen auf eine defensive Stellung, nahe der kleinen Stadt New Market, zurück. Am 15. Mai besetzten Breckinridge's Truppen eine Höhenstellung südlich und westlich der Stadt auf Shirleys Hill. Sigel's Truppen besetzten die Stadt und das hohe Gelände nördlich der Bushong Farm.

Ununterbrochener Regen brachte die schlimmsten Zustände zur Schlacht, die am 15. Mai ausgetragen wurde. Als Breckinridge's Hoffnung auf Sigel's Angriff sich nicht verwirklichte, entschloß er sich, die Unionstreitkräfte um 10.00 Uhr am Morgen anzugreifen. Er verteilte seine zwei Infanteriebrigaden - unter dem Kommando von Generalen Echols und Wharton - auf einer Linie, die von Shirley's Hill bis zum Smith Creek lief. Die Truppen formten in einer gestaffelten Linie, um die Unionstreitkräfte über die Strenge der Konföderierten zu täuschen.

Breckinridge's Truppen zogen vom nördlichen Teil des Hügel's herunter in die Stadt und das Tal. Bei 12.30 Uhr waren die Uniontruppen zurückgeschlagen und die Stadt war in den Händen der Konföderierten. Die Südstaatler drängten vorwärts gegen die Unionlinien, unmittelbar nördlich der Bushong Farm. Ihre Linien waren verstärkt und Breckinridge's Truppen hatten schwere Verluste von der Unionartillerie. Aber ohne Erfolg versuchten die Unionsoldaten, die erschöpften Konföderierten anzugreifen. Die VMI Kadetten wurden zur Verstärkung der Konföderierten Linien eingesetzt und Sigel's Truppen weiter nach Norden getrieben, in die Nähe von Cedar Creek Church. Die Verfolgung bei den Konföderierten wurde durch das Feuer einer Artilleriebatterie aufgehalten. Breckinridge versuchte, seine Truppen wieder zu gruppieren, aber bei 19.00 Uhr waren Sigel's Truppen über den Shenandoah Fluß entkommen, und hatten die Brücke hinter sich zerstört.

BEDEUTUNG

Die Unionstreitkräfte wurden für eine kurze Zeit länger aus dem Shenandoah Tal zurückgehalten.

247 VMI Kadetten nahmen an der Schlacht teil. 10 waren gefallen oder tödlich verwundet, und 50 verwundet.

Sigel's Niederlage erlaubte Breckinridge vorübergehend Lee's Armee zu verstärken.

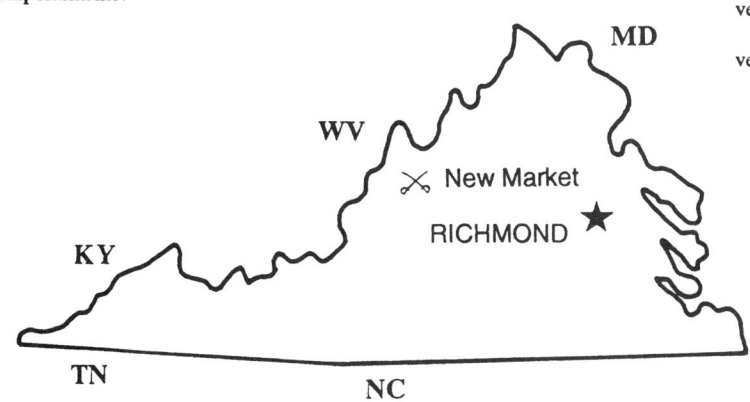

State: Georgia

U.S.

Commander:
Maj. Gen. William T. Sherman
U.S. Army: Military Division of the
Miss., Armies of the Cumberland,
Tennessee, and Ohio
No. of Troops: 81,000-112,000
Casualties:
Killed: 4,400
Wounded: 22,800
Captured or missing: 4,400

C.S.

Commanders:
Gen. Joseph Johnston
Gen. John B. Hood
C.S. Army: Army of Tennessee
No. of Troops: 59,000
Casualties:
Killed: 3,000
Wounded: 19,000
Captured or missing: 13,000

COMMENTS

The Union objective during the Atlanta Campaign was the destruction of Johnston's Army and to inflict as much damage as possible against their war resources. By early May Sherman's force had begun moving from Chattanooga. Sherman's 98,000 mean force split into three armies under Thomas, McPherson, and Schofield. Opposing him was Johnston's 53,000 Confederates in northwest Georgia. Through May and June Sherman steadily advanced toward Atlanta. The battles during this time were very similar as Sherman constantly sidestepped Johnston's fortified positions forcing the Southerners to fall back upon new lines. From May 9-June 27 Johnston was forced to retreat from positions at Snake Creek Gap, Resaca, Adairsville, Cassville, Allatoona Pass, New Hope Church, and Marietta. The action at all of these places was the same. The opposing armies made contact, whether an engagement followed or not, Sherman eventually initiated a movement to flank the Confederate position causing Johnston to fall back. On June 27, however, Sherman tired of flanking movements and tried a frontal assault on Johnston's most formidable position to date at Kennesaw Mountain.

The Confederates then fell back to the Chattahoochee River, but on July 8 Johnston withdrew to the south side. Tired of Johnston's constant retreats, Jefferson Davis replaced him with General Hood. On the 20th, Hood attacked the Federals north of Atlanta at Peachtree Creek. The Confederates were repulsed with heavy casualties and Hood was forced back into the city's defenses. Two days later Hood attacked McPherson's separated column east of Atlanta. Although McPherson was killed and his troops shaken, the assault gained nothing.

During the rest of July and August, Sherman attempted to circle around the city to the west. His goal was to sever the railroads supplying Atlanta. On Aug. 31-Sept. 1 Hood again assaulted Sherman's forces. At the Battle of Jonesborough Hood struck the Union right flank in an effort to protect his supply lines. The Confederates were repulsed and Atlanta was doomed. During the night the Confederates pulled out and on Sept. 2 Sherman marched to Atlanta.

SIGNIFICANCE

With the capture of Atlanta, Sherman was free to march to the sea.

Atlanta's fall devastated Southern morale.

Atlanta's fall hurt the Southern war effort as the city was an industrial, supply, and communications center.

Etat: Georgie

Etats-Unis

Commandant:
Général de Division William T.
Sherman
Armées: Division militaire du
Mississipi, Armées du
Cumberland, du Tennessee et de
l'Ohio
81 000-112 000 soldats
Pertes:
Tués: 4 400
Blessés: 22 800
Prisonniers ou disparus: 4 400

Etats Confédérés

Commandants:
Général Joseph Johnston
Général John B. Hood
Armée: du Tennessee
59 000 soldats

Pertes:
Tués: 3 000
Blessés: 19 000
Prisonniers ou disparus: 13 000

COMMENTAIRE

Pendant la campagne d'Atlanta, le but de l'Union était de détruire l'armée de Johnston, et d'infliger le plus de dommages possibles aux industries et aux communications des sudistes. Début mai, les forces de Sherman avaient commencé à se déplacer depuis Chattanooga. Les 98 000 hommes de Sherman furent partagés en trois armées entre Thomas, McPherson et Schofield. En face de lui se trouvaient les 53 000 Confédérés de Johnston dans le nord-ouest de la Georgie. En mai et juin, Sherman avança fermement vers Atlanta. Les diverses batailles furent ici très similaires. Sherman contournait constamment le long des positions fortifiées de Johnston, forçant les Sudistes à se replier sur de nouvelles lignes. Du 9 mai au 27 juin, Johnston fut obligé de battre en retraite depuis ses positions à Snake Creek Gap, Resaca, Adairsville, Cassville, Allatoona Pass, New Hope Church, et Marietta. Le scénario était partout le meme. Les armées opposées se rencontraient, s'engageaient ou non puis Sherman prenait l'initiative d'un mouvement au flanc de la position confédérée, causant le repli de Johnston. Le 27 juin, cependant, Sherman se fatigua des mouvements de flancs et tenta un assaut de front sur la position la plus forte de Johnston à Kennesaw Mountain.

Les Confédérés se replièrent ensuite sur la rivière Chattahoochee, mais le 8 juillet Johnston se retira vers le sud. Irrité par les retraites de Johnston, Jefferson Davis le remplaça avec le Général Hood. Le 20, Hood attaqua les Fédéraux au nord d'Atlanta à Peachtree Creek. Les Confédérés furent repoussés avec de lourdes pertes et Hood dut se replier dans les défenses de la ville. Deux jours plus tard, Hood attaqua la colonne séparée de McPherson à l'est d'Atlanta. Cet assaut n'eut aucun résultat en dépit de la mort de McPherson et de l'ébranlement de ses troupes.

Pendant le reste de juillet et août, Sherman essaya d'encercler la ville à l'ouest. Il voulait couper les lignes de chemin de fer qui desservaient Atlanta. Le 31 août et le 1er septembre, Hood attaqua de nouveau les forces de Sherman. Dans l'espoir de protéger ses lignes d'approvisionnement, Hood frappa le flanc droit de l'Union à la bataille de Jonesborough. Les Confédérés furent repoussés; Atlanta était perdu. Pendant la nuit, les Confédérés évacuèrent et le 2 septembre Sherman entrait dans la ville.

CONSEQUENCES

Ayant pris Atlanta, Sherman avait le route libre vers la'mer.

La tombée d'Atlanta démolit le moral des Sudistes.

La ville d'Atlanta étant un centre d'industries, d'approvisionement et de communication, sa chute portait un coup sérieux aux tentatives de la guerre sudiste.

Important Landmarks	Important Buildings
Rockey Face Ridge	New Hope Church
Pumpkin Vine Creek	Howard House
Bald Hill	Union Depot
Western and Atlantic R.R.	Troop Hurt House
Camp Creek	Ezra Church
Kennesaw Mountain	Atlanta City Hall
Fort Hood	Potter House
Allatoona Pass	Atlanta Arsenal
Chattahoochee River	
Peach Tree Creek	

Estado: Georgia

U.S.	C.S.
Comandante:	Comandante:
Maj. Gen. William T. Sherman	Gen. Joseph Johnston
U.S. Ejército: Military Division of the Miss., Armies of the Cumberland, Tennessee and Ohio	Gen. John B. Hood
	C.S. Ejercito: Army of Tennessee
No. de tropas: 81,000-112,000	No. de tropas: 59,000
Perdidas:	Perdidas:
Muertos: 4,400	Muertos: 3,000
Heridos: 22,800	Heridos: 19,000
Capturados o ausentes: 4,400	Capturados o ausentes: 13,000

COMENTARIO

El objetivo de la Unión durante la campaña de Atlanta era la destrucción del ejército de Johnston e infligir tanto daño como posible contra sus recursos de guerra. A principios de mayo la fuerza de Sherman había empezado a mudarse de Chattanooga. La fuerza de Sherman de 98,000 hombres se dividió en tres ejércitos bajo Thomas, McPherson y Schofield. Opuesto a él estaban los 53,000 Confederados bajo Johnston en el noroeste de Georgia. Durante mayo y junio Sherman firmemente avanzó hacia Atlanta. Las batallas durante esta época fueron parecidas puesto que Sherman constantemente se hacia a un lado de las posiciones fortificadas de Johnston, lo que forzó que los sureños se retiraran a líneas nuevas. Desde el 9 de mayo hasta el 27 de junio Johnston tuvo que retirarse de posiciones en Snake Creek Gap, Resaca, Adairsville, Cassville, Allatoona Pass, New Hope Church, y Marietta. La acción en todos estos sitios fue la misma. Los dos ejércitos hicieron contacto, y si una batalla tuvo lugar o no, Sherman eventualmente inició un movimiento para flanquear la posición Confederada causando que Johnston se retirara. El 27 de junio, sin embargo, Sherman se cansó de flanquear y trató un asalto en frente de la posición más formidable de Johnston hasta este punto en Kennesaw Mountain.

Los Confederados entonces retrocedieron al río Chattahoochee, pero el 8 de julio Johnston se retiró al lado sureño. Harto de las constantes retiradas de Johnston, Jefferson Davis lo reemplazó con el General Hood. El 20, Hood atacó a los Federales al norte de Atlanta en Peachtree Creek. Los Confederados fueron repulsados con muchas pérdidas y Hood tuvo que retirarse a las defensas de la ciudad. Dos días despues Hood atacó la columna seperada de McPherson al este de Atlanta. Aunque McPherson fue matado y sus tropas debilitadas, el asalto no ganó nada.

Durante el resto de julio y agosto, Sherman trató de circuir la ciudad al oeste. Su objeto era cortar los ferrocarriles que traían provisiones a Atlanta. El 31 de agosto y el 1 de septiembre Hood atacó las fuerzas de Sherman de nuevo. En la batalla de Jonesborough Hood golpeó el flanco derecho Federal en un esfuerzo para proteger sus líneas de provisiones. Los Confederados fueron repulsados y Atlanta estaba destinada a la ruina. Durante la noche los Confederados se retiraron y Sherman entró en Atlanta.

CONSECUENCIAS

Con la captura de Atlanta, Sherman tenía la oportunidad de marchar al mar.

La caída de Atlanta hizo sufrir la moral del Sur.

La caída de Atlanta hizo daño al esfuerzo de guerra sureño porque la ciudad tenía mucha industria, provisiones y comunicaciones.

Staat: Georgia

Befehlshaber der US:	Befehlshaber der CS:
Generalmajor William T. Sherman	General Joseph Johnston
Armee der US: Militärdivision von Mississippi, Armeen des Cumberlands, Tennessees und Ohios	General John B. Hood
	Armee der CS: Armee von Tennessee
Truppenstärke: 81,000 - 112,000	Truppenstärke: 59,000
Verluste:	Verluste:
Gefallen: 4,400	Gefallen: 3,000
Verwundet: 22,800	Verwundet: 19,000
Gefangengenommen oder vermißt: 4,400	Gefangengenommen oder vermißt: 13,000

KOMMENTAR

Das Ziel der Union während der Atlanta Kanpagne war, Johnston's Armee zu vernichten und seinem Nachschub soviel Schaden wie möglich anzurichten. Früh im Mai begannen Sherman's Streitkräfte ihren Abzug von Chattanooga. Sherman's 98,000 Truppenstärke teilte sich in drei Armeen unter Thomas, McPherson und Schofield auf. Sein Gegner waren Johnston's 53,000 Konföderierten im Nordwesten von Georgia. Mai und Juni fanden Shernan auf dem Vormarsch nach Atlanta. Während dieser Zeit war jede Schlacht der anderen ähnlich, indem Sherman stets Johnston's befestigten Stellungen auswich, was die Südstaatler zwang, auf neue Linien zurückzufallen. Vom 9. Mai bis 27. Juni wurde Johnston dazu gezwungen, sich aus Stellungen bei Snake Creek Gap, Resca, Adairsville, Cassville, Allatoona Pass, New Hope Church und Marietta zurückzuziehen. Die Aktion bei diesen Orten war immer die gleiche. Die feindlichen Armeen kamen in Kontakt, und, weder ein Angriff darauf folgte oder nicht, Sherman unternahm am Ende eine Flankierung der Konföderierten, was Johnston jedesmal veranlaßte, zurückzufallen. Sherman wurde überdrüßig dieser Flankenzüge und versuchte einen frontalen Angriff auf die bis dahin bedrohlichste Stellung von Johnston — Kennesaw Mountain.

Die Konföderierten fielen an den Chattahoochee Fluß zurück, aber am 8. Juli zog sich Johnston auf die südliche Seite zurück. Jefferson Davis hatte mehr als genug von Johnston's wiederholten Rückzügen und ersetzte ihn mit General Hood. Am 20. ging Hood gegen die Föderalisten von Atlanta am Peachtree Creek zum Angriff vor. Die Konföderierten wurden mit schweren Verlusten zurückgeschlagen und Hood wurde in die Stadtbefestigungen zurückgedrängt. Zwei Tage später griff Hood McPherson's abgetrennte Kolonne östlich von Atlanta an. McPherson fiel — tiefe Erschütterung ergriff seine Truppen — der Angriff war erfolglos.

Während der übrigen Tage im Juli, sowie im Monat August, versuchte Sherman die Stadt nach Westen zu umzingeln. Sein Ziel war, die Eisenbahnstrecken, die Atlanta versorgten, zu unterbrechen. Vom 31. August bis 1. September griff Hood wiederum Sherman's Truppen an. Bei der Schlacht von Jonesborough griff Hood die rechte Flanke der Union an, in der Bestrebung, seine Versorgungslinien zu schützen. Die Konföderierten wurden zurückgeschlagn und Atlanta war dem Schicksal überlaßen. Während der Nacht zogen sich die Konföderierten aus der Stadt zurück. Am 2. September marschierte Sherman in Atlanta ein.

BEDEUTUNG

Nach der Eroberung Atlanta's hatte Sherman eine freie Strecke zum Marsch an die See.

Die Eroberung Atlanta's brachte eine totale Entmutigung des Südens mit sich.

Die Eroberung Atlanta's war ein schwerer Schlag für die sudstaatlichen Kriegsanstrengungen. Die Stadt war ein Zentrum der Industrieversorgung und der Kommunikation.

Abandoned Confederate defenses on the site of the Battle of Atlanta, July 22, 1864.

State: Virginia

U.S.
Commanders: Lt. Gen. U.S. Grant
Maj. Gen. George G. Meade
U.S. Army: Army of the Potomac
No. of Troops: 114,000
Casualties:
Killed: 1,800
Wounded: 9,000
Captured or missing: 1,800

C.S.
Commander: Gen. Robert E. Lee
C.S. Army: Army of Northern
Virginia
No. of Troops: 56,000
Casualties:
4,000 total killed, wounded, and
missing

COMMENTS

Cold Harbor, an old tavern located at a crossroads 8 miles from Richmond, was the last major "open-field" battle before the two armies settled into the long siege of Petersburg.

Early on May 31 Confederate General Fitz Lee's cavalry arrived at the crossroads. Soon General Sheridan's Northern cavalry, armed with Spencer repeating carbines, drove the Southerners out and took possession of Cold Harbor.

On June 1, Lee ordered General Anderson's infantry to advance and dislodge the federal cavalry. Two Confederate attacks were repulsed due to the fast-firing Spencer repeaters. Around noon, the Union VI Corps arrived to relieve the cavalry. At 4 o'clock the XVIII Corps also arrived and both corps attacked the Confederates. The Southern line was pushed back in spots and was breached in one place. A Confederate counterattack finally repulsed the Northerners, but Grant believed that one more strong, coordinated attack would give him possession of the Cold Harbor area. General Grant ordered General Hancock's II Corps to march all night and be ready to attack in the morning. However, hunger, heat, and exhaustion slowed the march of the II Corps. This caused Grant to postpone the attack until 5 p.m. The condition of the soldiers again postponed the attack, now set for 4:30 a.m., June 3rd. Meanwhile, this extra day gave Lee the time he needed to reinforce his lines and dig trenches.

On June 3rd the time came to attack. The three Union corps, the II, VI, and XVIII, all stepped out on their way—a 2-1/2 mile long frontal attack. The Confederate veterans waited for the blue lines to get close. Then a "volcanic blast of sound and flame" erupted from the Southern line. The Union lines crumpled in heaps; only Hancock's men managed to reach the Confederate works, but they, too, were soon blown away by the rifle and canister fire.

The charge lasted less than half an hour. The battle was over, but the armies remained in the trenches until June 12 when Grant secretly slipped to the south—heading for Petersburg.

SIGNIFICANCE

War in the Eastern Theater turned into trench warfare as both armies dug in.

Grant would never again attempt a frontal attack on an entrenched enemy position.

Lee's last major victory in the field.

Etat: Virginie

Etats-Unis
Commandants:
Lieutenant Général U. S. Grant
Général de division George G.
Meade
Armée: du Potomac
114 000 soldats
Pertes:
Tués: 1 800
Blessés: 9 000
Prisonniers ou disparus: 1 800

Etats Confédérés
Commandant:
Général Robert E. Lee

Armée: de Virginie du Nord
56 000 soldats
Pertes totales:
Tués, blessés ou disparus: 4 000

COMMENTAIRE

Vieille taverne située à un carrefour à 12 kilomètres de Richmond, Cold Harbor fut la dernière bataille à champ ouvert avant que les deux armées se trouvent aux prises dans le long siège de Petersburg.

Au petit matin du 31 mai, la cavalerie du général Fitz Lee arriva au carrefour Bientôt, la cavalerie nordiste de général Sheridan, armée de carabines spencer à répétition, expulsa les Sudistes et s'empara de Cold Harbor.

Le 1 er juin, Lee donna ordre à l'infanterie du général Anderson d'avancer et de déloger la cavalerie fédérale. Les carabines à répétition permirent de repousser deux attaques des Confédérés. Vers midi, le quatrième corps d'armée arriva pour prendre la relève de la cavalerie. A 16 heures, aidé du corps XVIII, il attaqua les Confédérés. La ligne sudiste fut poussée par endroits et trouée en un point. Une contre-attaque confédérée repoussa les Nordistes. Grant pensa alors qu'une autre attaque très forte et bien coordonnée le rendrait maître de la région de Cold Harbor. Il donna ordre au deuxième corps d'armée du général Hancock de marcher toute la nuit pour être prêt à l'attaque au matin. Cependant, la faim, la chaleur et l'épuisement ralentirent la marche des troupes. A cause de l'état des soldats, Grant dut remettre l'attaque à 17 heures. Puis à 4h30 le matin du 3 juin l'attaque prévue au matin du 2 eut lieu. Ce delai donna à Lee tout le temps dont il avait besoin pour renforcer ses lignes et creuser des tranchées.

L'attaque commença enfin le 3 juin. Les corps d'armée II, VI et XVIII s'élancèrent, formant une ligne de front de 4 km. Les vétérans confédérés attendait jusqu'à ce que les lignes bleu furent tout prés. Puis une explosion de sons et de flammes surgit de la ligne sudiste. Les lignes de l'Union s'effritèrent, et tandis que les hommes d'Hancock réussissaient à atteindre les tranchées des Confédérés, ils furent réduits par le feu des fusils et de la mitraille.

La charge dura moins d'une demi-heure. La bataille était finie, mais les armées restèrent dans les tranchées jusqu'au 12 où Grant fila secrètement vers le sud, en route pour Petersburg.

CONSEQUENCES

Dans le théatre de l'est la lutte devint une guerre de tranchées pour les deux armées.

Grant apprit à ne jamais attaquer le front d'une armée en position de retranchement.

Cette bataille était la dernière victoire importante de Lee sur un champ de bataille.

Important Landmarks
Chickahominy River
Old Church Road
Cold Harbor Road
Crossroads at New & Old Cold Harbor

Important Buildings
Gaines House
Beulah Church
Old Cold Harbor Tavern
Garthright House
Bethesda Church

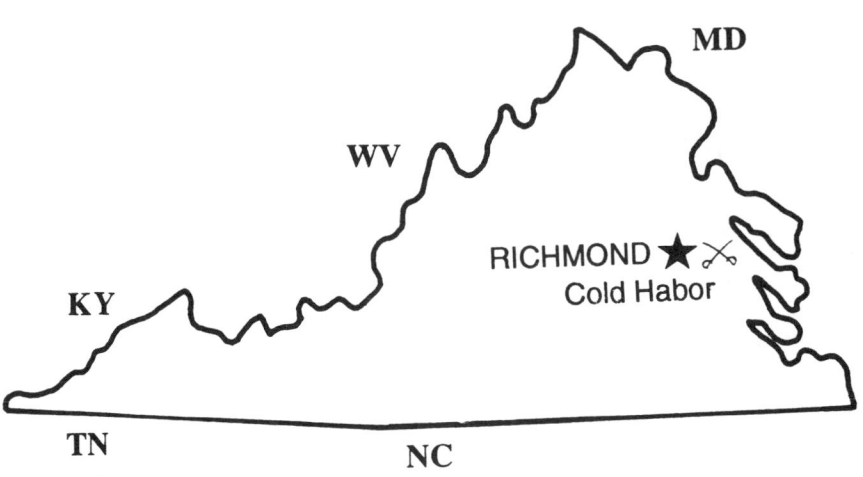

U.S.	C.S.
Comandante:	Comandante:
Lt. Gen. U.S. Grant	Gen. Robert E. Lee
Maj. Gen. George G. Meade	
U.S. Ejército: Army of the Potomac	C.S. Ejército: Army of Northern
No. de tropas: 114,000	Virginia
Pérdidas:	No. de tropas: 56,000
Muertos: 1,800	Pérdidas:
Heridos: 9,000	4,000 total en muertos, heridos,
Capturados o ausentes: 1,800	ausentes

Befehlshaber der US:	Befehlshaber der CS:
Generalleutnant U.S. Grant	General Robert E. Lee
Generalmajor George G. Meade	
Armee der US: Armee des Potomac	Armee der CS: Armee von
Truppenstärke: 114,000	Nordvirginia
Verluste:	Truppenstärke: 56,000
Gefallen: 1,400	Verluste:
Verwundet: 9,000	Insgesamt 4,000 gefallen,
Gefangengenommen oder	verwundet gefangengenommen
vermißt: 1,800	oder vermißt

COMENTARIO

Cold Harbor, una taberna antigua situada en un crucecaminos a 8 millas de Richmond, fue la última batalla en el campo abierto antes de que los dos ejércitos se asentaron al asedio largo de Petersburg.

Temprano en el 31 de mayo la caballería del General Confederado Fitz Lee llegó al crucecaminos. Poco después la caballería norteña del General Sheridan, armada con carabinas repetidoras del tipo Spencer, empujó fuera a los sureños y tomó posesión de Cold Harbor.

El 1 de junio, Lee mandó a la infantería del General Anderson que avanzara y desalojara a la caballería Yanqui. Dos ataques Confederados fueron repulsados por las carabinas que disparaban tan rápidamente. Cerca del mediodía, el cuerpo VI de la Unión llegó para relevar a los caballeros. A las 4 el cuerpo XVIII también llegó y los dos cuerpos atacaron a los Confederados. La línea sureña fue empujada para atrás en algunos sitios y en un sitio fue abierta una brecha. Un contraataque Confederado finalmente repulsó a los Federales, pero Grant creía que un ataque fuerte y bien coordinado más le daría posesión del área de Cold Harbor. Grant ordenó que el cuerpo II de Hancock marchara por toda la noche y que estuviera listo para atacar por la mañana. Sin embargo, el hambre, el calor, y el agotamiento retardaron la marcha del cuerpo II. Esto causó que Grant pospusiera el ataque hasta las 5 de la tarde. La condición de los soldados causó otra vez que se pospusiera el ataque, ahora fijado para las 4:30 de la mañana, el 3 de junio. Mientras tanto, este día extra le dio a Lee el tiempo que necesitaba para reforzar sus líneas y hacer trincheras.

En el día 3 llegó la hora para el asalto. Los tres cuerpos Federales, el II, el VI, y el XVIII empezaron su avance — un ataque frontal de 2 1/2 millas. Los veteranos Confederados esperaron hasta que las líneas azules llegaron cerca. Entonces una "rafaga de volcan de sonido y fuego" hizo erupción por toda la línea sureña. Las líneas Federales se desmenuzaron a montones. Sólamente las tropas de Hancock llegaron a las defensas Confederadas, pero ellos, también, fueron aplastados por el fuego de rifle y canister.

El asalto tardó menos de media hora. La batalla había terminado, pero los ejércitos se quedaron en sus trincheras hasta el 12 de junio cuando Grant, en secreto, salió para Petersburg al sur.

CONSECUENCIAS

La guerra en el este se hizo una guerra de trincheras.

Grant nunca haría otro asalto frontal a una posición del enemigo atrincherado.

Fue la última victoria para Lee en el campo.

KOMMENTAR

Cold Harbor, eine alte Taverne, die sich an einer Kreuzung 13 Kilometer von Richmond entfernt befand, war die letzte große Schlacht auf offenem Feld, ehe sich beide Armeen auf die lange Belagerung von Petersburg vorbereiteten.

Früh am 31. Mai erreichte die Kavallerie, unter Konföderations general Fitz Lee, die Kreuzung. General Sheridan's Nordkavallerie, bewaffnet mit Spencer Repetierkarabinern, trieb die Südstaatler heraus und nahm Cold Harbor in Besitz.

Am 1. Juni befahl Lee General Anderson's Infanterie vorzurücken, um die Föderalistenkavallerie aus der Stellung zu werfen. Der Rückschlag von zwei Angriffen der Konföderierten war den schnell feuernden Spencer Repetiergewehren zu verdanken. Gegen Mittag kam das 6. Korps der Union an, um die Kavallerie abzulösen. Mit der Ankunft des 18. Korps um 16.00 Uhr, griffen nun beide Korps die Konföderierten an. Hier und da wurde die Südlinie zurückgedrängt und an einer Stelle gelang es, eine Bresche zu schlagen. Endlich wurden die Nordstaatler durch einen Gegenangriff der Konföderierten abgewehrt. Jedoch Grant glaubte, daß ein letzter, stark koordinierter Angriff ihm das Gebiet um Cold Harbor in seine Gewalt bringen könnte. General Grant befahl dem 2. Korps von General Hancock, die ganze Nacht hindurch zu marschieren, um am frühen Morgen zum Angriff bereit zu sein. Hunger, Hitze und Erschöpfung verzögerten jedoch den Marsch des 2. Korps. Dies forderte Grant, den Angriff bis auf 17.00 Uhr zu verschieben. Später veranlaßte der Zustand der Soldaten den Angriff nocheinmal weiter zu verschieben, diesmal bis auf 4.30 Uhr am 3. Juni. Mittlerweile gab dieser zusätzliche Tag Lee die notwendige Zeit, seine Linien zu verstärken und Schützengräben auszuheben.

Am 3. Juni kam die Zeit zum Angriff. Die drei Unionkorps — das 2., 6., und 18. — traten auf einen frontalen Angriff mit einer Länge von 4 Kilometern an. Die Konföderierten warteten, bis die blauen Linien in unmittelbarer Nähe waren. Eine Explosion von Lärm und Flammen brach aus der Südlinie — die Unionlinien fielen reihenweise um. Nur Hancock's Truppen konnten die Gräben erreichen, aber auch sie wurden bald vom Feuer der Gewehre und Kartätschen zerfetzt.

Der Sturm dauerte weniger als eine halbe Stunde. Die Schlacht war vorüber, aber die Armeen verblieben bis 12. Juni in den Gräben, als Grant sich im geheimen nach Süden, in Richtung Petersburg, wegschlich.

BEDEUTUNG

Der Kriegsschauplatz im Osten wurde zum Stellungskrieg, als beide Armeen sich eingruben.

Grant würde nie wieder einen frontalen Angriff gegen einen eingegrabenen Feind versuchen.

Es war Lee's letzter, grosser Sieg auf dem Feld.

Collecting the remains of the dead on the battlefield for reinterment after the war.

State: Virginia

U.S.

Commanders: Lt. Gen. U.S. Grant
Maj. Gen. George G. Meade
U.S. Army: Army of the Potomac
No. of Troops: 112,000
Casualties:
Killed: 5,100
Wounded: 24,800
Captured or missing: 17,500

C.S.

Commander: Gen. Robert E. Lee
C.S. Army: Army of Northern
Virginia
No. of Troops: 65,000
Casualties:
28,000 total killed, wounded, and
captured

COMMENTS

After the disastrous defeat at Cold Harbor, Grant secretly moved his army south. On June 15th Gen. Smith and Hancock were ordered to attack the weak Confederate defenses around Petersburg. A few outer works were taken but the Federals fumbled the greater opportunity of capturing Petersburg before Lee's army arrived from Cold Harbor. By the 18th Lee's men were filling up the trenches around Petersburg. After Grant's first attempts at dislodging the Confederates (costing him over 11,000 men and gaining little) both armies settled in for a long siege.

Grant's strategy was to continue extending his lines south toward the roads and railroads that supplied Richmond and Petersburg. To oppose Grant, Lee would have to stretch his already thin lines. Grant started lengthening his lines in late June. From the 22nd to the 24th two Union infantry corps attempted to capture the Weldon Railroad which supplied Lee's army from North Carolina. The Confederates repulsed the Federals and remained in control of the railroad.

In July a regiment of Pennsylvania coal miners dug a mine under the Confederate lines. The tunnel was filled with gunpowder and exploded. But the Federal infantry attack following the blast was unorganized and was completely repulsed.

In August Grant turned to the west again. This time the Northerners captured the Weldon Railroad and further extended their lines to the south and west. In February 1865, Union troops advanced toward the Boydton Plank Road. At the Battle of Hatcher's Run the Confederates suffered heavy losses but defeated the Federals and kept Boydton Road open. On March 25th, in an attempt to relieve pressure on his lines, Lee took the offensive and seized Fort Stedman along with a mile of the Federal line. The Union troops counterattacked and after serious fighting regained control of the fort inflicting 3,500 casualties on the rebels.

On April 1 Grant again tried to out-flank the Confederates southwest of Petersburg. At the Battle of Five Forks his plans finally succeeded as cavalry and infantry under Gen. Sheridan smashed the defending Confederates. The next morning another Union assault caused Lee's defenses to crumble. The remnants of the Army of Northern Virginia withdrew from Petersburg and on the morning of April 3 the city was in federal hands.

SIGNIFICANCE

The siege of Petersburg prolonged the war.
The fall of Petersburg meant that Richmond would capitulate.

Etat: Virginie

Etats-Unis

Commandants:
Lieutenant Général U. S. Grant
Général de Division George G.
Meade
Armée: du Potomac
112 000 soldats
Pertes:
Tués: 5 100
Blessés: 24 800
Prisonniers ou disparus: 17 500

Etats Confédérés

Commandants:
Général Robert E. Lee

Armée: de Virginie du Nord
65 000 soldats
Pertes totales:
Tués, blessés ou prisonniers:
28 000

COMMENTAIRE

Après le désastre de Cold Harbor, Grant déplaça secrètement son armée vers le sud. Le 15 juin, les généraux Smith et Hancock reçurent l'ordre d'attaquer les défenses faibles des Confédérés près de Petersburg. Une petite quantité de matériel fut capturée, mais les Fédéraux perdirent leur meilleure occasion de prendre Petersburg avant que les armées de Lee arrivent de Cold Harbor. Le 18, les hommes de Lee remplissaient les tranchées autour de Petersburg. Après les premiers essais de Grant de les déloger en perdant 11 000 hommes, les deux armées s'installèrent pour un long siège.

La stratégie de Grant était de continuer à étendre ses lignes vers le sud en direction des routes et chemins de fer qui approvisionnaient Richmond et Petersburg. Pour faire face à Grant, Lee devrait allonger ses lignes déjà maigres. Fin juin, Grant commança à étendre ses lignes. Du 22 au 24, deux corps d'infanterie de l'Union essayèrent de prendre le chemin de fer de Weldon qui approvisionnait l'armée de Lee depuis la Caroline du Nord. Les Confédérés repoussèrent les Fédéraux et restèrent maîtres du chemin de fer.

En juin, un régiment de mineurs de charbon pennsylvaniens creusa une mine sous les lignes des Confédérés. Le tunnel, rempli de poudre à canon, explosa. L'attaque fédérale qui suivit fut cependant trop désorganisée pour réussir.

En août, Grant se tourna à nouveau vers l'ouest. Cette fois, les Nordistes prirent le chemin de fer de Weldon et étendirent leurs lignes au sud et à l'ouest. En février 1865, les troupes de l'Union s'approchèrent de Boydton Plank Road. A la bataille de Hatcher's Run les Confédérés souffrirent de grandes pertes mais ils défirent les Fédéraux et gardèrent la route de Boydton ouverte. Le 25 mars, pour essayer d'alléger la pression sur ses lignes, Lee prit l'offensive et s'empara du Fort Stedman et d'une partie de la ligne fédérale. Les troupes de l'Union contre-attaquèrent et reprirent le contrôle du fort, après une lutte serrée infligeant 3 500 morts aux rebelles.

Le 1er avril, Grant essaya à nouveau de prendre les Confédérés de flanc au sud-est de Petersburg. A la bataille de Five Forks, ses plans réussirent et la cavalerie et l'infanterie du général Sheridan écrasèrent les Confédérés. Le matin suivant, une autre attaque de l'Union démolit les défenses de Lee. Les restes de l'armée de Virginie du Nord se retirèrent de Petersburg et le matin de 3 avril la ville était aux mains des Fédéraux.

CONSEQUENCES

Le siège de Petersburg prolongea la guerre.
La capitulation de Petersburg préparait celle de Richmond.

Important Landmarks
Appomattox River
Boydton Plank Road
Fort Stedman
Fort Wadsworth
Fort Mahone
Hatcher's Run
Gracie's Dam
Fort Fisher
Weldon R.R.
Dimmock Line
Battery 5
Fort Gregg
The Crater
Fort Haskell
Fort Davis
Fort Lee

Important Buildings
Globe Tavern site
St. Paul's Episcopal Church
Poplar Grove Church site
Turnbull House site
Blandford Church
Peebles' Farm site

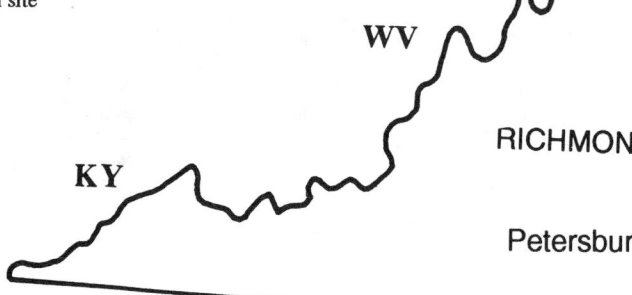

Estado: Virginia

U.S.	C.S.
Comandante:	**Comandante:**
Lt. Gen. U.S. Grant	Gen. Robert E. Lee
Maj. Gen. G.G. Meade	C.S. Ejército: Army of Northern
U.S. Ejército: Army of the Potomac	Virginia
No. de tropas: 112,000	No. de tropas: 65,000
Pérdidas:	Pérdidas:
28,000 muertos, heridos, y	Muertos: 5,100
capturados	Heridos: 24,800
	Capturados o ausentes: 17,500

COMENTARIO

Después del desastre de la derrota en Cold Harbor, Grant, en secreto, trasladó su ejército al sur. El 15 de junio los Generales Smith y Hancock fueron mandados a atacar las defensas débiles Confederadas alrededor de Petersburg. Algunas de las defensas exteriores fueron tomadas pero los Federales perdieron la oportunidad más grande de capturar Petersburg antes de que el ejército de Lee llegara desde Cold Harbor. El 18 las tropas de Lee ya llenaban las trincheras alrededor de Petersburg. Después de unos intentos por Grant de desalojar a los Confederados (costándole más de 11,000 hombres y ganando poco) los dos ejércitos se pusieron a un asedio largo.

La estrategia de Grant era seguir extendiendo sus líneas al sur hacia las carreterras y ferrocarriles que traían provisiones a Richmond y Petersburg. Para oponerse a Grant, Lee tendría que alargar sus líneas ya muy estrechas. Grant comenzó a extender sus líneas a finales de junio. Desde el 22 hasta el 24 dos cuerpos de infantería de la Unión intentaron capturar el ferrocarril Weldon que suplía al ejército de Lee desde North Carolina. Los Confederados repulsaron a los Federales y quedaron en control del ferrocarril.

En julio un regimiento de mineros de Pennsylvania excavaron una mina debajo de las líneas Confederadas. El túnel se llenó con pólvora y explotó. Pero el ataque hecho por la infantería Federal fue muy desorganizado y fue complétamente repulsado.

En agosto Grant se volvió al oeste de nuevo. Esta vez los Yanquis capturaron Weldon Railroad y extendieron sus líneas más al sur y al oeste. En febrero, 1865, tropas Federales avanzaron hacia el Boydton Plank Road. En la batalla de Hatcher's Run los Confederados sufrieron muchas pérdidas pero derrotaron a los Federales y mantuvieron abierto Boydton Plank Road. El 25 de marzo, en un intento de relevar presión en sus líneas, Lee tomó la ofensiva, y capturó Fort Stedman y una milla de la línea Federal. Los Yanquis contraatacaron y después de una lucha seria reganaron el control del fuerte infligiendo 3,500 pérdidas a los Rebeldes.

El 1 de abril Grant, de nuevo, trató de flanquear a los Confederados al sudoeste de Petersburg. En la batalla de Five Forks sus planes finálmente tuvieron éxito por la caballería e infantería del Gen. Sheridan que aplastaron a los Confederados que defendían. La próxima mañana otro asalto Federal causó que las defensas de Lee se cayeran. Lo que quedaba de Army of Northern Virginia se retiró de Petersburg y por la mañana del 3 de abril la ciudad estaba en las manos de la Unión.

CONSECUENCIAS

El asedio de Petersburg prolongó la guerra.

La caída de Petersburg significó que Richmond recapitulara.

Staat: Virginia

Befehlshaber der US:	Befehlshaber der CS:
Generalleutnant U.S. Grant	General Robert E. Lee
Generalmajor George G. Meade	
Armee der CS: Armee des Potomac	Armee der CS: Armee von Nord-
Truppenstärke: 112,000	virginia
Verluste:	Truppenstärke: 65,000
Gefallen: 5,100	Verluste
Verwundet: 24,800	Insgesamt 28,000 gefallen,
Gefangengenommen oder vermißt:	verwundet gefangengenommen
17,500	oder vermißt

KOMMENTAR

Nach der katastrophalen Niederlage bei Cold Harbor zog Grant seine Armee im geheimen nach Süden. Am 15. Juni wurden Generale Smith und Hancock befohlen, die schwachen Konföderierten Verteidigungsanlagen um Petersburg anzugreifen. Einige außerhalb liegenden Anlagen wurden erobert, aber die Föderalisten verpfuschten die beste Gelegenheit, vor Lee's Ankunft von Cold Harbor, Petersburg zu erobern, denn am 18. besetzten Lee's Truppen schon die Schutzengräben, die Petersburg umringten. Nach Grant's wiederholten Versuchen, die Konföderierten zu verdrängen (was ihm über 11,000 Mann kostete, aber wenig bewirkte), vorbereiteten sich beide Armeen auf eine lange Belagerung.

Grant's Strategie war, seine Linien immer weiter südwärts auszudehnen, bis an die Landstraßen und Eisenbahnstrecken, die Richmond und Petersburg versorgten. Um sich Grant entgegenstellen zu können, mußte General Lee seine eigenen, dünnen Linien noch weiter ausdehnen. Im späten Juni begann Grant, seine Linien zu verlängern. Vom 22. bis zum 24. versuchten zwei Infanteriekorps der Union den Weldon Railroad zu erobern. Diese Eisenbahnstrecke beförderte Nachschub von Nordcarolina für Lee's Armee. Die Konföderierten wehrten die Föderalisten ab und behielten die Kontrolle der Eisenbahnstrecke.

Im Juli grub ein Regiment von Bergarbeitern aus dem Staat Pennsylvania ein Tunnel unter den Linien der Konföderierten. Sie sprengten das Tunnel, nachdem sie es mit Pulver gefüllt hatten. Der Angriff der Föderalisteninfanterie, der auf die Explosion folgte, war nicht gut organisiert und wurde total zurückgeschlagen.

Im August wendete sich Grant wieder nach Westen. Die Nordstaatler eroberten diesmal die Weldon Eisenbahn und dehnten ihre Linien weiter nach Süden und Westen aus. Im Februar 1865 rückten Uniontruppen in Richtung Boydton Plank Road vor. Bei der Schlacht von Hatchers Run erlitten die Konföderierten schwere Verluste, trotzdem aber besiegten sie die Föderalisten und hielten Boydton Plank Road offen. Lee, um den feindlichen Druck auf seine Linien Zu erleichtern, ging am 25. März auf die Offensive und eroberte Fort Stedman und eine anderthalb Kilometer lange Strecke der Föderalistenlinie. Die Uniontruppen trugen einen Gegenangriff aus und, einen schweren kampf, der 3,500 Verluste forderte brachten sie das Fort wieder in ihre Gewalt.

Am 1. April versuchte Grant wiederholt, südwestlich der Stadt Petersburg die Flanke der Konföderierten zu umfassen. Bei der Schlacht von Five Forks hatten seine Pläne endlich Erfolg, als die Kavallerie und Infanterie, unter General Sheridan, die südstaatliche Verteidigung zerbrachen. Am folgenden Morgen zwang ein weiterer Unionangriff Lee's Verteidigung zur Auflösung. Der überrest der Armee von Nordvirginia zog sich von Petersburg zurück, und am Morgen des 3. April war die Stadt in den Händen der Föderalisten.

BEDEUTUNG

Die Belagerung von Petersburg verlängerte den Krieg.

Der Fall von Petersburg kündete die Kapitulation von Richmond an.

The interior of Confederate Fort Mahone after its evacuation.

C.S.S. ALABAMA vs. U.S.S. KEARSARGE
June 19th, 1864

Location: Atlantic Ocean near Cherbourg France		Local: Océan Atlantique près de Cherbourg, France	
U.S.	**C.S.**	**Etats-Unis**	**Etats Confédérés**
Commander:	Commander:	Commandant:	Commandant:
Capt. John Winsolw	Capt. Raphael Semmes	Capitaine John Winslow	Capitaine Rafael Semmes
U.S. Ship: U.S.S. Kearsarge	C.S. Ship: C.S.S. Alabama	Vaisseau: U.S.S. Kearsarge	Vaisseau: C.S.S. Alabama
Crew Compliment: 163	Crew Compliment: 145	Equipage: 163	Equipage: 145
Casualties:	Casualties:	Pertes:	Pertes:
Killed: 0	Killed: 26	Tués: 0	Tués: 26
Wounded: 3	Wounded: 21	Blessés: 3	Blessés: 21
Captured or Missing: 0	Captured or Missing: 64	Prisonniers ou disparus: 0	Prisonniers ou disparus: 64

COMMENTS

The Confederate States, with their limited ship building equipment and facilities, negotiated with English firms to build Confederate naval vessels. The Confederate screw sloop Alabama, built in Liverpool England, became the most famous of these. Alabama, also known as ship number 290 (being the 290th ship built in Liverpool ship yards), was designed to be a Confederate raider of commerce. She performed her duty well. In 23 months of service, she captured or destroyed no less than 63 naval vessels, including the Union warship U.S.S. Hatteras.

The Alabama left Liverpool on July 29, 1862, under an English flag and despite protest from the U.S. Government, she sailed for the Azores to be armed and supplied. She operated mostly in the Atlantic Ocean and never dropped anchor in a Southern port. She stopped at foreign ports where she could be provisioned.

The Union warship Kearsarge on June 14, 1864, took up position off the French port of Cherbourg and waited to destroy Alabama, in port for supplies. Capt. Semmes of the Alabama wanted to grant shore leave for his tired crew, but on seeing Kearsarge, he prepared to meet her in battle. Semmes, noting a challenge, sent a note to the Kearsarge requesting them to wait for him.

On the 19th the Alabama steamed out to sea. Capt. Winslow of the Kearsarge, not wanting to risk an international incident, positioned his ship between six and seven miles off shore. At 11:00 A.M. the firing began and the ships moved in a circular pattern with 900 yards separating them. The Kearsarge was stuck n 28 places by shot and shell, including a 100 pound shell which lodged in the stern post and did not explode! Covered by chain armor on the sides, Kearsarge suffered little damage. The Alabama was hit by many Union shells during the engagement until the hull was punctured and the ship began to sink. Capt. Semmes, seeing no alternative, ordered his men to abandon ship. Several Confederate sailors were picked up by the Kearsarge and made prisoners of war, while Capt. Semmes and others swam to the safety of several neutral boats nearby. One of these was the English steam yacht Deerhound and the others were French pilot boats. The Alabama was finally sunk and she would no longer pose a threat to Union merchant ships.

SIGNIFICANCE

Resulted in the destruction of the Confederacy's best known commerce raider.

COMMENTAIRE

Les Confédérés, leur capacité de construire des vaisseaux étant très limité, néqociaient avec des chantiers anglais pour la construction des vaisseaux pour leur marine. Le sloop confédéré à hélice Alabama, constuit à Liverpool en Angleterre, fut le plus célèbre. L'Alabama, dit aussi vaisseau 290, étant le 290ième Vaisseau construit à Liverpool, fut destiné à être un corsaire. Il fit bien son devoir. En 23 mois de service, il captura ou detruisit 63 vaisseaux, y compris le navire de guerre, l'U.S.S. Hatteras.

L'Alabama quitta Liverpool le 29 juillet hissant pavillon anglaise, et malgré les protestations du gouvenement des Etats-Unis, il fila vers les Açores où il reçut son armement et provisions. Il opérait principalement en Atlantique et ne mouillait jamais dans un port sudiste; il faisait escale aux ports étrangers où il pouvait s'approvisionner.

Le 14 juillet 1864, le navire de guerre U.S.S. Kearsarge prit position au large du port français de Cherbourg, où l'Alabama était en train de s'approvisionner. Le capitaine Semmes voulait permettre ses hommes fatigués de visiter la ville, mais en voyant le Kearsarge, il décida de le combattre. Semmes envoya une note à Winslow lui priant de l'attendre.

Le 19, L'Alabama quitta le port. Le caitaine Winslow, désireux déeviter un incident international l'attendait entre six et sept milles au large. A 11 heures la bataille commença. Les deux vaisseaux tournèrent en deux circles concentriques, ouvrant le feu à 900 mètres. Le combat durait une heure. Le Kearsarge reçut 28 impacts, y compris un obus de 100 livres qui, heuresement, n'explosa pas. Sa coque fut ccovverte d'un blindage de chaines, et par conséquent, le Kearsarge souffrit peu de dommage. L'Alabama encaissa beaucoup de coups et commença à couler. La capitaine Semmes fut forcé de donner l'ordre d'abandooner le vaisseau. Plusieurs marins confédérés fut ramassés par le Kearsarge et faits prisonniers de guerre pendant que le capitaine Semmes et autres se sauvèrent à la nage et se réfugièrent dans des bateaux à proximité. Un ce ces bateaux fut le yacht à vapeur anglais Deerhound. Les autres furent des bateaux de pilotage français. L'Alabamau ne menacerait plus les navires fédéraux.

CONSEQUENCE

Le meilleur corsaire confédéré fut au fond de la mer.

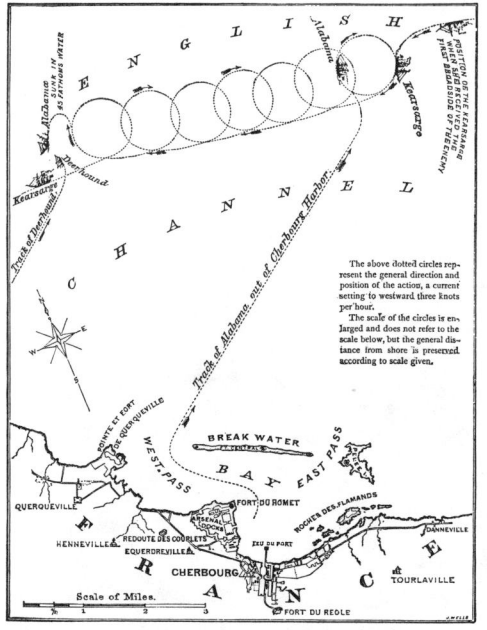

CHART OF THE ACTION OFF CHERBOURG.

Important Landmarks
The French coastline
The Cherbourg port

Ubicación: El Océano Atlántico cerca de Cherbourg, Francia

U.S.	C.S.
Comandante:	**Comandante:**
Capitán John Winslow	Capitán Raphael Semmes
Buque: U.S.S. Kearsarge	**Buque:** C.S.S. Alabama
Tripulación: 163	Tripulación: 145
Pérdidas:	**Pérdidas:**
Muertos: 0	Muertos: 26
Heridos: 3	Heridos: 21
Capturados o desaparecidos: 0	Capturados o desaparecidos: 64

COMENTARIOS

Los Estados Confederados con un equipo de construcción y facilidades limitadas, negociaron con firmas inglesas para construir buques de guerra confederados. El Confederado screw sloop Alabama, construído en Liverpool, Inglaterra llegó a ser el más famoso de estos. Alabama, también conocido como el barco número 290 (por ser el barco 290 construído en el arsenal de Liverpool), fue diseñado para ser el de las correrías comerciales. Hizo su trabajo bien. En 23 meses de servicio, capturó o destruyó no menos de 63 buques de guerra, incluyendo el buque de guerra U.S.S. Hatteras de la Unión.

El Alabama salió de Liverpool el 29 de julio de 1862 bajo una bandera inglesa y a pesar de la protesta del gobierno de los Estados Unidos, salió para las Azores para ser armado y abastecido. Casi siempre operó en el Océano Atlántico y nunco echó anclas en un puerto sureño. Paró en puertos extranjeros donde pdía ser surtido.

El buque de guerra Kearsarge de la Unión el 14 de junio de 1864 tomó posición fuera del puerto francés de Cherbourg y esperó para destruir el Alabama en el puerto para abastecimientos. El capitán Semmes de Alabama quería darle permiso a su cansada tripulación para ir a tierra, pero viendo el Kearsarge, él se preparó para encontrarlo en batalla. Semmes, viendo un desafío, mandó un mensaje al Kearsarge, pidiendo que lo esperaran.

El 19 el Alabama tomó rumbo hacia el mar. El capitán Winslow del Kearsarge, no queriendo correr el riesgo de un incidente internacional colocó su nave a 6 o 7 millas de la costa. A las 11:00 de la mañana el fuego empezó y los barcos se movieron en un patrón circular de 900 yardas separándolos. La hora de batalla costó cara a ambos barcos y a sus tripulaciones. El Kearsarge fur golpeado en 28 lugares por balas y bombas, incluyendo una bomba de 100 libras que se clavó en la posta de la popa y no explotó. Cubierto por una coraza a los lados, Kearsarge sufrió poco daño. El Alabama fue golpeado por tantas bombas de la Unión durante el encuentro hasta que el casco fue agujereado y el buque empezó a hundirse. El capitán Semmes, no viendo ninguna alternativa, ordenó a sus hombres que abandonaran el buque. Varios marineros confederados fueron recogidos por el Kearsarge y fueron hechos prisioneros de guerra, mientras que el capitán Semmes y otros nadaron a la seguirdad de algunos botes neutrales cercanos. Uno de estos fue el yate de vapor inglés Deerhound y los otros fueron botes franceses de cabotaje. El Alabama fue finalmente hundido y nunca más sería una amenaza a los barcos mercantes de la Unión.

CONSECUENCIAS

Resultó en la destrucción del más conocido de correría comerciales.

Lokale: Atlantischer Ozeab in der Nähe von Cherbourg, Frankreich

US Kommandant:	CS Kommandant:
Kapitän John Winslow	Kapitän Raphael Semmes
U.S. Ship: U.S.S. Kearsarge	CS Ship: C.S.S. Alabama
Schiffsmannschaft: 163	Schiffsmannschaft: 145
Verluste:	Verluste:
Gefallen: 0	Gefallen: 26
Verwundet: 3	Verwundet: 21
Gefangengenommen oder vermißt: 0	Gefangengenommen oder vermißt: 64

KOMMENTAR

Die Konföderierten Staaten, begrenzt im Schiffbau und notwendigen Schiffsanlagen, verhandelten mit Englischen Firmen in Bezug auf den Bau von Konföderierten Marineschiffen. Die Konföderierte Korvette Alabama, in England gebaut, bekam die berühmteste von ihrer Klasse. Alabama, also bekannt als Schiff No. 290 (was bedeuted, daß dieses Schiff das 290te war, das beim Liverpool Schiffsbau gebaut wurde), hatte die Aufgabe als Handelszerstörer auf See für die Konföderations zu wirken. Sie führte ihre Pflichten exemplarisch aus. In 23 Monaten im Dienst, erbeutete oder zerstörte sie 63 Marineschiffe, einbegriffen das Union Kriegsschiff U.S.S. Hatteras.

Die Alabama, unter Englischer Flagge, verließ am 29. Juli 1862 Liverpool und, trotz Protesten der US Regierung, steuerte auf die Azoren, wo sie Bewaffnung und Provianten erhielt. Ihre Operationen waren zum größten Teil auf dem Atlantischen Ozean ausgetragen - sie ankerte niemals in einem südlichen Hafen. Für Provisionen lief sie in ausländischen Hafen ein.

Am 14. Juni 1864 nahm das Unionkriegsschiff Kearsarge ihre Stellung ausserhalb des Cherbourg Hafens, um die Alabama, welche Provisionen im dortigen Hafen aufnahm, zu überraschen und sie zu zerstören. Kapitän Semmes hatte geplant, seinen müden Mannschaften Landurlaub zu gewähren, sah die Kearsarge und traf Vorbereitungen zur Schlacht. Semmes, der Kearsarge's Stellung als ein Zeichen zur Herausforderung annahm, sandte eine Note zur Kearsarge, mit der Aufforderung, auf ihn zu warten.

Am 19. zog die Alabama auf See. Um einen internationalen Skandal zu vermeiden, nahm Kapitän Winslow seine Stellung etwa 10 km von der Küste entfernt auf. Um 11:00 Uhr begann das Feuer - die Schiffe manövrierten kreisförmig, 850 Meter Entfernung zwischen den Gegnern. Der stundenlange Kampf brachte Verluste zu Schiffen und Mannschaften auf beiden Seiten. Die Kearsarge wurde in 28 Stellen von Granaten und Geschoßen getroffen, einbegriffen einer 90 Pfd schweren Granate, die im Achtersteven steckenblieb und nicht explodierte! Kearsarge, deren Seiten mit Kettenarmour bedeckt waren, erlitt wenig Schaden. Die Alabama nahm viele Volltreffer von Uniongeschützen - ihr Rumpf war durchlöchert und sie begann zu sinken. Kapitän Semmes, ohne einen weiteren Ausweg zu finden, befahl seiner Mannschaft, das Schiff zu verlaßen. Etliche Konföderierte Matrosen wurden von Kearsarge als Kriegsgefangene vom Wasser aufgenommen. Kapitän Semmes und ein Teil seiner Mannschaften schwam men zur Sicherheit von neutralen Booten in der Nähe. Eines dieser Boote war die Englische Dampf Jacht Deerhound, die anderen waren Französische Pilotenboote. Endlich war die Alabama gesunken und keine Bedrohung ihrerseits war weiterhin zu befürchten.

BEDEUTUNG

Diese Seeschlacht endete mit der Zerstörung des berühmtesten Handelszerstörers der Konföderierten.

The U.S.S. Kearsarge preparing to fire on the C.S.S. Alabama.

State: Georgia

U.S.

Commander:
  Maj. Gen. William T. Sherman
U.S. Army: Military Division of the
  Mississippi
No. of Troops: 100,000
Casualties:
  3,900 total killed, wounded, and
  captured

C.S.

Commander:
  Gen. Joseph E. Johnston
C.S. Army: Army of Tennessee
No. of Troops: 50,000

Casualties:
  2,800 total killed, wounded, and
  captured

(June 14—Pine Mtn. to June 27—Kennesaw Mtn.)

COMMENTS

During the first seven weeks of the Atlanta Campaign, Gen. Sherman had been constantly sidestepping the Southern army in an attempt at attacking Johnston's flanks. But the Confederates kept slipping away, moving to new entrenched positions every time.

By late June Johnston was positioned on high ground two miles from Marietta, GA. His lines were stretched seven miles. The Confederate left rested on Olley's Creek while the center and right ran north along a ridgeline culminating at Kennesaw Mountain. This position featured steep slopes covered with trees and large boulders with the Confederates entrenched at the summit. Gen. Sherman, unable to attempt another movement around the enemy's flank because recent rains turned the roads to mud, was induced to try a frontal assault.

On the 26th Gen. Schofield was ordered to "demonstrate" against the Confederate left at Olly's Creek. To everyone's surprise, Schofield gained a foothold on the south bank of the stream. But Sherman didn't exploit these gains; he decided to stay with his original plan of attacking the center and right.

The next day at 6:00 a.m. Sherman's army started up the slopes. At Kennesaw Mountain troops from the 15th Army Corps skirmished for two hours with Confederates of Gen. Loring's Corps. Then the Federals rushed up the hill and, after rough hand-to-hand fighting with bayonets and clubbed muskets they captured the first line of works. But rushing up to Loring's main position, the Yankees were met with a blaze of musket and cannon fire. Hundreds of soldiers fell, the survivors huddled behind trees and rocks, unable to advance or retreat without being exposed to the deadly fire.

Meanwhile the Confederate center was assaulted in two spots by troops under Generals Davis and Newton. Gen. Davis' men advanced up the slope and captured a line of trenches only to be slaughtered as they headed for the main enemy works. Newton fared no better as his men were raked by canister and were forced to flee on this and a second assault. By noon the Union defensive was over.

SIGNIFICANCE

The Confederates handed Sherman his worst defeat of the Atlanta Campaign at Kennesaw Mountain. They also delayed Sherman's advance on Atlanta for a few days, but in the end Sherman's superior numbers made up for this single defeat.

Etat: Georgie

Etats-Unis

Commandant: Général de Division
  William T. Sherman
Armée: Division du Mississipi
  100 000 soldats
Pertes totales:
  Tués, blessés et prisonniers: 3 900

Etats Confédérés

Commandant:
  Général Joseph E. Johnston
Armée: du Tennessee
  50 000 soldats
Pertes totales:
  Tués, blessés et prisonniers: 2 800

(Batailles du 14 juin à Pine Mountain au 17 juin à Kennesaw Mountain)

COMMENTAIRE

Pendant les sept premières semaines de la campagne d'Atlanta, le général Sherman avait constamment esquivé l'armée sudiste pour tenter de prendre Johnston de flanc. Mais les Confédérés s'éclipsaient toujours, se déplaçant à chaque fois dans de nouvelles tranchées.

Fin juin, Johnston était posté sur une hauteur, à environ trois kilomètres de Marietta en Georgie. Ses lignes s'étiraient sur une dizaine de kilomètres. La gauche des Confédérés était à Olley's Creek tandis que le centre et la droite montaient au nord le long de crêtes culminant à Kennesaw Mountain. Cette position était caractérisée par des pentes raides couvertes d'arbres et de gros rochers; les Confédérés étaient au sommet dans leurs tranchées. A cause des pluies récentes qui avaient transformé les routes en boue, le général Sherman dut renoncer à son attaque de flanc et il fut réduit à attaquer de front.

Le 26, le général Schofield dut faire une démonstration contre les Confédérés à Olley's Creek. A la surprise de tous, Sholfield gagna la rive sud d'Olley's Creek. Mais, décidant de s'en tenir à sa décision d'attaquer au centre et à droite, Sherman ne put profiter de cet avantage.

Le jour suivant à 6 heures, l'armée de Sherman commença à grimper. A Kennesaw Mountain, il y eut une escarmouche de deux heures entre les troupes du quinzième corps d'armée et les Confédérés du corps du général Loring. Puis les Fédéraux se précipitèrent vers le sommet; après de féroces luttes d'homme à homme à coups de baionnettes et de mousquets, ils prirent la première ligne. En atteignant la position principale de Loring, les Yankees furent pris dans une flambée de feu de canons et de mousquets. Des centaines de soldats tombèrent; les survivants s'aggripaient derrière les rochers, ne pouvant ni avancer ni reculer sans s'exposer aux feux meurtriers.

Pendant ce temps, le centre des Confédérés était assailli en deux points par les troupes des généraux Davis et Newton. Les hommes de Davis montèrent et prirent une ligne de tranchée avant d'etre massacrés alors qu'ils allaient atteindre l'essentiel des ouvrages défensifs confédérés. Newton n'alla pas loin non plus; ses hommes furent pris sous la mitraille et forcés à un second assaut. A midi, l'offensive de l'Union était terminée.

CONSEQUENCE

A Kennesaw Mountain, les Confédérés infligèrent à Sherman sa plus terrible défaite de la campagne d'Atlanta. Ils retardèrent aussi de quelques jours l'avance vers Atlanta. Cependant, sa supériorité en nombre permit à Sherman de rattraper cette seule défaite.

Important Landmarks
Pine Mountain
Mud Creek
Pigeon Hill
Horseshoe Bend
Hardee's Salient
Kennesaw Mountain
Cheatham Hill
Bald Knob
Lost Mountain
Little Kennesaw Mountain
Burnt Hickory Road

Important Buildings
Darby House
Gilgal Church
Oakton Kolb Farm
Oatman House
Lester House
Latimer Place
Fair Oaks

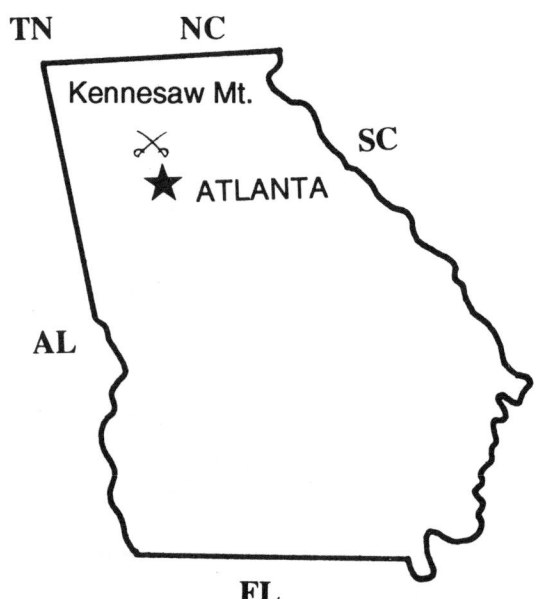

Estado: Georgia

U.S.	C.S.
Comandante:	Comandante:
Maj. Gen. William T. Sherman	Gen. Joseph E. Johnston
U.S. Ejército: Military Division of the Mississippi	C.S. Ejército: Army of Tennessee
No. de tropas: 100,000	No.de tropas: 50,000
Pérdidas:	Pérdidas:
3,900 muertos, heridos y capturados	2,800 muertos, heridos, y capturados

(14 de junio-Pine Mountain hasta el 27 de junio Kennesaw Mountain)

COMENTARIO

Durante las primeras siete semanas de la campaña de Atlanta, el General Sherman constántemente había estado haciéndose a un lado del ejército sureño en un intento de atacar los flancos de Johnston. Pero los Confederados continuámente desaparecían, moviéndose cada vez a unas nuevas posiciones entrincheradas.

A finales de junio Johnston estaba situado en tierra alta a dos millas de Marietta, Georgia. Sus líneas se extendían por siete millas. La izquierda Confederada descansaba en Olley's Creek mientras el centro y la derecha se extendían al norte por un terraplén culminando en Kennesaw Mountain. Esta posición tenía cuestas empinadas cubiertas de árboles y piedras grandes con los Confederados entrincherados en la cima. El General Sherman, no pudiendo hacer otro movimiento alrededor del flanco enemigo por las lluvias que habían convertido los caminos en barro, tuvo que intentar un asalto frontal.

El 26 el General Schofield fue mandado a "demostrar" contra la izquierda Confederada en Olley's Creek. Sorprendiendo a todo el mundo, Schofield ganó una posición establecida en la orilla del arroyo. Pero Sherman no se aprovechó de estas ganancias, decidiendo quedarse con su plan original de atacar el centro y la derecha.

El próximo día a las 6 de la mañana el ejército de Sherman empezó a subir las cuestas. En Kennesaw Mountain tropas del cuerpo XV escaramuzaron por dos horas con Confederados del cuerpo del General Loring. Con prisa los Federales subieron la cuesta y, después de una lucha violenta de cuerpo a cuerpo, luchando con bayonetas y rifles usados como bates, capturaron la primera línea de las defensas. Pero, corriendo a la posición principal de Loring, los Yanquis se encontraron con fuego de rifles y cañones. Cientos de soldados cayeron, los sobrevivientes se escondían detrás de árboles y piedras, no pudiendo avanzar ni retirarse sin exponerse al fuego letal.

Mientras tanto, el centro Confederado fue asaltado en dos sitios por tropas bajo los Generales Davis y Newton. Los hombres del General Davis subieron la cuesta y capturaron una línea de trincheras sólo para estar matados cuando se dirigieron para las defensas principales del enemigo. Newton no tuvo mejor resultado. Sus tropas fueron barridas por canister y tuvieron que huir en éste y un segundo asalto. Al mediodía la ofensiva Federal ya se acabó.

CONSECUENCIAS

Los Confederados le dieron a Sherman su peor derrota de la campaña de Atlanta en Kennesaw Mountain. También retrasaron el avance de Sherman a Atlanta por unos días, pero al final los números superiores de Sherman compensaron por esta derrota.

Staat: Georgia

Befehlshaber der US:	Befehlshaber der CS:
Generalmajor William T. Sherman	General Joseph E. Johnston
Armee der US: Militärdivision des Mississippi	Armee der CS: Armee von Tennessee
Truppenstärke: 100,000	Truppenstärke: 50,000
Verluste:	Verluste:
Insgesamt: 3,900 gefallen, verwundet gefangengenommen oder vermißt	Insgesamt: 2,800 gefallen, verwundet gefangengenommen oder vermißt

(14. Juni, Pine Mountain bis 27. Juni, Kennesaw Mountain)

KOMMENTAR

Während der ersten sieben Wochen der Atlanta Kampagne wich General Sherman fortwährend der Südarmee aus, in einem Versuch, Johnston's Flanken angreifen zu können. Die Konföderierten schlichen sich aber immer wieder weg und bezogen jedesmal neue, verschanzte Stellungen.

Spät im Juni befand sich Johnston auf einer Höhe, drei Kilometer von Marietta entfernt. Seine Linien erstreckten sich 11 Kilometer. Die linke Seite der Konföderierten lag am Olly's Creek, während der Mittelabschnitt und die rechte Seite nördlich an einem Kamm entlang liefen, der rechts auf dem Kennesaw Mountain auslief. Diese Stellung zeichnete sich durch steile Hänge aus, bedeckt nit Bäumen und grossen Felsen, mit den Konföderiertn auf dem Gipfel verschanzt. Landstraßen, die durch Regen verschlammt geworden waren, verhinderten weitere Umflankierungsversuche bei General Sherman. Dies bewegte ihn zu einem Frontalangriff.

Am 26. wurde General Schofield befohlen, am Olley's Creek gegen die Konföderierten zu "demonstrieren." Zu jedermanns Überraschung falße Schofield an südlichen Ufer Fuß. Sherman nutzte diesen Vorteil aber nicht aus, sondern entschloß sich, bei seinem ursprünglichen Plan zu bleiben, die Mitte und rechte Flanke anzugreifen.

Am folgenden Morgen, um 6.00 Uhr, begann Sherman's Armee den Aufstieg über die Hänge. An Kennesaw Mountain plänkelten Truppn vom 15. Armeekorps zwei Stunden lang mit Konföderierten von General Loring's Korps. Dann stürzten sich die Föderalisten auf den Berg. Nach einem rohen Nahkampf mit Bajonetten und Musketenkolben, eroberten sie die vorderste Linie der Schanzwerke. Als die Yankees sich aber auf Loring's Hauptstellung stürzten, rannten sie in einen Hagel von Musketen- und Kanonenfeuer. Hunderte von Soldaten fielen, die Überlebenden kauerten sich hinter Bäumen und Felsen, denn sie konnten weder vorrücken noch sich zurückziehen, ohne sich dem tödlichen Feuer auszusetzen.

Die Konföderiertenmitte wurde inzwischen an zwei Stellen von Truppen unter Generalen Davis und Newton angegriffen. General Davis' Truppen rückten mühsan den Abhang hinauf und eroberten eine Schanzlinie, aber wurden niedergemäht, als sie sich auf das Hauptschanzwerk drängten. Der Kampf ging nicht besser für Newton, denn seine Truppen wurden von Kartätschenfeuer bestrichen und beim ersten und zweiten Ansturm waren sie in die Flucht getrieben. Um 12.00 Uhr mittags war die Unionoffensive vorüber.

BEDEUTUNG

Am Kennesaw Mountain fügten die Konföderierten Sherman seine größte Niederlage in der Atlanta Kampagne zu. Sie hielten Sherman's Vormarsch nach Atlanta einige Tage auf, aber letzten Endes glich Sherman's zahlenmässige Überlegenheit diese Niederlage aus.

Federal trenches near the Burnt Hickory Road facing Little Kennesaw Mountain (left) and Pigeon Hill (right).

State: Virginia

U.S.	C.S.
Commander:	Commander:
Maj. Gen. Philip Sheridan	Lt. Gen. Jubal Early
U.S. Army: Army of the Shenandoah	C.S. Army: independent command
Army of West Virginia	No. of Troops: 20,000
No. of Troops: 43,000	
Casualties:	Casualties:
Killed: 644	Killed: 320
Wounded: 3,430	Wounded: 1,540
Captured or missing: 1,591	Captured or missing: 1,050

COMMENTS

Gen. Early and Sheridan had been "fighting it out" for months in the Shenandoah Valley. Sheridan had defeated the Confederates in the last three engagements (Winchester, Fishers Hill, and Tom's Brook). These losses had seriously reduced Early's army. But Gen. Early, always eager for a fight, approved a bold plan developed by Generals Gordon and Hotchkiss.

On Oct. 19th, five divisions of Early's army charged through thick fog, striking the Federal camp as the soldiers slept. In the early morning confusion, small groups of Union soldiers tried to stand and resist the oncoming Confederates, only to be swept away. The Union 6th Corps and the cavalry managed to form a line and repulsed several Confederate charges, but they were finally forced to retire. By 10:00 a.m. the Federals had been pushed to a position three miles from their camps.

Gen. Early was unable to pursue the Federals. Many of his troops stopped in the Federal camps to "enjoy the fruits of their victory." Also, Early needed time to regroup his scattered divisions. Finally he reformed his lines sensing victory.

Meanwhile the Yankees regrouped. Soon Gen. Sheridan arrived at the battlefield and, riding among his troops, reinstilled the fighting spirit in his men. At 4:00 p.m. the Northerners launched a counterattack. The Confederate battle line was pierced and soon crumbled. The Confederates fled southward in full retreat.

SIGNIFICANCE

This Federal disaster turned into a victory and ended the major fighting in the Shenandoah Valley.

The opposing forces returned to the Petersburg lines.

Etat: Virginie

Etats-Unis	Etats Confédérés
Commandant: Général de Division	Commandant: Lieutenant Général
Phillip Sheridan	Jubal Early
Armées du Shenandoa et de Virginie	Armée commandement indépendant
de l'Ouest	20 000 soldats
43 000 soldats	
Pertes:	Pertes:
Tués: 644	Tués: 320
Blessés: 3 430	Blessés: 1 540
Prisonniers ou disparus: 1 591	Prisonniers ou disparus: 1 050

COMMENTAIRE

Les généraux Early et Sheridan s'étaient battus pendant plusieurs mois dans la vallée du Shenandoah. Sheridan avait défait les Confédérés dans les trois dernièrs combats de Winchester, Fishers Hill et Tom's Brook. Ces pertes avaient prodigieusement réduit l'armée d'Early. Mais toujours pret à se battre, celui-ci approuva le plan audacieux organisé par les généraux Gordon et Hotchkiss.

Le 1 octobre, cinq divisions de l'armée d'Early chargèrent à travers un épais brouillard, et attaquèrent le camp fédéral où les soldats dormaient. Dans la confusion du petit matin, quelques groupes de l'Union essayèrent sans succès de s'opposer au attaquants. Le sixième corps d'armée et la cavalerie réussirent former une ligne et à repousser plusieurs assauts des Confédérés. Pourtant, ils finirent par etre forcés à la retraite. A 10 heures, ce matin-là, les Fédéraux avaient été repoussés à cinq kilomètres de leur camp.

Le Général Early fut incapable de puorsuivre les Fédéraux. Ses troupes voulaient rester dans le camp fédéral pour jouir du fruit de leur victoire. De plus, Early avait à regrouper ses divisions éparpillées. Finalement, sentant la victoire, il reforma ses lignes.

Pendant ce temps, les Yankees récupéraient. Le général Sheridan arriva bientot sur le champ de bataille, redonnant l'espoir à ses hommes. A 16 heures, les Nordistes lancèrent une conte-attaque. La ligne confédérée fut démantelée et perdue. Battus, les Confédérés filèrent de sud.

CONSEQUENCES

Ce désastre fédéral changé en victoire mit fin au combats du Shenandoah Valley.

Les forces opposées revinrent aux lignes de Petersburg.

Important Landmarks

Valley Turnpike
Cedar Creek
Middle Marsh Brook
Meadow Brook
North Branch of Shenandoah River
Hupp's Hill
Back Road
Three Top Mountain

Important Buildings

Belle Grove
Burnt Mills
Cooley House

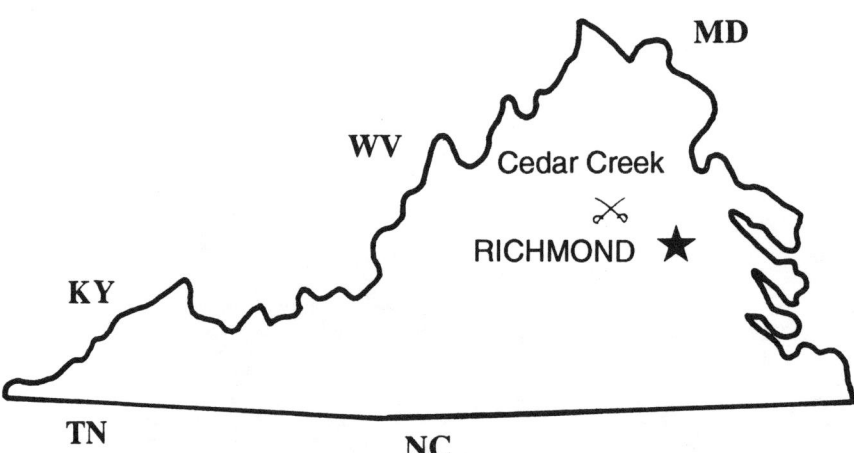

Estado: Virginia

U.S.
Comandnate:
 Maj. Gen. Phillip Sheridan
U.S. Ejército: Army of the Shenandoah
 Army of West Virginia
 No. de tropas: 43,000
Pérdidas:
 Muertos: 640
 Heridos: 3,430
 Capturados o ausentes: 1,591

C.S.
Comandante: Lt. Gen. Jubal Early

C.S. Ejército: comandancia
 independiente
 No. de tropas: 20,000
Pérdidas:
 Muertos: 320
 Heridos: 1,540
 Capturados o ausentes: 1,050

COMENTARIO

Los Generales Early y Sheridan habían estado luchando por meses en el valle Shenandoah. Sheridan había derrotado a los Confederados en las últimas tres batallas (Winchester, Fishers Hill y Tom's Brook). Estas derrotas habían reducido sériamente el ejército de Early. Pero el General Early, siempre ávido para una lucha, aprobó un plan intrépido desarollado por los Generales Gordon y Hotchkiss.

El 19 de octubre, cinco divisiones del ejército de Early atacaron a través de una niebla espesa, golpeando el campo Federal mientras los soldados dormían. En la confusión de la mañana temprana, pequeños grupos de soldados trataron de resistir a los Confederados, pero fueron barridos. El cuerpo VI Federal y la caballería hicieron una línea y repulsaron algunos asaltos, pero al final tuvieron que retirarse. A las 10 de la mañana los Federales ya habían sido empujados a una posición a tres millas de sus campos.

El General Early no pudo perseguir a los Federales. Muchas de sus tropas pararon en los campos Federales para "disfrutar de las frutas de su victoria." También, Early necesitaba tiempo para reorganizar sus divisiones dispersadas. Finálmente él reformó sus líneas sintiendo la victoria.

Mientras tanto los Yanquis se reorganizaron. Poco después el General Sheridan llegó al campo de batalla y, montando caballo entre sus tropas, reinstaló el espíritu en sus hombres. A las 4 de la tarde los Norteños lanzaron un contraataque. La línea de batalla Confederada se perforó y se derrumbó. Los Confederados huyeron para el sur en una retirada completa.

CONSECUENCIAS

Este desastre Federal convertido en una victoria terminó la lucha principal en Shenandoah Valley.

Las fuerzas opuestas volvieron a las líneas de Petersburg.

Staat: Virginia

Befehlshaber der US:
 Generalmajor Phillip Sheridan
Armee der US: Armee des Shenandoah,
 Armee von Westvirginia
 Truppenstärke: 43,000
Verluste:
 Gefallen: 644
 Verwundet: 3,430
 Gefangengenommen oder vermißt:
 1,591

Befehlshaber der CS:
 Generalleutnant Jubal Early
Armee der CS:
 Unabhängiges Kommando
 Truppenstärke: 20,000
Verluste:
 Gefallen: 320
 Verwundet: 1,540
 Gefangengenommen oder vermißt:
 1,050

KOMMENTAR

Die Generale Early und Sheridan hatten es seit Monaten untereinander "ausgefochten." Sheridan hatte die Konföderierten in den letzten drei Aktionen besiegt (Winchester, Fischer's Hill und Tom's Brook). Diese Niederlagen hatten Early's Armee stark reduziert, aber der immer kampflustige General Early genehmigte einen Plan, den die Generale Gordon und Hotchkiss entworfen hatten.

Am 19. Oktober stürzten sich fünf Divisionen von Early's Armee durch dichten Nebel auf das Föderisten Lager, als die Truppen noch im Schlaf waren. In der Verwirrung der frühen Stunde versuchten kleine Gruppen von Unionsoldaten sich zu stellen und den anstürmenden Konföderierten Widerstand zu leisten, aber sie wurden weggefegt. Es gelang dem 6. Korps der Union und der Kavallerie, eine Linie aufzustellen und einige Anstürme zurück zuschlagen, aber sie mußten sich schließlich zurückziehen. Um 10.00 Uhr fanden sich die Föderalisten 5 Kilometer von ihren Lagern getrieben.

General Early war nicht imstande, die Föderalisten zu verfolgen, da viele seiner Truppen sich noch in den Föderalistenlagern aufhielten, um die "Siegesfrüchte" zu geniessen. Auch brauchte Early Zeit, seine zerstreute Division wieder zu gruppieren. Endlich gelang es ihm, seine Linien wieder aufzustellen — ein Siegesgefühl überkam ihn.

In der Zwischenzeit hatten sich die Yankees wieder gruppiert. Bald erreichte General Sheridan das Schlachtfeld. Er ritt durch seine Truppen und flößte ihnen den Kampfgeist wieder ein. Um 16.00 Uhr gingen die Nordstaatler zum Gegenangriff über. Die Linie der Konföderierten wurde durchdrungen und löste sich bald danach auf. Die Konföderierten strömten in voller Flucht nach Süden.

BEDEUTUNG

Diese Katastrophe der Föderalisten endete siegreich und brachte die Hauptaktionen im Shenandoahtal zu Ende.

Die feindlichen Streitkräfte kehrten zu den Petersburg Linien zurück.

Post-war view of the battlefield; Belle Grove, used as Sheridan's headquarters, is on the rise of ground in the center of the photo.

State: Tennessee

U.S.
Commander:
  Maj. Gen. John Schofield
U.S. Army: 4th & 23rd Corps of the
  Army of the Tennessee
No. of Troops: 28,000
Casualties
  Killed: 189
  Wounded: 1,033
  Captured or missing: 1,104

C.S.
Commander:
  Gen. John B. Hood
C.S. Army: Army of Tennessee
  No. of Troops: 27,000

Casualties:
  Killed: 1,750
  Wounded: 3,800
  Captured or missing: 702

COMMENTS

In an attempt to draw military attention away from the deep south, destroy Sherman's supply routes, and possibly take the war through Kentucky and into the north, General Hood's 39,000 Confederates invaded Tennessee.

To counter this threat, General Sherman dispatched the 4th, 16th, & 23rd Corps toward Nashville. Sherman believed that with these reinforcements Thomas would be able to stop Hood.

The Confederate plan was to attack and destroy these reinforcements before they reached Thomas. The Union 4th & 23rd Corps, commanded by Gen. Schofield, was closely pursued for several days. On November 30th Schofield, at Franklin, TN, stopped to rest his troops and to repair the bridges his army needed to cross the Harpeth River north of town. The Federals quickly threw up a line of earthworks around Franklin. Shortly after noon Hood's columns appeared in front of the Federals.

Hood planned a frontal assault despite objections from Generals Forrest and Cheatham. At 4 p.m. the Confederates advanced along a broad front. Two Union brigades, in front of the main works, were easily overwhelmed and raced back toward the trenches. The Confederates followed closely, causing the Union infantry and artillery to hold their fire until their fleeing comrades were safely out of the way. Then the Federal line exploded with musket and cannon fire, leveling several rows of Confederates. But despite this, the Southerners were so close that the momentum of the charge carried them over the Union works, forcing the defenders back. A Union reserve brigade rushed up to meet the Confederates and managed to push them back to the trenches where they were pinned down. The fighting raged around the earthworks until 9 p.m. when the Confederates withdrew. General Schofield hurried his men across the Harpeth River at 11 p.m. and reached Nashville by noon the next day.

SIGNIFICANCE

Hood's frontal attack was a major disaster losing him an irreplaceable 6,200 casualties.

The loss of 12 generals (6 killed, 5 wounded, and 1 captured) ruined the command of the Confederate Army of Tennessee.

Schofield's arrival at Nashville brought Thomas' strength up to 70,000 men. Although Hood still planned to fight Thomas at Nashville, his chances of a successful campaign were now diminished.

Etat: Tennessee

Etats-Unis
Commandant: Général de
  Division John Schofield
Armées: 4ème et 23ème corps de
  l'armée du Tennessee
  28 000 soldats
Pertes:
  Tués: 189
  Blessés: 1 033
  Prisonniers ou disparus: 1 104

Etats Confédérés
Commandant:
  Général John B. Hood
Armée: du Tennessee
  27 000 soldats

Pertes:
  Tués: 1 750
  Blessés: 3 800
  Prisonniers ou disparus: 702

COMMENTAIRE

Ave 39 000 Confédérés, le général Hood envahit le Tennessee. Il voulait distraire l'attention militaire du Sud, barrer les routes d'approvisionnement de Sherman, et si possible déplacer la guerre vers le Nord via le Kentucky.

Pour contrecarrer ces plans, le général Sherman envoya les quatrième, seizième et vingt-troisième corps d'armée vers Nashville. Sherman pensait que ces renforts permettraient à Thomas d'arreter Hood.

Le plan des Confédérés était d'attaquer et de détruire ces renforts avant qu'ils atteignent Thomas. Les quatrième et vingt-troisième corps de l'Union, commandés par le général Schofield, furent poursuivis de près pendant plusieurs jours. A Franklin, dans le Tennessee, le 3 novembre, Schofield fit reposer ses troupes et se mit à réparer les ponts pour que son armée puisse traverser la rivière Harpeth au nord de la ville. Les Fédéraux construisirent rapidement une ligne de tranchées autour de Franklin. Peu après midi, les colonnes de Hood apparurent devant eux.

En dépit des objections des généraux Forrest et Cheatman, Hood opta pour une attaque de front. A 16 heures, les Confédérés avancèrent sur un large front. Deux brigades de l'Union furent aisément battues et renvoyées vers leurs tranchées. Les Confédérés les suivirent de si près que l'infanterie et l'artillerie de l'Union attendirent pour ouvrir le feu que leurs camarades soient hors de danger. Alors la ligne fédérale explosa du feu de ses mousquets et canons, rasant plusieurs rangs de Confédérés. Cependant, les Sudistes étaient si proches que l'élan de la charge les transporta sur les Fédéraux forcés de reculer. Une brigade de réserve de l'Union se jeta sur les Confédérés et réussit à les repousser et les maintenir dans les tranchées. Le combat fit rage jusqu'à 2 heures quand les Confédérés se retirèrent. Le général Shofield pressa ses hommes de traverser la rivière Harpeth à 2 heures. A midi le jour suivant, il avait atteint Nashville.

CONSEQUENCES

L'attaque de front du général Hood fut un désastre qui lui fit perdre 6 200 hommes irremplaçables.

La perte de douze généraux (6 tués, blessés et prisonnier ruina le commandement de l'armée confédérée de Tennessee.

L'arrivée de Schofield à Nashville monta la force de Thomas à 70 000 hommes. En dépit de la volonté persistante du général Hood de combattre Thomas à Nashville, ses chances de succès étaient maintenant réduites.

Important Landmarks
Harpeth River
Winstead Hills
Roper's Knob
Carter's Creek Pike
Nashville & Decatur R.R.
Franklin & Columbia Turnpike
Lewisburg Turnpike

Important Buildings
Carter House
Widow Bostick House
Gin-house

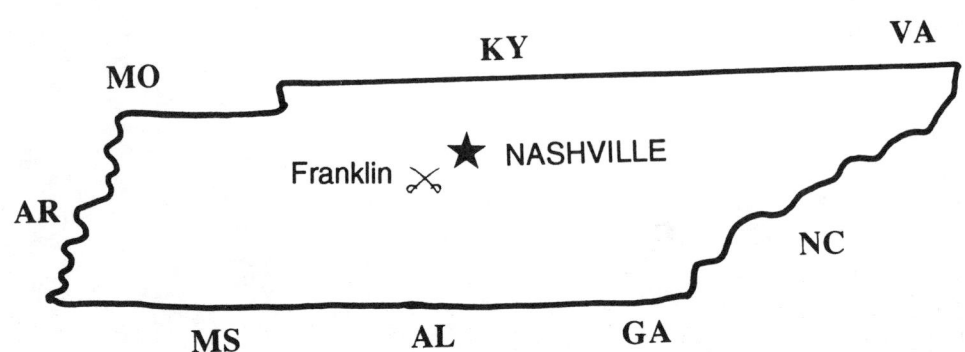

Estado: Tennessee

U.S.	C.S.
Comandante:	**Comandante:**
Maj. Gen. John Schofield	Gen. John B. Hood
U.S. Ejército: 4th & 23rd Corps of Army of the Tennessee	U.S. Ejército: Army of Tennessee
No. de tropas: 28,000	No. de tropas: 27,000
Pérdidas:	**Pérdidas:**
Muertos: 189	Muertos: 1,750
Heridos: 1,033	Heridos: 3,800
Capturados o ausentes: 1,104	Capturados o ausentes: 702

COMENTARIO

En un intento para distraer la atención militar del Sur hondo, destruir las rutas de provisiones de Sherman y posíblemente llevar la guerra por Kentucky y entrar en el Norte, los 39,000 Confederados de Hood invadieron Tennessee.

Para responder a esta amenaza, el General Sherman mandó los cuerpos IV, XVI y XXIII hacia Nashville. Sherman creía que con estos refuerzos Thomas podría parar a Hood.

El plan Confederado era atacar y destruir estos refuerzos antes de que llegaran a Thomas. Los cuerpos IV y XXIII, bajo el General Schofield, fueron perseguidos estréchamente por varios días. El 30 de noviembre Schofield en, Franklin, Tennessee, paró a sus tropas para descansar y reparar los puentes que su ejército necesitaba para cruzar el río Harpeth al norte del pueblo. Los Federales rápidamente hicieron trincheras y otras defensas alrededor de Franklin. Un poco después del mediodía las columnas de Hood aparecieron en frente de los Federales.

Hood planeó un asalto frontal a pesar de las objeciones de los Generales Forrest y Cheatham. A las 4 de la tarde los Confederados avanzaron en una línea ancha. Dos brigadas Federales, en frente de las defensas principales, fueron fácilmente aplastadas y se retiraron a las trincheras. Los Confederados los persiguieron estréchamente causando que la infantería y artillería Federal no pudieran disparar hasta que sus compañeros que huían estuvieran fuera del camino. Entonces la línea Federal explotó con fuego de los rifles y cañones, derribando a varias líneas de Rebeldes. Pero a pesar de esto, los sureños estaban tan cerca que su ímpetu los llevó encima de las defensas, forzando a los defensores para atrás. Una brigada Federal en reserva rápidamente avanzó para encontrar a los Confederados y los empujó hasta las trincheras donde estaban inmovilizados. La lucha siguió alrededor de las trincheras hasta las 9 de la noche cuando se retiraron los Rebeldes. El General Schofield apresuró a sus tropas a través del río Harpeth a las 11 de la noche y llegó a Nashville al mediodía el próximo día.

CONSECUENCIAS

El ataque frontal de Hood fue un desastre perdiéndole 6,200 pérdidas irreemplazables.

La pérdida de 12 Generales (6 muertos, 5 heridos, y 1 capturado) arruinó la comandancia de Army of Tennessee Confederado.

La llegada de Schofield en Nashville aumentó la fuerza de Thomas a 70,000 hombres. Aunque Hood todavía planeaba luchar contra Thomas en Nashville, sus probabilidades de tener éxito ya fueron disminuidas.

Staat: Tennessee

Befehlshaber der US:	Befehlshaber der CS:
Generalmajor John Schofield	General John B. Hood
Armee der US: 4. und 23. Korps der Armee des Tennessee	Armee der CS: Armee von Tennessee
Truppenstärke: 28,000	Truppenstärke: 27,000
Verluste:	**Verluste:**
Gefallen: 189	Gefallen: 1,750
Verwundet: 1,033	Verwundet: 3,800
Gefangengenommen oder vermißt: 1,104	Gefangengenommen oder vermißt: 702

KOMMENTAR

General Hood marschierte seine 39,000 Konföderierte in den Staat Tennessee, in einem Versuch, nicht nur das Interesse des Militärs vom tiefen Süden abzulenken, sondern auch Sherman's Versorgungslinien zu vernichten, und möglichrwise den Krieg durch Kentucky bis in den Norden zu bringen.

Um diese Gefahr zu kontern, entsandte General Sherman das 4., 16. und 23. Korps in Richtung Nashville. Sherman glaubte, daß Thomas, zusammen mit diesen Verstärkungstruppen, Hood aufhalten könnte. Die Konföderierten jedoch hatten vor, diese Verstärkungstruppen anzugreifen und zu vernichten, ehe sie Thomas erreichen konnten. Das 4. und 23. Korps, unter dem Kommando von General Sherman, wurden über etliche Tage von den Konföderierten scharf verfolgt.

Am 30. November hielt Sherman seine Truppen bei Franklin, in Tennessee, auf, um sich ruhen zu können. Die Brücken, über welche die Armee plante, den Harpeth Fluß nördlich der Stadt zu überqueren, mussten während dieser Zeit ebenfalls repariert werden. Die Föderalisten hoben eiligst ein Schanzwerk um Franklin aus. Kurz nach 12.00 Uhr mittags erschienen Hoods Kolonnen vor den Föderalisten.

Trozt Einwände von den Generalen Forrest und Cheatham, bereitete sich Hood auf einen Frontalangriff vor. Um 16.00 Uhr rückten die Konföderierten an einer breiten Front vor. Zwei Unionbrigaden, die vor dem Hauptschanzwerk Stellung hielten, wurden mühelos überwältigt und sie zogen sich in Eile zu ihren Gräben zurück. Die Konföderierten folgten dicht hinter ihnen, aber die Unioninfanterie und Artillerie hielten ihr Feuer, bis ihre fliehenden Kameraden sicher außerhalb Schußweite waren. Dann explodierte von der Föderalistenlinie Musketen- und Kanonenfeuer, das etliche Reihen der Konföderierten abmähte. Die Südstaatler waren nun aber so nahe an die Schanze herangekommen, das Momentum ihres Sturmes trug sie über die Stellungswerke und die Verteidiger wurden zurückgedrängt. Eine Unionreservebrigade eilte zur Stelle, um sich den Konföderierten entgegenzusetzen. Es gelang ihnen, die Konföderierten in die Schützengräben zurückzutreiben und sie dort festzuhalten. Der Kampf tobte um das Schanzwerk, bis die Konföderierten sich um 21.00 Uhr zurückzogen. Um 23.00 Uhr brachte General Schofield seine Truppen schleunigst über den Harpeth Fluß, und sie erreichten Nashville vor 12.00 Uhr mittags am nächsten Tag.

BEDEUTUNG

Hood's Frontalangriff war katastrophal- er verlor dadurch 6,200 unersetzliche Truppen.

Der Verlust von 12 Generalen (6 gefallen, 5 verwundet und einer gefangengenommen) ruinierte das Kommando der Konföderiertenarmee von Tennessee.

Schofield's Ankunft in Nashville brachte Thomas' Truppenstärke auf 70,000 Mann. Obwohl Hood weiterhin plante, Thomas bei Nashville anzugreifen, seine Chance für eine erfolgreiche Kampagne hatte sich jetzt vermindert.

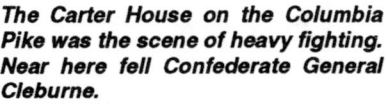
The Carter House on the Columbia Pike was the scene of heavy fighting. Near here fell Confederate General Cleburne.

State: Tennessee

U.S.

Commander:
  Maj. Gen. George Thomas
U.S. Army: Dept. of the Cumberland
  No. of Troops: 55,000
Casualties:
  Killed: 387
  Wounded: 2,558
  Captured or missing: 112

C.S.

Commander:
  Gen. John B. Hood
C.S. Army: Army of Tennessee
  No. of Troops: 39,000
Casualties:
  Killed & wounded: 1,500
  Captured or missing: 4,462

COMMENTS

After the battle of Franklin, Gen. Thomas concentrated his Union forces within the Nashville defenses. Gen. Hood placed the city under siege in the hope he might receive reinforcements or defeat a Federal attempt to break out. With vastly superior numbers, Washington became impatient with Thomas' indecisive actions and Grant threatened his removal. However, after several delays, Thomas was ready with his masterly plan.

Early on the morning of Dec. 15 he hit Hood's left with the XVI and IV Corps and held Schofield's XXIII Corps in reserve positioned to aid the drive. A secondary attack struck Hood's right and Wilson's cavalry screened Thomas' right. Hood had insufficient strength to accept battle, no reserves and with no interior lines to shift reinforcements he was, by nightfall, driven back to a line extending from Overton Hill to Shy's Hill.

Unable to determine whether Hood would retreat during the night, Thomas issued no orders to continue the attack, but the Corps commanders reorganized their lines and made contact with Hood's new defenses at dawn on Dec. 16. Little action occurred until 3 p.m. when a Federal attack on Overton Hill was driven back with heavy losses. At about 3:30 p.m. Wilson's cavalry began driving in Hood's left. Federal artillery was very effective and at 4 p.m. an infantry assault crushed Hood's left and made his entire line untenable. Gen. Edward Johnson and nearly all of his division and artillery were captured. The Army of Tennessee abandoned the field in confusion and Thomas followed with a vigorous pursuit.

SIGNIFICANCE

Hood's invasion of Tennessee ended in disaster and he was soon relieved of the command of the Army of Tennessee at his own request.

The fragments of the Army of Tennessee were again assigned to the command of Gen. Joseph E. Johnston with the impossible task of stopping Sherman in the Carolinas.

Considered by many to be the decisive battle of the Civil War because of Hood's utter rout.

Etat: Tennessee

Etats-Unis

Commandant: Général de Division
  George Thomas
Armée: Département du Cumberland
  55 000 soldats
Pertes:
  Tués: 387
  Blessés: 2 558
  Prisonniers et disparus: 112

Etats Confédérés

Commandant:
  Général John B. Hood
Armée: du Tennessee
  39 000 soldats
Pertes:
  Tués et blessés: 1 500
  Prisonniers et disparus: 4 462

COMMENTAIRE

Après la bataille de Franklin, Thomas concentra ses forces unionistes à l'intérieur des défenses de Nashville. Le général Hood mit le siège sur la ville avec l'espoir de recevoir des renforts ou de ruiner toute tentative des Fédéraux de prendre l'offensive. Dans sa supériorité numérique, Washington s'impatienta devant l'indécision de Thomas et Grant menaçait de le remplacer. Cependant, après plusieurs jours, Thomas était pret avec son plan de maître.

Au petit matin du 1 décembre, il frappa la gauche de Hood ave les corps d'armée XV et IV et gardait en réserve le corps XXII de Schofield pret à attaquer. Une attaque secondaire atteint la droite de Hood et la cavalerie de Wilson dissimulait la droite de Thomas. Hood se trouvait en infériorité dans cette bataille; il n'avait ni réserves ni lignes internes pour passer des renforts. A la tombée de la nuit, il avait été repoussé sur une ligne s'étendant d'Overton's Hill à Shy's Hill.

Ne sachant pas si Hood se retirerait pendant la nuit, Thomas ne donna pas d'ordres pour continuer la bataille. Cependant, les corps d'armée réorganisèrent leurs lignes et contactèrent les nouvelles défenses de Hood à l'aube du 16 décembre. Il ne se passa pas grand chose jusqu'à 15 heures où les Fédérau souffrirent de lourdes pertes et furent repoussés après leur attaque sur Overton Hill. Vers 15h30, la cavalerie de Wilson fonça dans la gauche de Hood. L'artillerie fédérale fut très efficace. A 16 heures, un assaut de l'infanterie écrasa la gauche de Hood et démolit toute sa linge. Le général Johnson fait prisonnier avec presque toute sa division et son artillerie. Dans la confusion, l'armée du Tennessee abandonna le champ et fut vigoureusement poursuivie par Thomas.

CONSEQUENCES

L'invasion du Tennessee par Hood s'avéra être un désastre. Le général demanda lui-meme a etre relevé de ses fonctions.

Ce qui restait de l'armée de Tennessee revint sous la commande de Johnston qui se retrouva aveo l'impossible tache d'arreter Sherman dans les Carolines.

La bataille de Nashville est souvent considérée comme déterminante dans la Guerre Civile à cause de la déroute de Hood.

Important Landmarks
Cumberland River
Shy's Hill
Franklin Pike
Brentwood Hills
Overton Hill
Montgomery Hill
Nolesville Pike
Rains Hill
Hardin Pike
Brown's Creek
Granny White Pike
Hillsboro Pike
Tenn. & Ala. R.R.

Important Buildings
Granny House
Overton's House

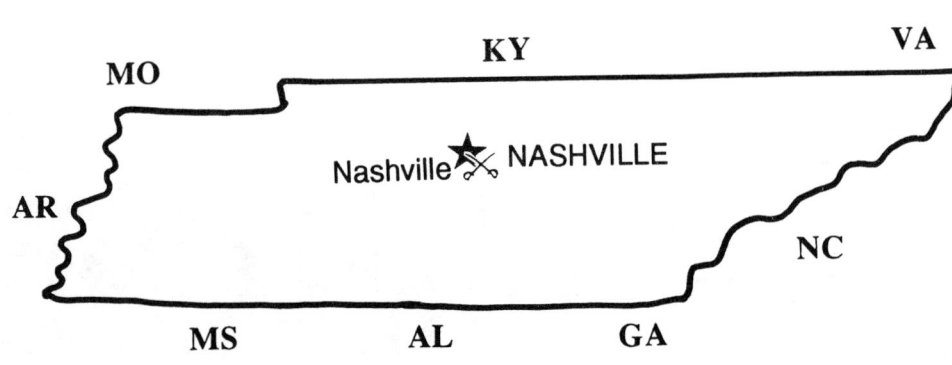

Estado: Tennessee

U.S.	C.S.
Comandante:	Comandante:
Maj. Gen. George Thomas	Gen. John B. Hood
U.S. Ejército: Dept. of the Cumberland	C.S. Ejército: Army of Tennessee
No. de tropas: 55,000	No. de tropas: 39,000
Pérdidas:	Pérdidas:
Muertos: 387	Muertos y Heridos: 1,500
Heridos: 2,558	Capturados o ausentes: 4,462
Capturados o ausentes: 112	

COMENTARIO

Después de la batalla de Franklin, el General Thomas concentró sus fuerzas en las defensas de Nashville. El General Hood puso la ciudad bajo un asedio con la esperanza de recibir refuerzos o derrotar un intento de los Federales de estallar. Washington se impacientó con las acciones indecisivas de Thomas y Grant pensó en removerlo. Sin embargo, después de varias dilaciones, Thomas estuvo listo con su plan.

Temprano por la mañana del 15 de diciembre golpeó la izquierda de Hood con los cuerpos XVI y IV y mantuvo el cuerpo XXIII de Schofield en reserva situado para apoyar el empuje. Un ataque secundario golpeó la derecha de Hood y la caballería de Wilson protegía la derecha de Thomas. Hood no tenía suficientes tropas para luchar, ninguna reserva y sin líneas internas para trasladar refuerzos él fue, al anochecer, forzado a retirarse a una línea que se extendía desde Overton Hill a Shy's Hill.

No pudiendo determinar si Hood se retiraría durante la noche, Thomas no dio órdenes para siguir con el ataque, pero los comandantes de los cuerpos reorganizaron sus líneas e hicieron contacto con las defensas nuevas de Hood en el alba del 16 de diciembre. Poca acción ocurió hasta las 3 de la tarde cuando un ataque Federal en Overton Hill fue repulsado con muchas pérdidas. Cerca de las 3:30 de la tarde la caballería de Wilson empezó a empujar la izquierda de Hood. La artillería Federal fue muy eficaz y a las cuatro un asalto de infantería aplastó la izquierda de Hood e hizo que toda su línea fuera insostenible. El General Edward Johnson y casi toda su división y artillería fueron capturados. El Army of Tennessee abandonó el campo en confusión y Thomas lo persiguió vigorósamente.

CONSECUENCIAS

La invasión de Tennessee hecha por Hood acabó en desastre y él fue relevado de la comandancia del Army of Tennessee por su propia solicitud.

Los fragmentos del Army of Tennessee fueron dados a la comandancia del General Joseph E. Johnston con el quehacer imposilbe de parar al General Sherman en las Carolinas.

Considerado por muchos de ser la batalla decesiva de la Guerra Civil por la derrota completa de Hood.

Staat: Tennessee

Befehlshaber der US:	Befehlshaber der CS:
Generalmajor George Thomas	General John B. Hood
Armee der US: Department des Cumberland	Armee der CS: Armee von Tennessee
Truppenstärke: 55,000	Truppenstärke: 39,000
Verluste:	Verluste:
Gefallen: 387	Gefallen und Verwundet: 1,500
Verwundet: 2,558	Gefangengenommen oder vermißt: 4,462
Gefangengenommen oder vermißt: 112	

KOMMENTAR

Nach der Schlacht von Franklin konzentrierte General Thomas seine Unionstreitkräfte innerhalb den Verteidigungsanlagen von Nashville. General Hood belagerte die Stadt in der Hoffnung, Verstärkungstruppen zu bekommen, oder daß er einen Ausbruchsversuch erfolgreich bekämpfen könnte. Obwohl Thomas über eine weitaus überlegene Truppenstärke verfügte, Washington bekam ungeduldig über seine Unentschlossenheit, und Grant drohte mit Thomas' Absetzung. Jedoch nach mehreren Verzögerungen war Thomas mit seinem meisterhaften Plan bereit.

Früh am Morgen des 15. Dezember, mit dem 23. Korps von Schofield zur Unterstützung des Vorstoßes in einsatzbarer Reserve gehalten, griff er mit dem 16. und 4. Korps Hood's linke Flanke an. Ein zweiter Angriff traf Hood's rechte Flanke, während Wilson's Kavallerie Thomas' rechte Flanke abschirmte. Hood's Truppenzahl war von Anfang an unzureichend, um den Kampf aufzunehmen - er hatte keine Reserven und war ohne innere Linien, die seine Stellungen hätten verstärken können. Bei Einbruch der Nacht wurde er auf eine Stellung zurückgetrieben, die sich vom Overton Hill bis Shy's Hill streckte.

Es war nicht möglich festzustellen, ob Hood sich während der Nacht zurückziehen würde, und daher gab Thomas keine Befehle, den Kampf fortzusetzen. Die Korpskommandanten organisierten jedoch ihre Linien wieder und machten bei Tagesanbruch, am 16. Dezember, Kontakt mit Hoods neuer Abwehr. Bis 15.00 Uhr war wenig Aktion zu verzeichnen. Dann wurde ein Angriff der Föderalisten am Overton Hill mit schweren Verlusten für den Gegner zurückgetrieben. Um etwa 15.30 Uhr begann Wilson's Kavallerie, Hood's linke Flanke einzudrücken. Die Nordartillerie war sehr effektiv, und um 16.00 Uhr vernichtete ein Infanterieangriff Hood's linke Flanke, wodurch seine ganze Linie unhaltbar wurde. General Edward Johnson, mit beinahe seiner ganzen Division, wurden gefangengenommen und seine Artillerie erobert. Die verwirrte Armee von Tennessee räumte das Feld mit Thomas' Verfolgung dicht auf ihren Fersen.

BEDEUTUNG

Hood's Einmarsch in Tennessee endete in einer Katastrophe. Seine Bitte, ihn vom Komando der Armee von Tennessee zu entheben, wurde ihm umgehend gewährt.

Die Fragmente der Armee von Tennessee wurden wieder unter das Kommando von General Joseph E. Johnston gestellt, der die unmögliche Aufgabe hatte, Sherman in den Carolinas aufzuhalten.

Hood's wilde Flucht wird von vielen als die entscheidende Schlacht im Bürgerkrieg betrachtet.

The Tennessee State Capitol building was fortified by General Thomas, indicating his intention to contest every foot of ground.

State: Virginia

U.S.
Commanders:
  Gens. Warren & Humphreys
U.S. Army: V & II Corps + Cavalry
  Army of the Potomac
No. of Troops: 34,500
Casualties:
  Killed: 171
  Wounded: 1,181
  Captured or missing: 187

C.S.
Commanders:
  Gens. Hill & Gordon
C.S. Army: Army of Northern
  Virginia
No. of Troops: 15,000
Casualties:
  1,200 total killed, wounded, and
  captured

COMMENTS
The Battle of Hatcher's Run was the result of Grant's drive to encircle Petersburg. Grant used 35,000 men in this operation aimed at the Boydton Plank Road, believed by him to be a Confederate supply route.

On the morning of February 5th General Davies' cavalry division raced ahead of the advancing II and V Infantry Corps. The Federal troopers, despite the bad weather, made good progress occupying Dinwiddie Court House on the Boydton Plank Road. After taking some prisoners, the Federal horsemen were ordered back to the supporting infantry.

Meanwhile, the Union infantry reached Hatcher's Run and began deploying. General Humphreys' II Corps was lined up 1,000 yards from the Confederate works with Warren's V Corps to the south. At 5 p.m. the Confederates attacked Humphreys' line but were repulsed. By morning of the 6th Davies' cavalry had rejoined the Union infantry. At 1 p.m. Warren's men went out on reconnaissance. To counter Warren's advance the Confederates sent a division crashing into them. But again the superior numbers of the Federals won out as they beat back the assault, killing Brig. General John Pegram.

On the 7th the Federals, discovering that the Boydton Plank Road wasn't used to supply Lee's army, abandoned their hold on the road, content on occupying and fortifying the newly extended line to Hatcher's Run.

SIGNIFICANCE
The Union line again successfully pushed to the west, causing Lee to lengthen his ever thinning defenses. Lee's thinly defended lines were now stretched to the breaking point.

Etat: Virginie

Etats-Unis
Commandants:
  Généraux Warren et Humphreys
Armées: Corps V et II avec la
  Cavalerie; armée du Potomac
34 500 soldats
Pertes:
  Tués: 171
  Blessés: 1 181
  Prisonniers ou disparus: 187

Etats Confédérés
Commandants:
  Généraux Hill et Gordon
Armée: de Virginie du Nord
  15 000 soldats

Pertes totales:
  Tués, blessés et prisonniers: 1 200

COMMENTAIRE
Grant voulait enclercler Petersburg; le résultat fut la bataille de Hatcher's Run. Grant utilisa 35 000 hommes pour cette opération dirigée sur le Boydton Plank Road parce qu'il croyait que cette route était une route de ravitaillement Confédérée.

Le matin du février, la division de cavalerie du général Davies fonça sur les corps d'infanterie II et V. En dépit du mauvais temps, les troupes des Fédéraux arrivèrent à occuper Dinwiddie Court House sur la route Boydton Plank. Après avoir pris quelques prisonniers, les cavaliers fédéraux revinrent soutenir l'infanterie.

Pendant ce temps, l'infanterie de l'Union atteignit Hatcher's Run et commença à déployer ses troupes. Le corps d'armée I du général Humphreys étendit sa ligne à environ 90 mètres des tranchées des Confédérés; le corps V de Warren était placé au sud. A 17 heures, les Confédérés attaquèrent la ligne de Humphreys et furent repoussés. Le matin du 6, la cavalerie de Davies avait rejoint l'infanterie de l'Union. A 13 heures, les hommes de Warren sortirent en reconnaissance. Pour contrecarrer l'avance de Warren, les Coféderés envoyèrent une division contre eux. Mais une fois de plus, la supériorité en nombre des Fédéraux eut raison de l'adversaire, et le général John Pegram fut tué dans la contre-attaque.

Le 7 février, découvrant que Boydton Plank Road ne servait pas à l'approvisionnement de l'armée de Lee, les Fédéraux l'abandonnèrent pour occuper et fortifier la nouvelle ligne qui s'étendait jusqu'à Hatcher's Run.

CONSEQUENCE
La ligne de l'Union avait gagné du terrain vers l'ouest en obligeant Lee à étendre ses défenses déjà minces. Les lignes de Lee n'avaient plus la force de faire face à l'Union.

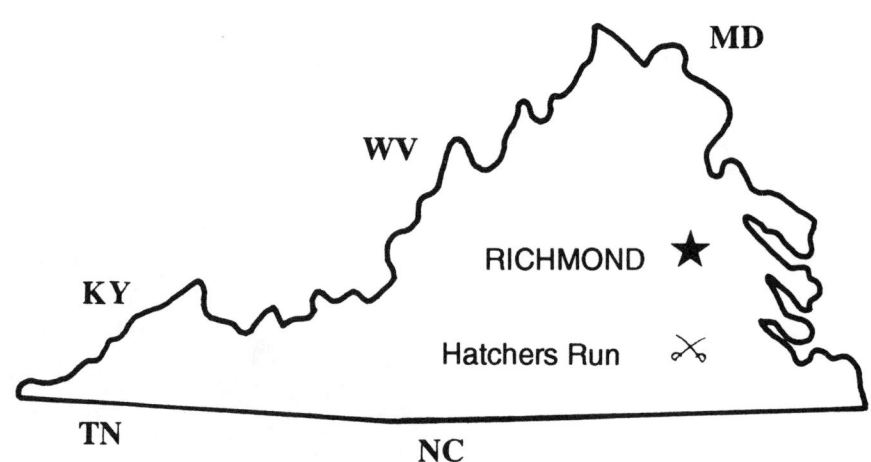

Important Landmarks
Boydton Plank Road
Rowanty Creek
Hatcher's Run
Vaughan Road
Gravelly Run

Important Buildings
Dabney's Steam Saw-mill
Armstrong's Mill

Estado: Virginia

U.S.	**C.S.**
Comandante:	Comandante:
Gens. Warren y Humphreys	Gens. Hill y Gordon
U.S. Ejército: V y II Corps y Cavalry, Army of the Potomac	C.S. Ejército: Army of Northern Virginia
No. de tropas: 34,500	No. de tropas: 15,000
Pérdidas:	Pérdidas:
Muertos: 171	1,200 muertos, heridos y capturados
Heridos: 1,181	
Capturados o ausentes: 187	

COMENTARIO

La batalla de Hatcher's Run fue el resultado del empuje de Grant de rodear Petersburg. Grant usó 35,000 hombres en esta operación dirigidos al Boydton Plank Road, creyendo él que era una ruta de provisiones Confederada.

Por la mañana del 5 de febrero la división de caballería del General Davies iba en frente de los cuerpos II y V de infantería que avanzaban. Las tropas Federales, a pesar del tiempo malo, hicieron buen progreso en ocupar Dinwiddie Court House en Boydton Plank Road. Después de capturar algunos prisioneros, los caballeros Federales fueron mandados atrás a la infantería.

Mientras tanto, la infantería Federal llegó a Hatcher's Run y empezó a desplegarse. El cuerpo II del General Humphreys estaba en la línea a 1,000 metros de las defensas Confederadas con el cuerpo V de Warren más al sur. A las 5 de la tarde los Confederados atacaron la línea de Humphreys pero fueron repulsados. Por la mañana del 6 la caballería de Davies ya se había juntado con la infantería de la Unión. A la una de la tarde los hombres de Warren fueron en reconocimiento. Para oponer el avance de Warren los Confederados mandaron una división que los atacó. Pero otra vez los números superiores de los Federales ganaron así como repulsaron el asalto, matando al General John Pegram.

El día 7 los Federales, dándose cuenta de que Boydton Plank Road no se usaba para poveer el ejército de Lee, abandonaron su posición en la carreterra, contentos de ocupar y hacer fortificaciones en la línea nuevamente establecida a Hatcher's Run.

CONSECUENCIAS

La línea Federal empujó otra vez con éxito al oeste, causando que Lee alargara sus defensas que ya estaban muy delgadas. Estas líneas, ya estréchamente defendidas, ahora estaban extendidas al punto de derrumbarse.

Staat: Virginia

Befehlshaber der US:	Befehlshaber der CS:
Generalmajor G.K. Warren und Generalmajor A.A. Humphreys	Generalleutnant A.P. Hill und Generalmajor John Gordon
Armee der US: 5. und 2. Korps und Kavallerie – Armee des Potomac	Armee der CS: Armee von Nordvirginia
Truppenstärke: 34,500	Truppenstärke: 15,000
Verluste:	Verluste:
Gefallen: 171	Insgesamt 1,200 gefallen, verwundet, gefangengenommen oder vermißt
Verwundet: 1,181	
Gefangengenommen oder vermißt: 187	

KOMMENTAR

Die Schlacht von Hatcher's Run war das Resultat von Grant's Offensive und deren Ziel, Petersburg zu umkreisen. Grant hatte 35,000 Truppen in dieser Operation eingesetzt, die auf Boydton Plank Road gerichtet war, eine Landstraße, die Grant für eine Versorgungslinie der Konföderierten hielt.

Am Morgen des 5. Februar galoppierte General Davies' Kavalleriedivision dem vorrückenden 2. und 5. Infanteriekorps voraus. Trotz schlechten Wetters machten die Kavalleristen gute Fortschritte und besetzten das Dinwiddie Court House an der Boydton Plank Landstraße. Nachdem die Kavalleristen einige Gefangene genommen hatten, erhielten sie den Befehl, zu der Unterstützung der Infanterie zurückzukehren.

In der Zwischenzeit erreichte die Unioninfanterie Hatcher's Run und begann, sich aufzustellen. General Humphreys' 2. Korps stellte sich in einer Linie, einen Kilometer von dem Schanzwerk der Konföderierten entfernt, auf, mit Warren's 5. Korps südlich davon. Um 17.00 Uhr griffen die Konföderierten Humphrey's Linie an, aber sie wurden abgewehrt. Am Morgen des 6. hatte sich Davies' Kavallerie der Unioninfanterie wieder angeschlossen. Um 13.00 Uhr gingen Warren's Truppen auf Aufklärung. Um Warren's Vorrücken zu kontern, schickten die Konföderierten eine Division gegen ihn. Die zahlenmäßige Überlegenheit der Föderalisten brachte ihnen wiederum den Sieg, als sie den Ansturm zurückwarfen. Während des Kampfes fiel Brigadegeneral der Konföderierten, John Pegram.

Als die Föderalisten am 7. entdeckten, daß die Boydton Plank Landstraße keine Versorgungsroute für Lee war, zogen sie sich von der Straße zurück und gaben sich mit der Besetzung und Befestigung der vor Kurzem nach Hatchers Run verlängerten Linien zufrieden.

BEDEUTUNG

Die Unionlinie drängte sich wieder mit Erfolg nach Westen, was Lee dazu veranlaßte, seine immer dünner werdende Verteidigung auszudehnen. Lee's schwach verteidigten Linien erlaubten keine weitere Ausdehnung.

By the fall of 1864, Grant's encirclement plans called for severing the remaining arteries leading from Petersburg to the south. Thrusts aimed at the South Side Railroad (seen here crossing a stream on a trestle) were largely unsuccessful until after the Battle of Five Forks.

State: North Carolina

U.S.
Commander:
  Maj. Gen. Henry W. Slocum
U.S. Army: Army of Georgia
  No. of Troops: 16,000
Casualties:
  Killed: 191
  Wounded: 1,168
  Captured or missing: 287

C.S.
Commander:
  Gen. Joseph E. Johnston
C.S. Army: Army of Tennessee
  No. of Troops: 17,000
Casualties:
  Killed: 239
  Wounded: 1,694
  Captured or missing: 673

COMMENTS

General Sherman's huge army, moving north, reached Fayetteville, NC, by mid-March 1865. From there Sherman's force moved on in two columns. One column, the Army of Tennessee under General Howard, marched northeast toward Goldsborough to join a Union force coming from the coast. The other column, the Army of Georgia commanded by General Slocum, marched to threaten Raleigh, NC.

The only chance for Confederate success was to attack the separate columns before they concentrated at Goldsborough.

On March 16th Slocum's column came up against a Confederate force at Averasborough. Although the Southerners were forced to retreat, they succeeded in delaying Slocum at Bentonville. On the morning of March 19th Slocum's leading elements ran into the Confederate cavalry south of Bentonville. The Union infantry pushed the horsemen back, but a Southern counterattack forced Slocum to pull his forces together in order to repulse several Confederate assaults. Johnston, unable to make any offensive gains, pulled back and took up a strong defensive position.

During the next day there was very little fighting. Slocum brought up more troops for an attack, while Johnston prepared his defenses. The Confederates hoped that Federal assaults on their strong works would so weaken Slocum's force that it could be destroyed by a Southern counterattack.

On the 21st Sherman, with his whole force present, struck Johnston's front while a division tried to get around the Confederate left cutting off their retreat route. The Southerners fought well, beating back the Federal attack in their front and blocking the flanking movement, but with their limited number of troops they were forced to withdraw toward Smithville.

SIGNIFICANCE

General Johnston, his force being only a third of Sherman's total strength, realized the hopelessness of any further fighting and soon started peace negotiations. On April 26 he surrendered his army to Sherman.

Etat: Caroline du Nord

Etats-Unis
Commandant:
  Général de Division Henry W. Slocum
Armée: de Georgie
  16 000 soldats
Pertes:
  Tués: 191
  Blessés: 1 168
  Prisonniers ou disparus: 287

Etats Confédérés
Commandant:
  Général Joseph E. Johnston
Armée: du Tennessee
  17 000 soldats
Pertes:
  Tués: 239
  Blessés: 1 694
  Prisonniers ou disparus: 673

COMMENTAIRE

L'énorme armée du général Sherman avança vers le nord et atteignit Fayetteville, en Caroline du Nord, au milieu du mois de mars 1865. Puis, les forces de Sherman furent divisées en deux colonnes. L'une celle de l'armée du Tennessee commandée par le général Howard, prit la direction nord-est vers Goldsboroug pour rejoindre les forces de l'Union venant de la côte. L'autre, l'armée de Georgie au ordres du général Slocum marcha sur Raleigh en Caroline du Nord.

La seule possibilité de victoire pour les Confédérés était d'attaquer les colonnes séparément avant qu'elles se rejoignent à Goldsborough.

Le 16 mars, la colonne de Slocum fit face à une force confédérée à Averasborough. Bien que les Sudistes soient forcés à la retraite, ils réussirent à retarder Slocum à Bentonville. Le matin du 19 mars, les troupes en tete de l'armée de Slocum affrontèrent la cavalerie des Confédérés au sud de Bentonville. L'infanterie de l'Union repousse les cavaliers; mais une contre-attaque des Sudistes força Slocum à rassembler ses forces pour vaincre plusieurs assauts des Confédérés. Dans l'impossibilité de réussir une offensive, Johnston recula et se mit en position défensive.

Le jour suivant, il n'eut pas de grand combat. Slocum renforça ses troupes pour une attaque et Johnston préparait ses défenses. Les Confédérés comptaient que les attaques des Fédérau contre leurs solides ouvrages défensifs affaibliraient les forces de Slocum qui pourraient ensuite être détruites par une contre-attaque des Sudistes.

Le 21, ave toute son armée rassemblée, Sherman frappa le centre de l'armée de Johnston pendant qu'une division essayait de contourner la gauche des Confédérés pour couper la route de leur retraite. Les Sudistes se battirent au front et tachèrent de défendre leur flanc, mais le nombre limité de leurs troupes les obligea à se retirer vers Smithville.

CONSEQUENCE

Ses forces étant l'équivalent d'un tiers de celles de Sherman, le général Johnston comprit que tout combat était désormais sans espoir. Il commença donc à négocier la paix et le 26 avril son armée se rendit à Sherman.

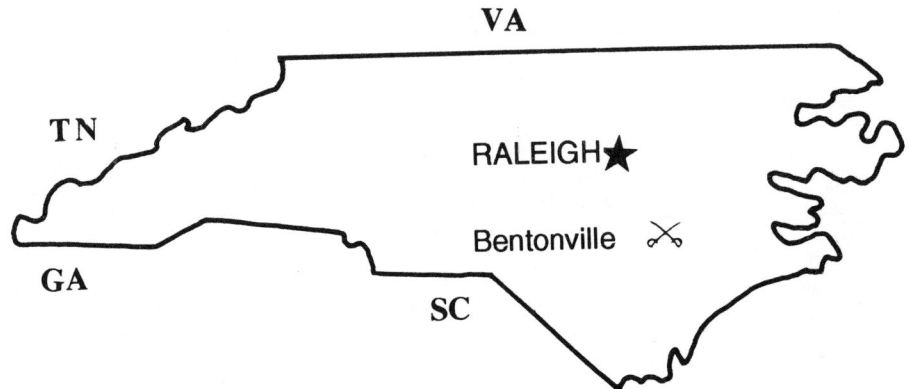

Important Landmarks
Mill Creek
Goldsboro Road
Averysboro Road

Important Buildings
Cole's House
Harper Home
S. Johnson House
Morris Home
N. & G. Flowers Homes

Estado: North Carolina

U.S.	C.S.
Comandante:	Comandante:
Maj. Gen. Henry W. Slocum	Gen. Joseph E. Johnston
U.S. Ejército: Army of Georgia	U.S. Ejército: Army of Tennessee
No. de tropas: 16,000	No. de tropas: 17,000
Pérdidas:	Pérdidas:
Muertos: 191	Muertos: 239
Heridos: 1,168	Heridos: 1,694
Capturados o ausentes: 287	Capturados o ausentes: 673

COMENTARIO

El ejército grandísimo de Sherman, trasladándose al norte, llegó a Fayetteville, North Carolina a mediados de marzo, 1865. Desde allí la fuerza avanzó en dos columnas. Una columna, Army of the Tennessee bajo el General Howard, marchó al noreste hacia Goldsborough para juntarse con la fuerza Federal que venía desde la costa. La otra columna, Army of Georgia bajo el General Slocum, marchó para amenazar Raleigh, N.C.

La única oportunidad de éxito para los Confederados era atacar a las columnas seperadas antes de que se concentraran en Goldsborough.

El 16 de marzo la columna de Solcum se encontró con una fuerza Confederada en Averasborough. Aunque los sureños tuvieron que retirarse, tuvieron éxito en retrasar a Slocum en Bentonville. Por la mañana del 19 de marzo la fuerza de Slocum que estaba en frente se encontró con la caballería Confederada al sur de Bentonville. La infantería empujó a los caballeros para atrás, pero un contraataque sureño forzó a Slocum a juntar sus fuerzas para repulsar varios asaltos Confederados. Johnston, no pudiendo ganar nada en la ofensiva, se retiró a una posición fuerte de defensa.

Durante el próximo día hubo poca batalla. Slocum trajo a más tropas para un ataque, mientras Johnston preparó sus defensas. Los Confederados esperaban que los asaltos Federales en sus defensas debilitaran tanto la fuerza de Slocum que podría ser destruída por un contraataque sureño.

El día 21 Sherman, con toda su fuerza presente, golpeó el frente de Johnston mientras una división trataba de ir atrás de la izquierda Confederada cortando su ruta de retirada. Los sureños lucharon bien, repulsando el ataque a su frente y bloqueando el movimiento de flanquear, pero con su número limitado de tropas tuvieron que retirarse hacia Smithville.

CONSECUENCIAS

El General Johnston, su fuerza siendo sólo la tercera parte de la fuerza entera de Sherman, se dio cuenta de la desesperanza de seguir con la lucha y pronto empezó negociaciones de paz. El 26 de abril él rindió su ejército a Sherman.

Staat: Nordcarolina

Befehlshaber der US:
    Generalmajor Henry W. Slocum
Armee der US: Armee von Georgia

    Truppenstärke: 16,000
Verluste:
    Gefallen: 191
    Verwundet: 1,168
    Gefangengenommen oder vermißt: 287

Befehlshaber der CS:
    General Joseph E. Johnston
Armee der CS:
    armee von Tennessee
    Truppenstärke: 17,000
Verluste:
    Gefallen: 239
    Verwundet: 1,694
    Gefangengenommen oder vermißt: 673

KOMMENTAR

General Sherman's riesige Armee zog sich nach Norden und erreichte Mitte März 1865 Fayetteville in Nordcarolina. Von dort zogen sich Sherman's Streitkräfte in zwei Kolonnen weiter. Eine Kolonne, General Howard's Armee von Tennessee, marschierte nordöstlich in Richtung Goldsboro, um sich dort Uniontruppen von der Küste anzuschließen. Die andere Kolonne, die Armee von Georgia unter General Slocum, marschierte um Raleigh in Nordcarolina zu bedrohen.

Die einzige Chance zum Erfolg für die Konföderierten lag darin, die getrennten Kolonnen einzeln anzugreifen, ehe sie sich bei Goldsboro konzentrierten.

Am 16. März stieß Slocum's Kolonne auf Konföderierte Truppen bei Averysboro. Obwohl die Südstaatler sich zurückziehen mußten, gelang es ihnen, Slocum bei Bentonville aufzuhalten. Am Morgen des 19. trafen Slocum's Vortruppen südlich von Bentonville überraschend auf Kavalleristen der Konföderierten. Die Unioninfanterie drängte die Kavalleristen zurück, aber ein Gegenangriff der Südstaatler zwang Slocum, seine Streitkräfte zusammenzuziehen, um weitere Stürme der Konföderierten abzuwehren. Johnston, der nicht imstande war, einen Erfolg in der Offensive zu gewinnen, zog sich zurück und bezog eine starke Defensivstellung.

Der nächste Tag sah wenig kämpfen. Slocum brachte weitere Truppen an für einen Angriff, während Johnston seine Verteidigungen vorbereitete. Die Konföderierten hofften, daß Angriffe der Föderalisten auf ihre starken Verteidigungsanlagen Slocum's Männer so schwächen würden, sie könnten dann durch einen südstaatlichen Gegenangriff vernichtet werden.

Sherman's volle Armee war auf dem Felde, und am 21. März stürmte er Johnston's Front, während eine Division versuchte, die linke Flanke der Konföderierten zu umkreisen, um ihnen den Fluchtweg abzuschneiden. Die Südstaatler kämpften tapfer - sie schlugen den Angriff auf ihrer Front zurück und blockierten den Flankierungsversuch. Jedoch ihre begrenzte Truppenzahl zwang sie am Ende sich nach Smithville zurückzuziehen.

BEDEUTUNG

General Johnston, mit Streitkräften die nur ein Drittel von Sherman's Truppenstärke umfaßten, sah die Hoffnungslosigkeit wiederholter Versuche, weiterzukämpfen, und nahm umgehend Friedensverhandlungen auf. Am 26. April übergab er Sherman seine Armee.

The battlefield on the morning after, the smoke is from resin that was fired by the Confederates.

State: Virginia

U.S.

Commander:
  Brig. Gen. Orlando Wilcox
U.S. Army: 9th Corps Army of the
  Potomac
No. of Troops: 5,000
Casualties:
  Killed: 75
  Wounded: 419
  Captured or missing: 523

C.S.

Commander:
  Maj. Gen. John Gordon
C.S. Army: Army of Northern
  Virginia
No. of Troops: 8,000
Casualties:
  Killed and wounded: 732
  Captured or missing: 1.949

COMMENTS

By mid-March 1865 the Confederacy's situation was terrible. To the south, Sherman was hammering Johnston, General Early had been defeated in the Shenandoah Valley, and around Richmond and Petersburg the troops were tired, hungry, and outnumbered.

Therefore, Lee planned to attack Grant. If successful, the attack might force Grant to shorten his lines around Petersburg allowing Lee to retreat into North Carolina where he could join forces with Johnston to make a last stand. Fort Stedman was chosen as the target for this last ditch assault. The Confederate plan was to capture the Union pickets and remove the abatis in front of the fort as quickly and as quietly as possible. They would then capture the fort and its supporting batteries while disrupting communications with Grant's supply base at City Point.

Nearly half of Lee's force would take part in the assault. At 4 a.m. on March 25th three 100-man columns quietly rushed out, capturing pickets and clearing a path to the fort. The Confederates then rushed into the fort, surprising the Federals, who surrendered without a fight. More Confederates poured through the hole in the Union line. Some headed in the direction of City Point, while other units turned north or south, capturing more of the Federal works. By 6 a.m. the Federals were finally able to stop the Confederate advance, but not until the Southerners held almost a mile of the Union line. A Federal counterattack pushed the Confederates back to Stedman where, for the next two hours, they were subjected to a murderous hail of musket and artillery fire. A withdrawal was ordered, but the line of retreat was covered by such a vicious cross fire that many of the Southerners preferred to surrender than to withdrawal. Another Federal counterattack recaptured Fort Stedman and shortly the Union line was restored.

SIGNIFICANCE

With this failure, Lee's only hope was to retreat toward North Carolina and unite with Johnston.

Etat: Virginie

Etats-Unis

Commandant: Général de Brigade
  Olando Wilcox
Armée: 9ème Corps de l'armée du
  Potomac
5 000 soldats
Pertes:
  Tués: 75
  Blessés: 419
  Prisonniers ou disparus: 523

Etats Confédérés

Commandant: Général de Division
  John Gordon
Armée: de Virginie du Nord
  8 000 soldats

Pertes:
  Tués: 732
  Blessés:
  Prisonniers ou disparus: 1 949

COMMENTAIRE

A la mi-mars, en 1865, la Confédération était dans un état pitoyable. Au sud, Sherman écrasait Johnston; le général Early avait été défait dans la valée du Shenandoah; autour de Richmond et Petersburg, les troupes étaient épuisées, affamées et surpassées en nombre.

Alors, Lee décida d'attaquer Grant. S'il réussissait, ilobligerait Grant à raccourcir ses lignes autour de Petersburg, ce qui lui permettrait de se retirer en Caroline où il pourrait rejoindre les forces de Johnston pour un dernier assaut. Il choisit Fort Stedman comme cible. Le plan des Confédérés était aussi de prendre les piquets de l'Union et d'enlever les abatis amassés devant le fort aussi rapidement et discrètement que possible. Enfin ils pourraient prendre le fort avec toutes ses batteries détruisant ainsi toutes les communications de Grant avec City Point, sa base d'approvisionnement.

Près de la moitié des forces de Lee devait participer à l'assaut. A 4 heures, le 2 mars, trois colonnes de 100 hommes chacune nettoyèrent vite et en silence le chemin du fort en prenant les piquets et enlevant les abattis. Ils assaillirent ensuite le fort, et les Fédéraux surpris se rendirent sans se battre. D'autres Confédérés passèrent par la brèche dans la ligne fédérale. Quelques uns foncèrent en direction de City Point, tandis que d'autres unités furent dirigées vers le nord et sud, capturant le encore plus de fortifications fédérales. A 6 heures, alors que les Sudistes tenaient déjà un kilomètre de la ligne de l'Union, les Fédéraux purent enfin arreter leur avance. Une contre-attaque fédérale repoussa les Confédérés jusqu'à Stedman où ils furent massacrés par les mousquets et l'artillerie pendant près de deux heures. Bien qu'ayant reçu l'ordre de faire retraite, beaucoup de Sudistes préférèrent se rendre à cause des feux croisés. Dès que l'Union eut restauré sa ligne, une autre contre-attaque fédérale lui permit de reprendre le fort Stedman.

CONSEQUENCE

Après cet échec, le seul espoir qui restait à Lee était de faire retraite vers la Caroline du Nord pour s'unir à Johnston.

Important Landmarks
Fort Stedman
Colquitt's Salient
Battery IX
Battery X
Battery XI
Battery XII
Prince George Court House Rd.
Fort Haskell
Cemetery Hill
Harrison's Creek

Important Buildings
Hare House site
Friend House
Taylor House site

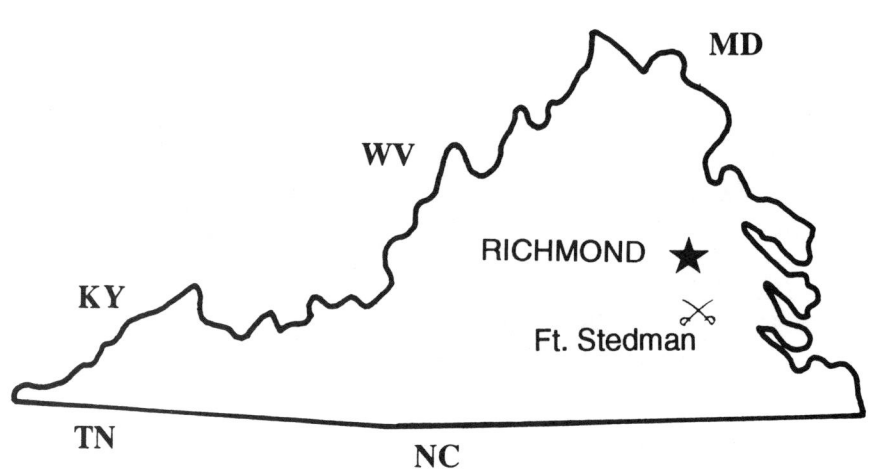

Estado: Virginia

	U.S.	C.S.

U.S.

Comandante:
 Brig. Gen. Orlando Willcox
U.S. Ejército: 9th Corps Army of the
 Potomac
No. de tropas: 5,000
Pérdidas:
 Muertos: 75
 Heridos: 419
 Capturados o ausentes: 523

C.S.

Comandante:
 Maj. Gen. John Gordon
C.S. Ejército: Army of Northern
 Virginia
No. de tropas: 8,000
Pérdidas:
 Muertos y heridos: 732
 Capturados o ausentes: 1,949

COMENTARIO

A mediados de marzo, 1865, la situación de la Confederación ya era terrible. Al sur, Sherman martillaba a Johnston, el General Early había sido derrotado en Shenandoah Valley, y alrededor de Richmond y Petersburg las tropas estaban cansadas, tenían hambre, y estaban excedidas en número.

Por eso Lee planeó atacar a Grant. Si tuviera éxito, el ataque quizás forzara a Grant a acortar sus líneas alrededor de Petersburg dejando que Lee se retirara a North Carolina donde pudiera juntarse con las fuerzas de Johnston para mantenerse firme por una última vez. Fort Stedman fue elegido para este último asalto. El plan Confederado era capturar a los piquetes Federales y remover la tala en frente del fuerte tan rápidamente y calládamente como posible. Después de capturar el fuerte y sus baterías mientras se rompían las comunicaciones con la base de provisiones de Grant en City Point.

Casi la mitad de la fuerza de Lee participaría en el asalto. A las 4 de la mañana el 25 de marzo tres columnas de 100 hombres en cada una salieron silenciosamente, capturando piquetes y haciendo un camino al fuerte. Los Confederados entonces entraron en el fuerte de prisa, sorprendiendo a los Federales, quienes se rindieron sin una lucha. Más Confederados pasaron por la brecha en la línea. Algunos se dirigieron a City Point, mientras otras unidades volvieron al norte o al sur, capturando más defensas norteñas. A las 6 de la mañana los Federales finalmente pararon el avance Confederado, pero no hasta que los Confederados ya tenían posesión de casi una milla de la línea Federal. Un contraataque Federal empujó a los Confederados a Stedman, donde durante las próximas dos horas, estuvieron sujetados a una tormenta de balas y bombas. Una retirada fue ordenada, pero la línea de retirada estaba cubierta por un fuego cruzado tan violento que muchos de los sureños prefirieron rendirse en vez de retirarse. Otro contraataque Federal recapturó Fort Stedman y poco después la línea Federal ya fue reestablecida.

CONSECUENCIAS

Con este fracaso, la única esperanza de Lee era retirarse hacia North Carolina y unirse con Johnston.

Staat: Virginia

Befehlshaber der US:
 Brigadegeneral Orlando Wilcox
Armee der US: 9. Korps der Armee des
 Potomac
Truppenstärke: 5,000
Verluste:
 Gefallen: 75
 Verwundet: 419
 Gefangengenommen oder vermißt:
 523

Befehlshaber der CS:
 Generalmajor John Gordon
Armee der CS:
 Armee von Nordvirginia
Truppenstärke: 8,000
Verluste:
 Gefallen und verwundet: 732
 Gefangengenommen oder vermißt:
 1,949

KOMMENTAR

Bei Mitte März 1865 hatte sich die Situation der Konföderierten sehr verschlechtert. Im Süden hämmerte Sherman auf Johnston ein, General Early wurde im Shenandoatal besiegt, und die Truppen in der Nähe von Richmond und Petersburg waren ermüdet, hungrig und zahlenmäßig unterlegen.

Aus diesen Gründen plante Lee, Grant anzugreifen. Ein erfolgreicher Angriff könnte Grant zwingen, seine Linie um Petersburg zu verkürzen. Dies wurde es für Lee ermöglichen, nach Nordcarolina zurückzuziehen, wo er sich Johnston anschließen könnte für einen letzten Widerstand. Fort Stedman wurde für diesen letzten Angriff gewählt. Der Plan war, die Unionvorposten gefangenzunehmen und die Baumbarrieren vor dem Fort so schnell und leise wie möglich zu beseitigen. Die Eroberung des Forts und seiner unterstützenden Batterien, sowie die Unterbrechung der Kommunikation mit Grant's Nachschublager in City Point, sollte nachfolgen.

Beinahe die Hälfte von Lee's Truppen waren für die Teilnahme am Angriff bestimmt. Um 4.00 Uhr am Morgen des 25. März eilten drei 100-Mann Kolonnen leise heraus, nahmen die Vorposten gefangen und räumten einen Weg auf das Fort. Die Konföderierten stürzten sich ins Fort und überraschten die Föderalisten, die sich ohne Kampf ergaben. Weitere Konföderierte strömten durch diese Lücke in die Unionlinie. Ein Teil ging nach City Point, während andere sich nach Norden oder Süden wendeten, und auf ihrem Weg weitere Verteidigungsanlagen der Föderalisten eroberten. Um 6.00 Uhr konnten die Föderalisten den Vormarsch der Südstaatler endlich aufhalten, aber erst nachdem die Konföderierten schon beinahe anderthalb Kilometer der Unionlinie beherrschten. Ein Gegenangriff der Föderalisten drängte die Konföderierten nach Stedman zurück, wo sie zwei Stunden lang einem tödlichen Hagel von Musketen- und Artilleriefeuer ausgesetzt wurden. Ein Rückzug wurde befohlen, aber die Rückzugslinie führte durch ein ungemein brutales Kreuzfeuer, was viele Südstaatler überzeugte, Kapitulation einem Rückzug vorzuziehen. Ein weiterer Föderalistenangriff eroberte Fort Stedman zurück, und kurz danach war die Unionlinie wieder hergestellt.

BEDEUTUNG

Nach diesem Fehlschlag war Lee's einzige Hoffnung, sich nach Nordcarolina zurückziehen zu können, um sich mit Johnston zu vereinigen.

The interior of the fort; scene of Lee's last offensive action.

State: Virginia

U.S.

Commander:
Maj. Gen. Philip Sheridan
U.S. Army: Army of the Potomac V Corps + Cavalry
No. of Troops: 21,000
Casualties:
Killed: 124
Wounded: 706
Captured or missing: 54

C.S.

Commander:
Maj. Gen. George E. Pickett
C.S. Army: Army of Northern Virginia
No. of Troops: 10,600
Casualties:
Killed: 450
Wounded: 750
Captured or missing: 3,244

COMMENTS

With the arrival of better weather, Grant planned another assault against Lee's strained defenses. Grant massed Federals on the extreme left of his line, hoping to deal the final blow to the Southern defenders. To meet this Union concentration, Lee dispatched men, one-third of his whole army, toward Five Forks to hold the line "at all hazards."

By this time Lee had already planned to withdraw. He was only waiting until he could collect a week's worth of supplies for the march. But, if Grant succeeded in turning the Confederate right at Five Forks, Lee's retreat route to Johnston in North Carolina might be cut.

Gen. Sheridan, in command of the forces on the left, planned to assault the Confederate front while Gen. Warren's V Corps would attack Pickett's flank. Throughout April 1 Pickett's men worked at building earthworks. At 4 p.m. the Federals attacked. Sheridan's cavalry occupied the Confederates along the front as Warren, after a delay, hit Pickett's weakly held left flank. In a storm of musket fire the Confederates holding the flank were forced back. Pickett tried to shift some of his troops to the left but his small force couldn't keep back the Federal waves. Meanwhile in the front at Five Forks, the Union cavalry stormed over the works shattering the Southern line and capturing flags, cannons, and over 3,000 prisoners. Pickett's fragmented force tried to retreat, but the road to Petersburg was blocked by Gen. MacKenzie's Union cavalry brigade. Darkness ended the fighting with Sheridan's troops in possession of Five Forks.

SIGNIFICANCE

The remnants of Pickett's command were cut off from Petersburg and the rest of the Army of Northern Virginia.

Lee's right flank was turned.

The Union victory at Five Forks forced Lee to evacuate Petersburg and Richmond immediately.

Etat: Virginie

Etats-Unis

Commandant: Général de Division Philip H. Sheridan
Armée: du Potomac Corps V + cavalerie
21 000 soldats
Pertes:
Tués: 124
Blessés: 706
Prisonniers ou disparus: 54

Etats Confédérés

Commandant: Général de Division George E. Pickett
Armée: de Virginie du Nord
10 600 soldats
Pertes:
Tués: 450
Blessés: 750
Prisonniers ou disparus: 3 244

COMMENTAIRE

Quand le temps s'améliora, Grant organisa une autre attaque contre les défenses affaiblies de Lee. Il concentra les forces fédérales à l'extreme gauche de sa ligne, espérant frapper le coup final sur les défenseurs sudistes. Pour faire face à la force unioniste, Lee détacha un tiers de son armée entière pour l'envoyer à Five Forks tenir la ligne "à tout hasard."

A ce moment Lee avait déjà prévu de se retirer. Il attendait seulement de pouvoir rassembler une semaine de provisions. Mais, si Grant réussissait à faire virer les Confédérés sur la droite à Five Forks, la retraite de Lee jusqu'à Johnston en Caroline risquait d'etre coupée.

Dirigeant les forces de l'aile gauche, le général Sheridan prévoyait d'assaillir les Confédérés de front tandis que le corps V de Warren prendrait Pickett de flanc. Toute la journée du premier avril fut employée par les hommes de Pickett à construire des travaux en terre. Les Fédéraux attaquèrent à 16 heures. La cavalerie de Sheridan occupa les Confédérés au front; un peu plus tard, Warren frappa la gauche faible de Pickett. Dans le tempete des feux de mousquets, les Confédérés furent repoussés. Pickett essaya de déplacer quelques unes de ses troupes sur la gauche, mais celles-ci furent trop faibles pour retenir les vagues des Fédéraux. Pendant ce temps, devant Five Forks, la cavalerie de l'Union chargea sur les défenses, ébranla la ligne sudiste et prit drapeaux, canons et plus de 3 000 prisonniers. La force émiettée de Pickett dut faire retraite; mais la route de Petersburg était bloquée par la cavalerie unioniste de la brigade de MacKenzie. A la nuit, le combat prit fin. Les troupes de Sheridan étaient en possession de Five Forks.

CONSEQUENCES

Les restes du commandement de Pickett furent coupés de Petersburg et de l'armée de Virginie du Nord.

Le flanc droit de Lee était défait.

La victorie de l'Union à Five Forks obligea Lee à faire évacuer Petersburg et Richmond immédiatement.

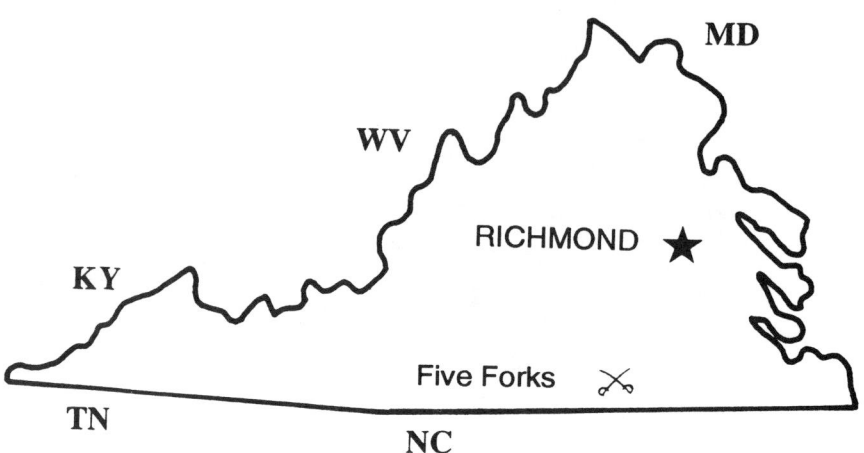

Important Landmarks
White Oak Road
South Side Railroad
Ford's Road
Scott's Road
Hatcher's Run
Gravelly Run

Important Buildings
"Burnt Quarter"/Gilliam Home
Gravely Run Church
Sidney Home

Estado: Virginia

U.S.

Comandante:
Maj. Gen. Philip H. Sheridan
U.S. Ejército: Army of the Potomac
  V Corps + Cavalry
  No. de tropas: 21,000
Pérdidas:
  Muertos: 124
  Heridos: 706
  Capturados o ausentes: 54

C.S.

Comandante:
Maj. Gen. George E. Pickett
U.S. Ejército: Army of Northern
Virginia
  No. de tropas: 10,600
Pérdidas:
  Muertos: 450
  Heridos: 750
  Capturados o ausentes: 3,244

COMENTARIO

Con la llegada de mejor tiempo, Grant planeó otro asalto contra las defensas debilitadas de Lee. Grant juntó a los Federales en la extremidad izquierda de su línea, esperando dar el golpe mortal a los defensores sureños. Para oponerse a esta concentración Federal, Lee mandó hombres, la tercera parte de su ejército, hacia Five Forks para mantener la línea en cualquier caso.

En este momento Lee ya planeó retirarse. Sólo esperaba hasta que pudiera coleccionar provisiones de una semana para la marcha. Pero, si Grant tuviera éxito en tornar la derecha Confederada en Five Forks, la ruta de la retirada a Johnston en North Carolina pudiera estar cortada.

El General Sheridan, en comandancia de las fuerzas de la izquierda, planeaba asaltar el frente Confederado mientras el cuerpo V del General Warren atacaría el flanco de Pickett. Durante todo el día del 1 de abril los hombres de Pickett trabajaron en construir defensas. A las 4 de la tarde los Federales atacaron. La caballería de Sheridan ocupaba a los Confederados en el frente mientras Warren, después de una tardanza, golpeó el flanco débil de Pickett. En una tormenta de balas los Confederados tuvieron que retirarse. Pickett trató de mudar a algunas de sus tropas a la izquierda pero su fuerza pequeña no pudo parar las olas Federales. Mientras tanto en frente de Five Forks, la caballería subió por encima de las defensas destruyendo la línea sureña y capturando banderas, cañones y más de 3,000 prisioneros. La fuerza fragmentada de Pickett trató de retirarse, pero la carreterra a Petersburg estaba bloqueada por la brigada de caballería del General MacKenzie. La oscuridad acabó la lucha con las tropas de Sheridan en posesión de Five Forks.

CONSECUENCIAS

Lo que quedaba de la comandancia de Pickett estaba aislada de Petersburg y el resto del Army of Northern Virginia.

El flanco derecho de Lee estuvo tornado.

La victoria Federal en Five Forks forzó a Lee a evacuar Petersburg y Richmond inmediátamente.

Staat: Virginia

Befehlshaber der US:
  Generalmajor Phillip Sheridan
Armee der US: Armee des Potomac
  Truppenstärke: 21,000

Verluste:
  Gefallen: 124
  Verwundet: 419
  Gefangengenommen oder vermißt:
  54

Befehlshaber der CS:
  Generalmajor George Pickett
Armee der CS:
  Armee von Nordvirginia
  Truppenstärke: 10,600

Verluste:
  Gefallen: 450
  Verwundet: 750
  Gefangengenommen oder vermißt:
  3,244

KOMMENTAR

Nach der Ankunft besseren Wetters, plante Grant einen weiteren Angriff gegen Lee's stark belastete Verteidigungen. In der Hoffnung, den südstaatlichen Verteidigern den entscheidenden Schlag zu versetzen, massierte Grant seine Föderalisten am äußersten Ende seiner linken Flanke. Um sich dieser Konzentration der Uniontruppen entgegenzustellen, entsandte Lee Truppen — ein Drittel seiner ganzen Armee — in Richtung Five Forks, um die Linie "trotz aller Gefahr" zu halten.

Inzwischen hatte Lee sich bereits entschloßen, zurückzuziehen. Er wartete nur auf den Zeitpunkt, bei dem er Vorräte für eine Woche des Rückmarsches aufgespeichert haben konnte. Lee's Rückzuglinie zu Johnston in Nordcarolina war in Gefahr, abgeschnitten zu werden, sollte es Grant rechtzeitig gelingen, die rechte Seite der Konföderierten bei Five Forks abzuwenden.

General Sheridan, der das Kommando über die Truppen auf der linken Flanke hatte, plante einen Angriff auf die Front der Konföderierten, während das 5. Korps, unter General Warren, Pickett's Flanke angreifen würde. Am 1. April arbeiteten Pickett's Truppen den ganzen Tag an Schanzwerken. Um 16.00 Uhr griffen die Föderalisten an. Sheridan's Kavallerie entwickelte die Konföderierten Truppen an der Frontlinie, während Warren, nach einer Verzögerung, Pickett's schwach aufgestellte linke Flanke angriff. In einem Hagel von Musketenfeuer wurden die Konföderierten an der linken Flanke zurückgedrängt. Pickett versuchte, einige seiner Truppen nach links zu versetzen, aber seine kleine Streitkraft konnte die Föderalistenwellen nicht zurückhalten. In der Zwischenzeit, an der Front bei Five Forks, stürzte sich die Unionkavallerie über die Schanzwerke, zerschmetterte die Linie der Südstaatler, eroberte Fahnen und Kanonen und nahm über 3,000 Truppen gefangen. Pickett's zersplitterte Streitkraft versuchte, sich zurückzuziehen, aber die Landstraße nach Petersburg war von der Unionkavalleriebrigade unter General MacKenzie, blockiert. Einbruch der Dunkelheit endete die Schlacht, mit Sheridan's Truppen in Gewalt von Five Forks.

BEDEUTUNG

Die Überreste von Pickett's Streitkraft waren von Petersburg, und der übrigen Armee von Nordvirginia, abgeschnitten.

Lee's rechte Flanke wurde abgewendet.

Der Sieg der Unionkavallerie bei Five Forks zwang Lee, Petersburg und Richmond sofort zu evakuieren.

Maj. Gen. Philip H. Sheridan, 1831-1888, was one of the premier Union generals during the Civil War.

Maj. Gen. George E. Pickett, 1825-1875, has been criticized for being at a fish bake in the rear as his defenses crumbled.

State: Virginia

Etat: Virginie

U.S.

Commander:
Lt. Gen. Ulysses S. Grant
U.S. Army: Armies of the Potomac,
James, and Shenandoah
No. of Troops: 76,113
Casualties:
Killed and wounded: 8,268
Captured or missing: 1,676

C.S.

Commander:
Gen. Robert E. Lee
C.S. Army: Army of Northern
Virginia
No. of Troops: 57,829
Casualties:
Killed and wounded: 6,266
Captured or missing: 19,132
Surrendered & Paroled: 28,231

Etats-Unis

Commandant: Lieutenant Général
Ulysses S. Grant
Armées: du Potomac, James et
Shenandoah
76 113 soldats
Pertes:
Tués et blessés: 8 268
Prisonniers ou disparus 676

Etats Confédérés

Commandant:
Général Robert E. Lee
Armée: de Virginie du Nord
57 829 soldats
Pertes:
Tués et blessés: 6 266
Prisonniers ou disparus: 19 132
Rendus ou prisonniers sur parole:
28 231

COMMENTS

After Sheridan's victory at Five Forks, Lee realized he had to evacuate his lines around Richmond and Petersburg if he wanted to save his army.

On April 2 the Confederates headed west. Hoping to join up with Johnston's forces in North Carolina, Lee planned to turn south when he reached Amelia Court House. But the Federals pressed their pursuit. One column closely followed Lee's course while another swung to the south, blocking his retreat route toward North Carolina. With no alternative the Army of Northern Virginia again headed west. On April 6 Lee's rear guard was attacked at Sayler's Creek. The exhausted Confederates were overwhelmed and over 6,000 were captured. This disaster, along with constant desertions, terribly weakened the Southern Army.

Lee's dwindling force headed toward Appomattox Station where much needed supplies were waiting for them.

On the night of April 8 the Confederates camped near Appomattox Court House. As darkness fell, the fate of the Army of Northern Virginia became visible. To their north and east the flicker of camp fires revealed Grant's position. To the south, the flash of artillery told the Southerners that Sheridan's cavalry had reached Appomattox Station first and their retreat route had again been blocked. Lee and his generals held a council of war. They decided to attack the cavalry, but agreed that if the cavalry was supported by a strong force of infantry the attack would probably fail.

On Palm Sunday, April 9, 1865, Lee attacked the Union cavalry. The Southerners easily pushed the horsemen aside, but behind them stood strong formations of blue infantry. Skirmishing continued until 10 a.m. when an informal truce ended the fighting. General Lee arranged for a meeting with Grant to discuss terms for surrender. Around 1:30 Grant arrived at the McLean house where Lee was waiting. By 3 p.m. Lee had surrendered the Confederate Army of Northern Virginia. On April 12 the Southerners laid down their arms and were paroled.

SIGNIFICANCE

With the surrender of the South's most successful army and its great leader, the war was finally ending. Other Confederate forces still operated, but upon hearing of Lee's surrender they soon began negotiations to surrender their diminished forces.

COMMENTAIRE

Aprés la victoire de Sheridan à Five Forks, Lee s'aperçut qu'il devait évacuer ses lignes autour de Richmond et de Petersburg s'il voulait sauver son armée.

Le 2 avril, les Confédérés prirent la direction ouest, espérant rejoindre les forces de Johnston en Caroline du Nord. Lee prévoyait de marcher vers le sud quand il atteindrait Amelia Court House. Mais les fédéraux les poursuivaient de près. Une colonne était sur les talons de Lee, tandis qu'une autre vola au sud pour bloquer sa retraite vers la Caroline du Nord. Alors l'armée de Virginie du Nord reprit la direction ouest. Le 6 avril l'arrière des troupes de Lee fut attaqué à Sayler's Creek. Les Confédérés épuisés étaient accablés et plus de 6 000 furent faits prisonniers. Ce désastre, et les désertions qui s'accumulaient, affaiblirent encore l'armée sudiste.

La force chancelante de Lee acheminait vers Appomattox où l'attendaient les provisions dont elle avait grand besoin.

La nuit d'avril, les Confédérés campèrent près du Appomattox Court House. Comme la nuit tombait, le sort de l'armée de Virginie du Nord devint clair. Au nord et à l'est, les lumières des feux de camp révélèrent la position de Grant. Au sud, les éclats de l'artillerie indiquaient aux sudistes que la cavalerie de Sheridan avait déjà atteint Appomattox Station et que la route de leur retraite était à nouveau bloquée. Lee tint un conseil de guerre avec ses généraux. Ils décidèrent d'attaquer la cavalerie, mais ils admettaient que si celle-ci était renforcée par une infanterie puissante, leur attaque échouerait probablement.

Le dimanche des Rameaux, avril 1865, Lee attaqua la cavalerie de l'Union. Les Sudistes écartèrent facilement les cavaliers; mais derrière eux, puissante et bleue, se tenait l'infanterie. Les escarmouches continuèrent jusqu'à 10 heures où une trêve informale y mit fin. Le général Lee engagea les pourparlers avec Grant pour discuter des termes de sa reddition. Vers 13h30 Grant arriva à McLean House où Lee l'attendait. A 15 heures Lee s'était rendu ave l'armée confédérée de Virginie du Nord. Le 12 avril, les Sudistes déposèrent les armes et furent libérés sur parole.

CONSEQUENCE

Avec la reddition de l'armée du Sud la plus victorieuse et de son chef prestigieux, la guerre finissait enfin. Lorsque les autres forces confédérées encore actives apprirent la nouvelle, elles entrèrent en négociations et se rendirent à leur tour.

Important Landmarks
Appomattox River
Plain Run
Prince Edward Court House Road
Richmond-Lynchburg Stage Road
Grant's HQ site
Lee's HQ site
Poplar Tree site
Apple Tree site
C.S. Cemetery

Important Buildings
Courthouse
Wright House
Peers House
McLean House
Kelly House
Clover Hill Tavern
County Jail
Bocock-Isbell House
Meeks Store

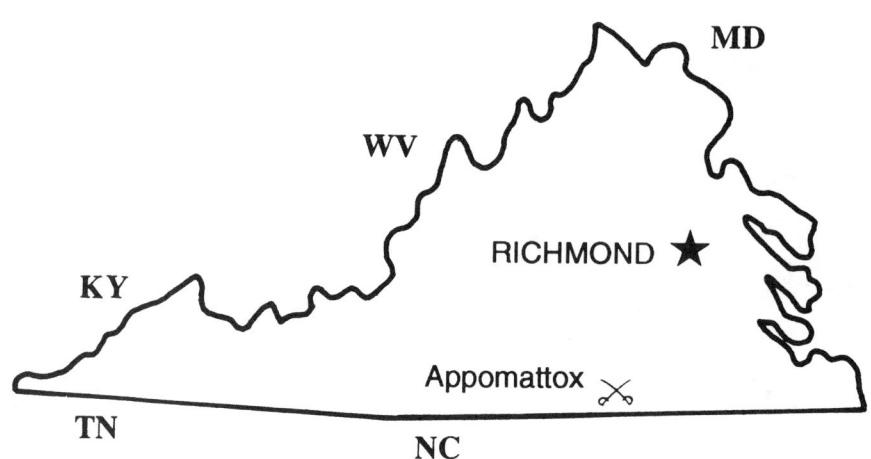

Estado: Virginia

U.S.

Comandante:
Lt. Gen. Ulysses S. Grant
U.S. Ejército: Armies of the Potomac, James, y Shenandoah
No. de tropas: 76,113
Pérdidas:
Muertos y Heridos: 8,268
Capturados o ausentes: 1,676

C.S.

Comandante:
Gen. Robert E. Lee
C.S. Ejército: Army of Northern Virginia
No. de tropas: 57,829
Pérdidas:
Muertos y Heridos: 6,266
Capturados o ausentes: 19,132
Rendidos y puestos en libertad bajo palabra de honor: 28,231

COMENTARIO

Después de la victoria de Sheridan en Five Forks, Lee se dio cuenta de que tenía que evacuar sus líneas alrededor de Richmond y Petersburg si quería salvar a su ejército.

El 2 de abril los Confederados se fueron para el oeste. Esperando juntarse con las fuerzas del General Johnston en North Carolina, Lee pensaba volver al sur cuando llegara a Amelia Court House. Pero los Federales lo perseguían estréchamente. Una columna seguía la ruta de Lee mientras otra iba para el sur, bloqueando la ruta de Lee a North Carolina. Sin alternativa Army of Northern Virginia fue más al oeste. El 6 de abril la retaguardia de Lee fue atacada en Sayler's Creek. Los Confederados fatigados fueron oprimidos y más de 6,000 fueron capturados. Este desastre con deserciones constantes terriblemente debilitó el ejército sureño.

La fuerza pequeña de Lee se dirigió para Appomattox Station donde había provisiones muy necesitadas.

Por la noche del 8 de abril los Confederados acamparon cerca de Appomattox Court House. Al anochecer el destino del Army of Northern Virginia llegó a ser visible. Al norte y este la vacilación de fuegos reveló la posición de Grant. Al sur, las ráfagas de luz de artillería les dijeron a los sureños que la caballería de Sheridan había llegado a Appomattox Station primero y su ruta de retirada había sido bloqueada otra vez. Lee y sus generales tuvieron un concilio de guerra. Decidieron atacar la caballería, pero acordaron que si la caballería estuviera apoyada por una fuerza fuerte de infantería, el ataque probáblemente fracasaria.

El domingo de palma, el 9 de abril, 1865, Lee atacó la caballería Federal. Los sureños fácilmente barrieron a los caballeros, pero detrás de ellos estaban formaciones de infantería azul. La escaramuza siguió hasta las 10 de la mañana cuando una tregua informal acabó la lucha. El General Lee acordó una reunión con Grant para discutir los términos de una rendición. A la 1:30 Grant llegó a la casa McLean donde Lee esperaba. A las 3 de la tarde Lee ya había rendido el Army of Northern Virginia. El 12 de abril los sureños rendieron sus armas y fueron puestos en libertad bajo palabra de honor.

CONSECUENCIAS

Con la rendición del ejército logrado de Lee y su gran líder, la guerra finalmente se acababa. Otras fuerzas Confederadas todavía operaban, pero al oír de la rendición de Lee pronto comenzaron a hacer negociaciones para rendir a sus propias fuerzas disminuidas.

Staat: Virginia

Befehlshaber der US:
Generalleutnant Ulysses S. Grant
Armee der US: Armeen des Potomac, James und Shenandoah
Truppenstärke: 76,113
Verluste:
Gefallen und verwundet: 8,268
Gefangengenommen oder vermißt: 1,676

Befehlshaber der CS:
General Robert E. Lee
Armee der CS:
Armee von Nordvirginia
Truppenstärke: 57,829
Verluste:
Gefallen und verwundet: 6,266
Gefangengenommen oder vermißt: 19,132
Kapituliert und auf Ehrenwort entlassen: 28,231

KOMMENTAR

Nach Sheridan's Sieg bei Five Forks sah Lee ein, daß er seine Linien um Richmond und Petersburg evakuieren mußte, um seine Armee zu retten.

Am 2. April zogen die Konföderierten nach Westen ab. In der Hoffnung, sich mit Johnston's Truppen in Nordcarolina zusammenzuschließen, plante Lee nach Süden abzubiegen, nachdem er das Amelia Court House erreicht hatte. Aber die Föderalisten drängten ihre Verfolgung. Eine Kolonne folgte dicht hinter Lee, während eine andere nach Süden abbog, und blockierte damit seine Rückzugroute nach Nordcarolina. Die Armee von Nordvirginia hatte keine andere Wahl, als einen westlichen Marsch anzutreten. Am 6. April wurde Lee's Nachhut bei Sayler's Creek angegriffen. Die erschöpften Konföderierten wurden überwältigt, und über 6,000 gefangengenommen. Diese Katastrophe, verbunden mit ständiger Fahnenflucht, schwächten die Südarmee außerordentlich.

Lee's schwindende Armee ging in Richtung Appomattox Station, wo dringend notwendige Vorräte sie erwarteten.

In der Nacht vom 8. April lagerten die Konföderierten in der Nähe von Appomattox Court House. Bei Einbruch der Dunkelheit bekam das Schicksal der Armee von Nordvirginia sichtbar. Nördlich und östlich von ihnen markierte das Flackern von Lagerfeuern die Stellungen von Grant's Truppen. Das Aufblitzen der Artillerie in südlicher Richtung verkündete, daß Sheridan's Kavallerie Appomattox Station vor den Konföderierten erreicht hatte, und somit ihre Rückzugroute wiederum blockiert war. Lee und seine Generale hielten einen Kriegsrat. Sie entschloßen sich, die Kavallerie anzugreifen, aber verstanden, daß, im Falle starke Infanterie die Kavallerie unterstützte, der geplante Angriff scheitern konnte.

Am Palmsonntag, dem 9. April 1865, griff Lee die Unionkavallerie an. Die Südstaatler stießen die Reiter ohne Mühe beiseite, aber hinter der Kavallerie standen starke Formationen von blauen Infanteristen. Vereinzelte Kämpfe setzten sich fort, als um 10.00 Uhr ein inoffizieller Waffenstillstand den Kampf beendete. General Lee vereinbarte eine Zusammenkunft mit Grant, um die Kapitulationsbedingungen festzulegen. Ungefähr um 13.30 Uhr kam Grant im McLean Haus in Appomattox Station an, wo Lee ihn erwartete. Um 15.00 Uhr übergab Lee die Konföderationsarmee von Nordvirginia. Am 12. April legten die Südstaatler ihre Waffen nieder, und sie wurden auf Ehrenwort entlassen.

BEDEUTUNG

Als Folge der Kapitulation der erfolgreichsten Südarmee und deren Führer, ging der Krieg nun dem Ende zu. Einige Streitkräfte der Konföderation operierten noch, aber sobald sie von Lee's Kapitulation hörten, begannen sie umgehend mit Verhandlungen zur Übergabe ihrer schwindenden Streitkräfte.

The Wilmer McLean House where Lee surrendered the Army of Northern Virginia to General U.S. Grant.

Photo Credits

Unless otherwise indicated, all of the photographs and drawings are courtesy of the U.S. Army Military History Institute, Carlisle Barracks, PA.

Battles and Leaders of the Civil War, pp. 62, 70, 71, 83.

Frank Leslie's Illustrated Newspaper, p. 45.

THOMAS PUBLICATIONS publishes books about the American Colonial era, the Revolutionary War, the Civil War, and other important topics. For a complete list of titles, please write to:

THOMAS PUBLICATIONS
P.O. Box 3031
Gettysburg, PA 17325